"American colleges and universities are being tested like never before in their commitment to inquiry and dialogue that is as open as it is diverse. As the son of a Jewish refugee who fled Poland in 1939, Ronald Daniels' insights on the essential role of colleges in a democracy ring with particular power. He offers a compelling history of the important relationship between higher education and democratic values—and a path forward to strengthen both."—Michael R. Bloomberg, founder of Bloomberg LP and Bloomberg Philanthropies, and Mayor of New York, 2002–2013

"Weaving personal history with his passion for democracy, Daniels has crafted a beautifully written story of the essential role of universities in maintaining and reinforcing fairness and justice in America. To discover the new role universities must play in the contest between liberal and illiberal ways of thought, and how institutions of higher learning need reform, read this essential book. There is no other like it."—Jonathan R. Cole, author of *The Great American University*

"Ron Daniels is a pioneer. In this critically important work, he examines the systemic and systematic reforms we need to achieve equity in US higher education. There has never been a more urgent moment for change."—Mellody Hobson, Co-CEO and President, Ariel Investments, LLC

"In this timely and compelling book, Ronald Daniels makes a powerful argument for the central role universities must have in ensuring the public good and fostering liberal democracy. Readers will appreciate his careful analysis, his global perspective, and his inspiring personal story, and they will come away understanding the urgency of his message."—Freeman A. Hrabowski III, author of *The Empowered University: Shared Leadership, Culture Change, and Academic Success*

"One of America's outstanding university presidents dares to tackle what ails US higher education. His recommendations are radical, exciting, and doable. This is one of those books that will define the conversation on campuses across the country."—Michael Ignatieff, President and Rector of Central European University

What
Universities
Owe
Democracy

>>>><<<<

What Universities Owe Democracy

RONALD J. DANIELS

WITH GRANT SHREVE
AND PHILLIP SPECTOR

Johns Hopkins University Press

BALTIMORE

Johns Hopkins University Press
2715 North Charles Street
Baltimore, Maryland 21218-4363
www.press.jhu.edu

Library of Congress Cataloging-in-Publication Data

Names: Daniels, Ronald J. (Ronald Joel), 1959– author. |
Shreve, Grant, 1984– author. | Spector, Phillip, 1976– author.
Title: What universities owe democracy / Ronald J. Daniels ;
with Grant Shreve and Phillip Spector.
Description: Baltimore : Johns Hopkins University Press, 2021. |
Includes bibliographical references and index.
Identifiers: LCCN 2021017904 | ISBN 9781421442693 (hardcover) |
ISBN 9781421442709 (ebook)
Subjects: LCSH: Education, Higher—Aims and objectives—United States. |
Democracy and education—United States.
Classification: LCC LA227.4 .D36 2021 | DDC 378.73—dc23
LC record available at https://lccn.loc.gov/2021017904

A catalog record for this book is available from the British Library.

*Special discounts are available for bulk purchases of this book. For more information,
please contact Special Sales at specialsales@jh.edu.*

CONTENTS

PREFACE   vii

Introduction   1

ONE | American Dreams   29
Access, Mobility, Fairness

TWO | Free Minds   86
Educating Democratic Citizens

THREE | Hard Truths   131
Creating Knowledge and Checking Power

FOUR | Purposeful Pluralism   187
Dialogue across Difference on Campus

Conclusion   239

ACKNOWLEDGMENTS   253
NOTES   255
INDEX   313

v

PREFACE

I AM THE SON of a European Jewish refugee who, along with his parents and two siblings, entered Canada from Warsaw, Poland, in March 1939, narrowly escaping the cataclysm that engulfed European Jewry. Not one of the scores of my father's relatives who remained in Europe—grandparents, aunts and uncles, cousins—survived. What makes the story of my father's great good fortune all the more remarkable was the studious indifference of the Canadian government toward European Jews from the time of Hitler's seizure of power in 1933 to the end of the Second World War in 1945. This indifference was memorably captured in the curt, chilling reply of a government official to the question of how many European Jews Canada would allow into the country: "None is too many." In total, during this twelve-year period, Canada accepted only five thousand Jewish refugees, which historians Irving Abella and Harold Troper deemed the worst record of any refugee-admitting country in the world. My family constituted five of those five thousand.

The framed passport of my father and grandfather, along with their entry visa to Canada, continues to hang in my parents' home in Toronto. It stands as a powerful reminder of the terrifying nightmare my family left behind in a continent riven by despotism, violence, and organized hatred; of the blissful succor they eventually found in Canada; and of the disquieting knowledge that autocracy underpinned by bigotry and an indifference to human life is never as far away as we would like to believe. A reminder, in short, that liberal democracy can never be taken for granted.

For my family, life in democratic Canada became inseparable from the bounties of higher education. It was here that my father, my aunt, and my uncle obtained degrees at the University of Toronto. I would later receive my undergraduate and law degrees from there, too. Universities made possible the promises of democracy. It is, in part, why I have dedicated my career to them.

It is hard for me not to wax quixotic about the role of universities. For more than four decades, I have inhabited several universities in different capacities—student, professor, dean, provost, and, most recently, president. In each of these roles, I have felt privileged to be able to work in an institution that is truly a place apart. A place where, at its best, reason and fact are venerated; where individual acts of imagination and insight that challenge orthodoxies receive support and encouragement; where ideas are hatched that change our understanding of the world around us, bring us closer to truth, and offer the prospect of human advancement. It is a place where fellow citizens from all walks of life can transcend their circumstances through the acquisition of knowledge and the cultivation of mastery, and where scientific investigation generates technologies and therapies that materially improve human flourishing. And so it will come as little surprise that there is seldom a moment of doubt around my decision to devote my life to this most extraordinary institution.

It is not that I am impervious to the idiosyncrasies, excesses, and petty absurdities that can afflict the university. More than once, I have been exposed to (or been forced to manage) the small *p* university politics over issues of office space, seating arrangements, or honorific titles that undergird Henry Kissinger's famous quip that "university politics are vicious precisely because the stakes are so small." I have experienced times where an institution that is supposed to be scrupulously devoted to rationality—to the careful probing and evaluation of claims of truth—has succumbed to the thrall of movements or enthusiasms of questionable validity that are only reappraised and repudiated with the passage of time. And I have seen the extent to which our espoused devotion to merit has been challenged, and perhaps even deformed, by admissions patterns in so many elite universities, both private and public, that only serve to further advantage the already advantaged. Despite these flaws, however, I continue to believe that the university stands as one of our most important social institutions, a noble institution imbued with a noble calling.

Over the past several years, my long-standing faith in the university has been fortified and enriched by a growing recognition of how this singular institution is intimately—and ineluctably—bound to the project of building and nourishing the system and habits of government that we call liberal democracy: the idea that democratic rule cannot be unbridled and must submit to clearly prescribed constraints, like the rule of law, that protect individual freedom and stand as a necessary counterbalance to the excesses of majority rule. Recognition of the university's indispensable role in modern liberal democracy, coupled with my strong concern over the precarity of liberal democracy in the United States and in other established democratic states, is what motivated me to write this book. Universities are not merely bystander institutions to democracy but deeply implicated in, and essential for, its success. It is imperative in this moment of democratic backsliding that our universities more self-consciously vindicate their obligations to this most precious and fragile form of self-governance.

What
Universities
Owe
Democracy

>>>><<<<

>>>><<<<

Introduction

The University is an institution of the people, an institution born of
the democratic spirit.   —WILLIAM RAINEY HARPER, 1899

Universities . . . like other refuges of truth, have remained exposed
to all the dangers arising from social and political power. Yet the chances
for truth to prevail in public are, of course, greatly improved by the mere
existence of such places.   —HANNAH ARENDT, 1967

JUST A FEW BLOCKS east of the Danube River on Arany János Street
in Budapest sits the Goldberger House. This magnificent premod-
ern building, with its ornamented façade of towering pillars and
delicate rosettes, was built in 1911 to serve as the warehouse and
administrative offices for Samuel Goldberger and Sons, one of
Hungary's oldest textile companies as well as one of its most storied Jewish-owned businesses. Although the company collapsed
after Hungary nationalized its textile industry in the late 1940s,
the building has survived, withstanding nearly a century's worth
of wars and political upheaval. Today, it is a monument to historical memory, housing one of the world's most vital archives on

the history of post–World War II human rights. And these archives are controlled by an institution that has for three decades been a vital actor in that history: Central European University (CEU), an international American research university founded by Hungarian American philanthropist George Soros after the fall of the Berlin Wall to assist former Soviet states in their transition to liberal democracy.

The person responsible for overseeing these archives is István Rév, a historian, native Hungarian, and one of CEU's first faculty members. In January 2019, I spoke to Rév in his modest, spare office on the uppermost floor of the Goldberger House. I was in Budapest as part of a review of CEU's accreditation, a typically uneventful and routine process. The circumstances this time, however, were anything but routine.

CEU was in the final throes of a long-underway political face-off with Hungary's prime minister, Viktor Orbán. Almost two years earlier, in April 2017, Orbán's government had passed a law prohibiting any foreign university without a physical campus in its home nation from operating in Budapest.[1] CEU was the only university without such a campus, and the law quickly became known as "Lex CEU."[2] The university made every effort to comply with the government's demands, including a last-minute run at negotiations between New York State and Hungary to establish a home campus in the United States. By the end of 2018, Orbán had prevailed, and the school was forced to prepare plans to decamp 150 miles west, in Vienna. CEU became only the second university to be expelled from a country's borders on political grounds since World War II.[3]

In my conversation with Rév, the soulful and soft-spoken historian was unflinching in his assessment of what was happening to his university under Orbán. "President Orbán has murdered my institution," he told me. "He has ripped it from its historical and geographic context, and stripped it of its identity."[4] Rév's reaction was reflective of a growing sense among fellow scholars, students, and citizens across the world that something foundational was at stake.

From its earliest days, CEU proved instrumental in restoring the social sciences and humanities—gutted during Communist rule—to a place of prominence in central Europe. It cultivated a new corps of diplomats and civil servants who were advancing the aims of a stable democratic Europe through sound public policy, and it investigated and propagated the values of liberalism, democracy, and open societies.[5] CEU's students have gone on to become presidents, cabinet officials, and members of parliament across Europe.[6] To be at CEU was (and still is) to be part of an endeavor in democratic institution-building in a region still reeling from an autocratic past. But in the early days of 2019, this university, which had come to symbolize the loftiest promises of higher education within Hungary, within central and Eastern Europe, and within the liberal democratic world writ large, was under attack—and, through no fault of its own, sadly succumbing to the campaign orchestrated against it.

When I left Hungary that winter to return to my home in Baltimore, Maryland, where I serve as the president of Johns Hopkins University, the writing was on the wall. Nothing CEU or its rector at the time, the former Canadian politician and academic Michael Ignatieff, could do would ever be enough to satisfy the Hungarian government. The following November, the university traversed the border between Hungary and Austria—which only two years before CEU's founding had been separated by hundreds of miles of barbed wire—to open its doors officially in Vienna.[7] But the school has not been intimidated. As Ignatieff has said, it is committed to "winnow[ing] the grain of knowledge from the chaff of ideology, partisanship, rhetoric and lies."[8]

Nevertheless, the saga of CEU underscores how unnerved autocrats are by the presence of vibrant, independent universities and how readily these institutions become early and attractive targets for harassment, restriction, or closure by the authoritarian state. Universities are not the only institutional targets for the autocrat's antipathy, of course: the courts, media, competitive political parties, and independent professionalized bureaucracies all share the distinction of being bulwarks of liberal democracy. That universities so swiftly draw the ire of autocrats, however, offers strong circumstantial evidence that these institutions are more intimately implicated in the enterprise of building and fostering liberal democracy than is typically acknowledged.

Born of the Democratic Spirit

Attacking universities is a time-worn page in the authoritarian's playbook, from Benito Mussolini's extraction of loyalty oaths from university faculty and expulsion of Jews from campuses in the 1920s and '30s, to Adolf Hitler's shuttering of Czechoslovakian universities and his execution of nine students, to the Communist government of Poland's crackdown on academic freedom in the 1970s that gave rise to a nomadic, underground "flying university" whose faculty and students held clandestine classes in private homes to escape arrest by the secret police.[9]

A similar pattern is playing out today. In Hungary, the assault on CEU was just the tip of the iceberg. Since ascending to power in 2010, Orbán has steadily chipped away at the autonomy of the nation's universities and scholars by installing overseers to manage all financial decisions at public universities, aggressively censoring academic conferences, placing the historically independent Hungarian Academy of Sciences under strict government control, and even launching a shadow network of research centers to prop up what one Hungarian political scientist called "the ideological façade" of the Orbán regime.[10] In Turkey, President Recep Tayyip Erdoğan has used executive decrees to arrest or fire thousands of academics, and he has granted himself complete power to appoint the heads of public and private universities.[11] In Russia, the state-sponsored watchdog agency, Rosobrnadzor, has exploited minute rules and regulations—including everything from improperly formatted course syllabi to having the wrong kind of windows installed in a building—to revoke universities' authority to operate.[12] And in Brazil, Jair Bolsonaro has slashed university budgets and threatened to demolish programs deemed too leftist.[13]

In the United States during the tumultuous four years of Donald J. Trump's presidency, there were doubtless many moments when universities felt as though they were in the crosshairs of the president and his surrogates. Trump's son, Donald Jr., in 2017 summed up the administration's public-facing attitude toward universities: "[They'll] take $200,000 of your money; in exchange [they'll] train your children to hate our country."[14] Echoing this sentiment was *The 1776 Report*, a lightly sourced call for patriotic education released in the waning days of the Trump presidency in which universities were described as "hotbeds of anti-Americanism, libel, and censorship that combine to generate in students and in the broader culture at the very least disdain and at worst outright hatred for this country."[15]

More than rhetorical contempt, universities during the Trump era were subject to specific actions that seemed gratuitous and vindictive, like the ill-fated effort to terminate the F1 visas of more than one million international students, or the initiation of a civil rights investigation against Princeton University in 2020 for its president's acknowledgment of the persistence of racism throughout our society in the aftermath of the killing of George Floyd in Minneapolis.[16] In truth, though, the actions taken by the Trump administration that universities found most injurious were not those targeted specifically at universities, but those that cut across the country as a whole. Here I think, in particular, of the administration's crude efforts to impose a ban on Muslim immigration and to terminate, without any meaningful alternative, the Obama administration's DACA (Deferred Action for Childhood Arrivals) program. These decisions arguably had a disparate impact on our faculty and students, but we were by no means the only institution in America diminished by these actions.

This is an important point: insofar as universities are concerned, the Trump administration's policies and actions were never as extreme as those taken by overt authoritarians like Orbán and Erdoğan. Indeed, despite the broadsides leveled against universities, President Trump signed spending bills that increased the level of federal research support and secured more permanent funding for historically Black colleges and universities.[17] And to the extent that other actions taken by the Trump administration—like the sweeping reformulation of the Department of Education's sexual assault guidelines under Title IX or the Justice Department's support for constitutional challenges aimed at abrogating affirmative action preferences in university admissions—provoked intense controversy and criticism, it is hard to characterize them as being squarely outside of the boundaries of what have, for many years, been long-standing conservative policy positions.

Nevertheless, the Trump years did see a widening rift in partisan perceptions of the value of higher education. In 2015, Pew reported that 54 percent of Republicans and 70 percent of Democrats viewed universities and colleges as having a positive impact on the country. Four years later, in 2019, the portion of Democrats who believed the same remained almost unchanged, while Republicans who viewed universities positively had collapsed to 33 percent.[18] The yawning gap between Republicans and Democrats in their views on universities and the national interest is just one of many divisions that mark and define our highly polarized country today. It is probably too soon to ascribe to former President Trump—despite his gleeful disdain for universities—the lion's share of responsibility for the shift in public sentiment. More likely, his success was in attracting non-college-educated voters to the Republican Party, many of whom are hostile to the significant economic and status benefits (real and perceived) that inure to those possessing university education over those who do not.[19] Of course, the American university is no stranger to controversy or calumny, and it has weathered periods of fierce attack in the past. But with liberal democracies flagging around the world, and hostility to institutions rising at home, this moment feels perilous, maybe singularly so. We can no longer pretend that the United States is immune from the gale winds of illiberalism, or its universities from the suppression that often follows.

Trump may have given voice to, and perhaps reinforced, the critical sentiments that his base had toward higher education, but those sentiments were already well established before he famously descended the escalator in Trump Tower in 2015 to announce his campaign for national office. His genius was in understanding and then exploiting the resentments, the anxieties, and the vulnerabilities of these voters, many of whom have been on the losing side of globalization's steady march over the past several decades. The forces of toxic populism and unabashed anti-intellectualism that he and so many other leaders around the globe have channeled and amplified will continue to persist. From sad experience, we know that sooner or later, such forces will not be able to bear the presence of an unfettered university.

The authoritarian allergy to universities is no mystery. Everything that universities embody is inimical to the autocrat's interest in the untrammeled exercise of arbitrary public power. They are institutions committed to freedom of inquiry, to the contestation of ideas through conversation and debate, to the formation of communities that gather and celebrate a diverse array of experiences and thought, and to individual flourishing achieved through diligent study. They rest upon a foundation of reliable knowledge and facts, which are antidotes to the uncertainty and dissimulation peddled by authoritarian regimes. They are, to quote William Rainey Harper, the first president of the University of Chicago, an "institution born of the democratic spirit."[20]

No truly great university can flourish in a society where the specter of autocratic power sows fear and distrust among its members. One country putting this proposition to the test is China, which has expanded its investments into higher education at an extraordinary pace in recent years. According to the BBC, China's higher education sector is growing at a rate equivalent to adding a new university each week.[21] The nation's universities have begun to ascend global university rankings, too, and they have managed to do so with minimal protections for academic freedom. In many cases, the government has limited researchers' access to archives, foreign scholars, and other sources of information that are essential to pioneering scholarly production; in others, faculty and students are intimidated, censored, or punished for their ideas.[22] These crackdowns on academic freedom are a central part of China's vision for its higher education system: President Xi Jinping has explicitly called for China to "build universities into strongholds that adhere to Party leadership."[23] As the Chinese state has further narrowed the space for free inquiry, though, scientists report that Internet restrictions have made working in China "a total disaster," and one study showed that while Chinese students outpace American students in critical thinking skills, when they get to college, Chinese students fall significantly behind their American counterparts.[24] The question looming before Chinese higher education, then, is whether, in the words of one report, it can "continue to build and maintain world-class institutions while relying on academic freedom practiced elsewhere."[25]

The Chinese case exemplifies the axiom that autocratic regimes extinguish the expressive freedom and organic flourishing of students and scholars. For those who love and believe in the university, we cannot be agnostic about, or indifferent to, the vibrancy of liberal democracy.

But this book is about more than the self-interest of universities; it also makes a broader claim about the role of universities in advancing the public good. Liberal democracy is the system of government best equipped to mediate among the different, competing, and often irreconcilable conceptions of the good and to ensure appropriate care for individual autonomy and dignity. The values of the university, in particular, are aligned with this system, given the premium each places on freedom of speech and thought, tolerance for dissent and heterodoxy, the free flow of information and ideas, and shared and distributed authority. Universities are places of such influence that they will, either through action or inaction, shape the society around them, and it would be a scandal for them to sit passively by as the political structures aligned with their mission degrade around them. They cannot be complacent: they must look hard at who they admit, how they teach, how they explore and share knowledge, and how they connect their discoveries with the teeming, diverse world beyond their walls. In this light, the relevant question is not, *How do we shape society to nourish the university?* but rather, *How does the university best foster democracy in our society?*

Answering this question calls for an explicit interrogation of the ways in which the university can serve and enrich liberal democracy. To the extent that the university is found to be significant—or, even more dramatically, indispensable—for liberal democracy, then it is necessary to evaluate, with rigor and courage, how well it is discharging that role and to consider reforms that make it a better steward. The university should brook no difference in obligation from that which is borne by other key institutions—the elected branches of government, the courts, media, and the vast political bureaucracy—at a time when liberal democracy is under profound stress.

This is, I believe, what the university owes democracy.

A Necessary Tension

One of the first times the term *liberal democracy* was printed in English to refer to a distinctive form of popular government was in an expansive 1867 essay on the meaning of the American Civil War.[26] Although published in an American periodical, its author was the French Catholic aristocrat Charles de Montalembert, who had followed the war from Paris with close interest and who believed the Union's victory signaled something truly exhilarating—it had made democracy a historical inevitability. Every nation stood at a crossroads to decide what sort of democracy it would be.

For Montalembert, the choices were stark. On the one side was *Caesarean democracy*, in which political authority was concentrated "in one all powerful."[27] Montalembert and his contemporaries—who had experienced the revolutions of 1848 in France and watched with horror as the democratically elected president Louis Napoléon swiftly consolidated power and established the Second French Empire—knew such regimes intimately. The alternative was *liberal democracy*, a form of popular rule that maintained a precarious balance between "unlimited public opinion," or popular sovereignty, and "individual liberty."[28] Montalembert believed that the United States, which had managed to abolish slavery and had evaded dictatorship even in the throes of a political emergency, was the country with the greatest chance to realize this balance.[29] It could truly be, as Abraham Lincoln had described it in the Gettysburg Address, "a nation conceived in Liberty, and dedicated to the proposition that all men are created equal."[30] From its earliest articulation, then, liberal democracy was defined by what political philosopher Gordon Graham has described as a "necessary tension" between two very different political and philosophical traditions: democracy and liberalism.[31]

Democracy, of course, reflects a commitment to political equality and popular sovereignty. The idea of a society governed by an enlightened citizenry first took root in ancient Greece, when the Athenian leader Cleisthenes instituted reforms that redistributed political power from a concentrated group of aristocratic families to male citizens from every village (*deme*) in the city-state by involving them directly in the processes of law-making and legal judgment. In the more than twenty-five hundred years since, our idea of democracy has come to connote not the direct democracy of Cleisthenes's Athens but electoral democracy, in which citizens choose their leaders in regular elections.[32] Whatever specific form it takes, democracy has always privileged the will of the majority and the wisdom of crowds.[33]

Liberalism, by contrast, is a moral and political philosophy grounded in the idea of individual human freedom. While its genealogy can be traced to critiques of religious orthodoxy and arbitrary rule in the seventeenth and eighteenth centuries, it truly began to take shape as a coherent philosophical paradigm in the nineteenth century.[34] In the work of John Stuart Mill, Tocqueville, Montalembert, and others, liberalism evolved to champion personal autonomy and human dignity, freedom of thought and belief, and reasoned debate as a means of progress. In the political realm, these philosophical convictions have long led self-avowed liberals to cherish rule-based institutions, which, as Canadian Supreme Court Justice Rosalie Abella has said of the courts, "are not there to cater to the majority . . . [but] can be impartial, risk being unpopular, and be able to do things that protect minorities."[35]

Clearly, democracy and liberalism do not exist in easy alignment with one another. It is that collision of opposites that is a vital part of liberal democracy's genius, however. The fusion of these two ideas binds the notion of a government responsive to popular will to the imperative to protect individual rights and preserve rule of law. In fact, the push and pull between these structures can be regarded as one of its unique sources of strength. After all, liberal democracies don't have the dubious luxury of stagnation or complacency. They are dynamic and sometimes turbulent societies, always seeking and accommodating new generations of citizens to renew them.

These societies are worth protecting. Across its history, liberal democracy has ushered in historic advances in the vindication of popular needs and the protection of political rights, achievements against which other systems of governance pale. Beyond that, liberal democracies have promoted the flourishing of human potential more broadly. They are more peaceful than authoritarian regimes, less corrupt, and less subject to terrorism, internal strife, and violent overthrows or instability.[36] In the words of one scholar, the principle that democracies do not go to war against one another is "as close as anything we have to an empirical law in international relations."[37] Moreover, they experience lower levels of infant mortality, longer life spans, and have greater economic development and even higher standards of living.[38] As Nobel Prize–winning economist Amartya Sen memorably put it, "no substantial famine has ever occurred in a democratic country."[39]

None of these facts is meant to paper over the reality that the promises of liberal democracy have been realized imperfectly. Indeed, for all that liberal democracy has given the world, its aspirations all too often have exceeded its realities. Now, the gulf between expectation and reality has become especially pronounced. The mass protests in 2020 over the deaths of George Floyd, Breonna Taylor, Ahmaud Arbery, and so many other Black Americans at the hands of police were tragic reminders of the history of racial injustice in the United States and the long road left to walk toward true equity. The #MeToo movement has called painful attention to the violence and inequities facing women and LGBTQ people. And disparities in access to quality health care, housing, and treatment have led to worse health outcomes and shortened life spans for far too many, especially Black and Native American populations.[40] Meanwhile, the widening gaps between rich and poor across the liberal democratic world have made clear that our economic system too often privileges the few at the expense of the many. In so many instances, change has come far too slow and too late, and liberal democracies have too often been complacent in the face of disparities. With the full recognition of its failings, however, I believe sincerely that the role that liberal democracy has played in the improvement of the human condition is profound and unmistakable.

Liberal democracy's contributions are never permanent, and the balance between liberalism and democracy can be easily upset. When, for instance, the will of the majority becomes the author of its own demise by electing a tyrant willing to transgress democratic norms, to dismantle democratic institutions, to abandon the most basic tenets of political reciprocity, and to lock in electoral success by removing safeguards for long-term advantage, we see the emergence of what Fareed Zakaria called "illiberal democracy" (a close cousin of Montalembert's notion of "Caesarean democracy").[41] Less urgent but no less real is the danger of a nominally democratic state that preserves the institutions of political liberalism—such as regulatory agencies to protect the rule of law and courts to safeguard rights—but does so with such a dense accumulation of rules that popular input is inhibited and politics becomes the sole dominion of elites who can navigate those rules to their advantage. Yascha Mounk has called this "undemocratic liberalism," and Tocqueville called it "soft despotism," a form of social control that "does not tyrannize, but . . . compresses, enervates, extinguishes, and stupefies a people."[42]

Of course, the unmaking of a liberal democracy rarely plays out along such clearly defined lines; these are combustible processes that react in fluid and unexpected ways. Nevertheless, the critical point is that both liberalism and democracy are essential, they each require constant and watchful nurturing, and this schematic offers a glimpse of what is at stake when the uneasy union of liberalism and democracy is disrupted, and perhaps irreversibly damaged.

A Democratic Recession

Several years ago, a vast multidisciplinary coalition of scholars from around the world formed the Varieties of Democracy Project to take a precise measure of the health of democracy. Now one of the largest social science enterprises of its kind, this global network of more than three thousand experts has assembled data that show, in grand empirical sweep, the emergence and the erosion of liberal democracy. Their data confirm in painstaking detail what scholars have been eyeing anxiously for years: while liberal democracy had steadily spread across the globe from World War II through the end of the twentieth century, it has since entered a period of decline. In 1996, more than a quarter of the world's population lived in countries that were democratizing.[43] By 2020, that number had plummeted to almost 5 percent, while nearly 30 percent—or 2.6 billion people—live in countries that are becoming more autocratic.[44] The group reported that our world has now retreated "back to the global level of democracy recorded shortly after the end of the Soviet Union."[45] In the words of democracy scholar Larry Diamond, we are in the midst of a "democratic recession."[46]

Many of the forces driving this recession will be familiar to the reader. The economic fallout from the 2008 global financial crisis, rapid demographic changes, and massive transformations in media and communications technology have formed a toxic brew of ethno-nationalism, frustration at elites, and conspiratorial suspicion that have upended liberal democratic society.

For me, one of the defining traits of this retreat has been a stunning rise in anti-institutional sentiment. In the United States, trust in institutions ranging from Congress to the news media to organized religion—with the military as one notable exception—has fallen in recent years to, in some surveys, fifty-year lows.[47] A deep vein of suspicion around institutions has become an endemic source of frustration on all sides of the political divide. In many countries, authoritarian-leaning leaders are exploiting this weakness to accrue more power to themselves. Prime Minister Jarosław Kaczyński of Poland has turned state television networks into propaganda machines and has assumed control over the country's court system.[48] Rodrigo Duterte, president of the Philippines, has ruthlessly attacked the Catholic Church, even calling on the public to "kill those useless bishops."[49] And closest to home, Donald Trump routinely attacked every institution—from the legislature to the news media to the judiciary to agencies within the executive branch to the very electoral system that launched him to power in the first place—that challenged or checked him.[50]

Despite the aspersions cast over our institutions in recent years, they remain critical to the health of our democracy—to maintaining that delicate balance of liberalism and democracy, of rule of law and majority will—and ought to be reformed rather than abandoned. This is a conviction I hold deeply. It is one borne out of personal and professional experience. When my father's family fled Poland for Canada at the outset of the Second World War, they found a country that although not entirely hospitable was composed of institutions that made the opportunity to live a full and flourishing life available to them, their children, and, eventually, their grandchildren. I have also spent years not only leading academic institutions but also intensively studying how institutions evolve, change, and interface with the societies of which they are a part, which has led me to see in theory and practice the power of institutions to better lives and uphold the animating principles of democratic society. Our core democratic institutions are vital intermediaries between citizens and governments that preserve both the popular will and rule of law, performing that consequential work of fusing democracy and liberalism together.

Many institutions perform this work. Some are political, like legislatures that channel the popular will into public law, courts that protect individual liberty against the overweening exercise of power, or even political parties that—in the ideal, of course—temper the excesses of public opinion by packaging diverse views into broad governing coalitions. Existing alongside these are institutions that sit outside of politics, such as the independent media that cultivate an informed electorate and serve as a watchdog over those in power, and voluntary associations like churches and community organizations through which citizens develop the customs and habits of coming together and acting toward a shared interest or enterprise. These entities hold a special relevance in promoting the common good and protecting individual liberty, and in cushioning the tensions between the many and the few.[51] They are integral to the success or failure of liberal democracy.

The past several years have occasioned soul-searching within many of these institutions (the media, political parties, even religious organizations) as to whether they have fallen asleep at the wheel, whether they are culpable in some way for the decline of liberal democracy, and if so, how they might better acquit their roles.[52] But one critical institution has been absent from these conversations.

A Carrier of Democratic Values

Our colleges and universities are indispensable to liberal democracy.

As I will develop in this book, this is a capacity into which universities have grown over time, but it was present from the very beginnings of our democracy, a point sometimes obscured or minimized in histories of American higher education. Indeed, from the earliest days of the republic, universities were considered to be integral to the democratic project. At first, their role was seen to be limited to cultivating democratic citizens and to offering young people from a variety of backgrounds a chance at a liberal education and, perhaps, a better life. Yet the scale at which they executed these aims was vanishingly small. In 1851, there were fewer than five hundred colleges serving only about sixty thousand students (less than 1 percent of the population) throughout the entire United States.[53] That fact didn't prevent one contemporary observer from describing the United States as "a land of Colleges."[54]

One can only imagine what he would have said today. As of 2018, the United States boasted almost four thousand postsecondary institutions—from liberal arts colleges to sprawling private and public research universities to regional colleges to community colleges to institutions that exist entirely online—educating nearly 20 million students, employing 1.5 million faculty members, and receiving more than $40 billion in federal research funding.[55]

As they have widened their reach, our colleges and universities have acquired additional capacities. They have come to be not only the educators of well-rounded citizens, but also certifiers of expertise, gateways to opportunity, and places of pluralistic inclusion that mirror the nation itself. Further, they produce research and knowledge that are integral to the formation of reasoned public policy and essential to checking the excesses of power. And they have harnessed their resources for the betterment of society through medicine, public health, the economic development of cities, and partnerships with communities. Truly, colleges and universities are among liberal democracy's cornerstone institutions, and they play an indispensable role in the exercise of building, maintaining, and inspiring liberal democracy.[56]

This immense potential has been brought into clearest relief during America's most convulsive moments. When the democratic project felt most imperiled, the nation turned to its universities to enter the breach.

This was true at its founding, when George Washington called for the establishment of a national university to unite the fledgling nation under the banner of learning, and when colleges adapted their curricula and structures to the aims of forming what Thomas Jefferson called "the statesmen, legislators & judges, on whom public prosperity, & individual happiness are so much to depend."[57] It was true at the onset of the Civil War, when President Lincoln signed into law the first of the Morrill Land-Grant College Acts, setting into motion the creation of the sprawling system of land-grant universities that came to be known as "democracy's colleges" and would eventually include historically Black colleges in the South, opening up opportunity for advancement for students in all parts of a fractured country and from all walks of life. It was true during the height of the Gilded Age, when rampant corruption and abject inequality threatened to sabotage the promise of democracy, and politicians enlisted academics to help them shape sweeping political and economic reforms. It was true after World War II, when—with the nation reeling from democracy's near demise at the hands of fascism—President Harry S. Truman turned to the nation's universities, convening a national commission on democracy and higher education that declared "the first and most essential charge upon higher education is that at all levels and in all its fields of specialization, it shall be the carrier of democratic values, ideals, and process."[58]

We stand at another such point of vulnerability. Our institutions of higher education can be neither indifferent nor passive in the face of democratic backsliding.

I believe that universities should be recognized as standing firmly among the institutions critical to securing the full promise of liberal democracy and sharing in the responsibility to protect it when its legitimacy and its durability are at risk. In fact, I maintain that few other social institutions rival the university, at its best, in the sheer breadth of its vaunted contributions to liberal democracy's twin promises of equality and liberty. Economists have even now demonstrated through empirical study that—historically, at least—higher levels of college education have made democracies more likely to endure and autocracies more likely to democratize.[59] The fates of higher education and liberal democracy are deeply, inextricably intertwined. With strongmen either in power or waiting in the wings and democracy in question, now is a time at which universities must purposefully and self-consciously embrace their role as one of the stewards of the liberal democratic experiment.

The Plan of the Book

The core of my argument is as follows. First, colleges and universities are essential to the flourishing of liberal democracy. Second, these institutions have come to acquire this role over time, as they have gathered about them new functions and reimagined old ones. Third, over the past several decades, they too often have faltered in their role, becoming distracted and distended by the exigencies of the moment. And finally, they have a responsibility to act in defense of the liberal democratic experiment as institutions that enrich and are enriched by democracy, and are inextricably intertwined with democracy's values and ends.

As the president of Johns Hopkins University—America's first research university—for more than a decade and, before that, as provost of one its oldest universities, the University of Pennsylvania, I have had the privilege to witness time and again the immense and incredible contributions of the American university to democratic life. I have watched undergraduates from all backgrounds and all regions flourish on campuses and discover their potential as leaders and scholars. I have watched as discoveries made in laboratories and amidst library stacks are transformed into life-saving treatments for deadly diseases, or antidotes to the poison of our public discourse, or enduring policies that improve the equitable treatment of all. And I have watched people's minds (including my own) be changed through impassioned but reasoned debate.

But I have also experienced many of the alarming trends of our democratic moment: the admissions policies we have allowed to accrue that stack the deck against talented low- and middle-income students; the ways in which our curricula have abdicated responsibility for teaching the habits of democracy; the incentives that have unintentionally hobbled the research enterprise and fostered distrust; and the hyperpolarization and self-segregation that have undercut our ability as educational institutions devoted to expressive freedom to speak to one another in a way that promotes compromise and mutual understanding.

This book details many of those experiences (the successes as well as the failures), but it also takes a long and broad view of the history and sweep of higher education to offer achievable reforms for the future. It seeks to evaluate universities' role and assess their ability to enhance our capacity to contribute to liberal democratic flourishing by tracing those argumentative strands through four of the key functions American higher education has acquired in the course of its history: (1) launching meritorious individuals up the social ladder (social mobility), (2) educating citizens for democracy (civic education), (3) creating and disseminating knowledge (stewardship of facts), and (4) cultivating the meaningful exchange of ideas across difference (pluralism). These do not represent the extent of American higher education's connections to liberal democracy, but they are critical capacities in which our colleges and universities both have particular purchase, and in which they have unfortunately regressed.

In taking this expansive approach, I seek to broaden our conversation about the place of the university in a democracy. For too long, this conversation has mostly arisen in the context of long debates over campus culture, without a full consideration of all the other capacities of the modern university that impact and shape liberal democracy. This narrow aperture dates back, at least, to books like William F. Buckley Jr.'s *God and Man at Yale* in 1951 or, later, Allan Bloom's 1987 bestseller *The Closing of the American Mind*, which argued that colleges had "failed democracy and impoverished the souls of today's students" by ousting the search for the good life from the undergraduate curriculum.[60] Versions of this debate proliferate today in op-eds, reports, and books—including Anthony Kronman's *The Assault on American Excellence* and even titles that explicitly invoke Bloom, like Greg Lukianoff and Jonathan Haidt's *The Coddling of the American Mind*.[61] The issues these works raise are important, but undergraduate education is just one part of a much larger story, and it is time we widened our purview beyond higher education's responsibility to the American mind and to its responsibility to the liberal democratic project more broadly.

In the chapters that follow, I explore the nature and the consequences of the relationship between liberal democracy and universities through studies of each of the four functions I've identified above. Each chapter begins by considering the relationship between a given function of the university and liberal democracy.

I then sketch a history of how this function evolved and changed within American higher education, with the hope of capturing for readers the sweep, the texture, and the nuance of university contributions to American democracy. These histories lead naturally into expositions of how and why colleges and universities have lapsed in the execution of a given function. I conclude with one or more proposals for colleges and universities to recover from these lapses. The solutions I offer are informed by my experience of more than three decades as dean of the Faculty of Law at the University of Toronto, as provost of the University of Pennsylvania, and as president of Johns Hopkins University, alongside noteworthy developments occurring at other colleges and universities across our country. In some cases, they take the form of specific policy recommendations and, in others, of broader shifts in orientation.

The chapters adhere to a common structure, but the contours of each story I tell are unique and worthy of independent consideration. I have sought throughout this book to cull insights from disciplines and perspectives across the academic enterprise. My sincere hope for readers of this book is that in both its content and its form, it demonstrates how much the university has to offer to democratic society.

Chapter 1 focuses on social mobility. At this moment, the liberal democratic dream of equal opportunity is more elusive than ever for many in contemporary America. For most of their history, colleges and universities gradually expanded access to college for people of all socioeconomic backgrounds, a feat achieved through the creation of public university systems and community colleges, through visionary legislation like the G.I. Bill and the Higher Education Act, and through massive investments in financial aid. But in the past thirty to forty years, states have scaled back financial support for higher education, federal funding has stagnated and lost focus, and universities have embraced admissions practices that too often advantage wealthy students and disadvantage poor ones. These trends have accelerated the stratification of higher education. The solution for addressing this dire problem will need to be far-ranging, including robust financial aid initiatives to mitigate the burdens of student debt. To start, I call for the reinvestment in financial aid by governments and for the elimination of legacy preferences in college admissions.

In chapter 2, I turn to civic education. Since the founding of the United States, leaders have called for higher education to play a role in the formation of democratic citizens. For most of the nineteenth century, colleges and universities sought to develop students' moral faculties; throughout the late nineteenth and early twentieth centuries, they championed training in scientific reasoning as the cure for society's ills; and after World War II, they created ambitious general education programs to instill in students the knowledge and values of the often fraught and contested notion of a common cultural inheritance. Since the 1980s, however, the dominant paradigm for civic education at colleges and universities has been community service. This movement has been truly important and has done much to strengthen connections between students and the communities of which they are a part. But as the source of a civic education, it is incomplete because it leaves untouched a knowledge of democratic history and political institutions, as well as many of the skills necessary to engage those institutions effectively to create lasting change. To ensure that students encounter an education in democracy during their college years, I call for the establishment of a Democracy Requirement.

Chapter 3 considers universities as fact-producing and fact-checking institutions. Liberal democracies need reliable knowledge and a shared sense of truth for citizens to make informed decisions as voters and community members, for legislators to develop rational public policy, and for holding institutions like the free press, leaders, and governments to account. With the founding of our first research universities in the 1870s, American higher education has been among the most important institutions for credentialing expertise; for conducting advanced research; and for unearthing, preserving, and disseminating facts. In time, democratic societies came to embrace universities as beacons of factual truth, and government support of research across the natural sciences, social sciences, and humanities has unleashed countless discoveries and strengthened the university's role as an anchor for democratic life. Yet this relationship has frayed in recent years, as questions from within and without the university have accumulated about the objectivity, legitimacy, and accuracy of the academy as a locus of truth and facts. Among the most troubling causes of this is the reproducibility crisis (the growing evidence that much scientific research cannot be replicated) that is leaving no part of the academy unaffected. Looking at the recent experiences of universities and scientific expertise during the COVID-19 pandemic, I consider what lessons we can draw in harnessing technology to begin to address this crisis of trust.

In chapter 4, I turn toward the question of diversity and speech on campus. Colleges and universities are microcosms of pluralistic, multiethnic democracy that have the capacity to model for students how to interact with one another across a vast spectrum of experiences to forge democratic compromise, consensus, and will. Our campuses today are far more diverse than in past eras, yet we do not fully or adequately encourage the interactions and exchanges across differences that are foundational to a healthy democracy. In a multitude of ways, universities have essentially given students a pass to opt out of encounters with people dissimilar from themselves. Higher education has rightly focused on promoting diversity in admissions, but it has neglected to foster pluralism once students arrive, which has given rise to an undercurrent of silencing and a dearth of substantive debate. The answer to this dilemma, I argue, lies in a move toward a more purposeful pluralism on our campuses, undergirded by policies that drive students to have more encounters with those unlike themselves, and that then help deepen and enrich these interactions.

Not all of these functions developed in concert with one another, and not all are operative in the same way—or to the same degree—for every single institution of higher education. At points this book will draw from the broad mosaic of institutions that comprise higher education, from the selective research universities that play a central role in knowledge creation, to the liberal arts colleges that have been the beating heart of social experimentation and curricular innovation, to the two-year community colleges that enroll millions of students each year and propel so many Americans up the social ladder. Framing this discussion, however, is the research university, which, besides being the place where I have spent most of my career, occupies a large role in the public conscience on issues of culture and politics, and weaves together the four connections to democracy—social mobility, civic education, stewardship of facts, and pluralism—discussed in this book.

It is not easy to change an institution. This is especially the case for colleges and universities, which are by design conservative, heterogeneous, decentralized, and often cumbersome. They are a perfect example of path-dependent institutions, those human organizations that, once established, accrue self-reinforcing mechanisms that make the exploration of alternative arrangements increasingly costly. Within such institutions, meaningful transformation becomes truly possible only during periods of change and profound uncertainty. Economists call these "critical junctures." The history of the university has seen such moments before, whether with the birth of the research university in the wake of Reconstruction or with the rise of the multiversity during the aftermath of World War II. What makes critical junctures tricky, however, is that—in the words of Canadian legal and economics scholar Michael Trebilcock—they are extraordinarily difficult "to identify with high levels of confidence while they are happening, without the benefit of hindsight."[62] In other words, we tend not to know whether we are at a critical juncture until it's too late.

As I write this, the United States is facing a raging global pandemic, a fragile liberal international order, and an economic recession. These lead me to suspect that liberal democracy and our universities stand, once again, at a critical juncture. I am also convinced that there are actions we can take now in our admissions policies, housing policies, curricula, extracurricular programming, and faculty research that have the potential to direct our academic institutions more firmly along a democratic path and, in the process, buoy the democratic idea.

An American Experience

The last thing to mention is that this is a fundamentally American book. Of course, as this introduction reveals, the connection between universities and liberal democracy extends far beyond this country, and the discussion to come will occasionally take the reader to other countries. But the focus of the book will be on the American experience. This is in part for reasons of exposition— each nation's system of higher education is at least slightly different, and to traverse each of the discussions to come in the depth that is needed, it is sensible to home in on a single country. It is also an autobiographical decision. I am a Canadian by birth and previously served as a faculty member and dean at the University of Toronto. But for the past fifteen years of my career, I have had the privilege to serve as a leader in two great American universities. The American focus of this book allows me to bring my own experiences and insights from those positions to bear on the discussion where it is appropriate, and to reflect where necessary on how the university I now lead—the nation's first research university, which opened its doors a century after the signing of the Declaration of Independence—is realizing its own democratic calling.

But there is something else—something singular about the American experience—and the questions I asked myself in preparing this book kept bringing that experience front and center. Although there are universities that predated America's founding, and although that founding predated the birth of the modern university as we recognize it today, the two came of age alongside each other, guiding each other's trajectories in a manner that connects them not only in impact or mission, but also as a matter of historical fact. It is in America where colleges and universities most indelibly imprinted themselves on the history of liberal democracy and where the values of liberal democracy most intimately shaped the evolution of higher education. By investigating this shared history, I aim to show anew what this institution and this form of governance still have to offer one another.

I believe the university must seize this moment to confront directly and courageously the challenges before it (and others still on the horizon) to requite its responsibility to liberal democracy. Such a project has never seemed more urgent.

ONE

American Dreams

Access, Mobility, Fairness

IN THE LATE 1990S, I served as dean of the Faculty of Law at the University of Toronto. As Canada's most selective law school, the competition for admission was—and remains—fierce. Applicants were always in search of anything they could do or add to their résumé to secure an advantage in the application process. Sometimes their parents would intervene on their behalf. In my position as dean, it was not uncommon for alumni whose children were applying to the school to approach me and inquire what kind of admissions bump their students would receive by virtue of being a legacy. The answer I gave was always the same: none whatsoever.

One encounter stands out. A prominent and philanthropic alumnus whose child had been denied admission to the school contacted me in the hope that I would reconsider the application. After all, he reasoned, his relationship with the school must mean something. As I had done in many similar situations, I explained that there were clear guardrails in place that fettered my capacity to reverse this decision. I simply had no ability to admit his child. Before our phone call ended, he said something that has been etched in my memory ever since: "If you really want to stand shoulder to shoulder with the great Ivy League law schools in the United States, you better start acting like one."

When I came to work in the United States, I saw firsthand how true these words were. For all of the progress that highly selective universities have started to make in recruiting low-income and historically underrepresented students, they continue to cling tenaciously to admissions policies like legacy preferences that confer significant advantages on children of privilege. Legacy admissions, when coupled with the considerable advantages that many of these children already have—like stable families, engaged parents, high-quality K–12 schools, ample extracurricular opportunities for personal enrichment and development (not to mention résumé fodder)—set these applicants up to triumph over applicants from less fortunate circumstances, fueling the argument that universities have failed to honor the Jeffersonian ideal of equal opportunity and merit. Several years into my tenure as president of Johns Hopkins, we made the formal decision to strike at one particularly egregious instance of this by eliminating entirely the use of legacy preferences in our admissions.[1]

I will have more to say about this decision at the end of this chapter. It is undeniable, though, that highly selective colleges and universities in the United States continue to be perceived as bastions of elitism and hereditary privilege. Events like the "Varsity Blues" college admissions bribery scandal in 2019 only reinforce this theme. While the actions taken by the parents on behalf of their children in that case were unquestionably illegal and their prosecution entirely justified, they were nevertheless a stark reminder of the numerous lawful means (legacy preferences being but one) by which some affluent students gain entrance to the country's most prestigious universities at the expense of talented students who lack the same financial resources, social networks, and genealogical good fortune. In this, our universities have done, and continue to do, grave disservice to our commitment to serve as crucial sites for instantiating the American Dream for all based on merit and not on inherited privilege.

The American Dream means many things to many people, but at its core is the promise that all people, regardless of the station of their birth, may climb the socioeconomic ladder on the basis of their own innate endowments and efforts. The term was coined by historian James Truslow Adams in his sweeping history of the American continent from the Aztecs to the Jazz Age, *The Epic of America*.[2] For Adams, the animating principle and ideal of this history was the belief that all people should have the opportunity "to rise in the economic scale" and "to develop our capacities to the full, unhampered by unjust restrictions of caste or custom."[3] This American Dream, he argued, was intrinsic to American democracy.[4]

Numerous thinkers before and since have recognized socioeconomic or social mobility—the ability for people to move up (or down) the economic ladder—as a cornerstone of the American experience. In the nineteenth century, Alexis de Tocqueville saw the constant shuffling of people between classes as the quintessence of a "democratic, enlightened, and free" nation, in part because it promoted vital cross-class interactions with the potential to introduce "a host of ideas, notions, and desires to people that they would not have had if ranks had been fixed and society immobile."[5] More than a century later, prominent sociologists like Peter Blau and Otis Duncan argued that mobility contributed to the stability of democratic societies by enabling citizens to project future versions of themselves into classes other than the one they were born into, thus expanding their political sympathies beyond the bounds of their present circumstance.[6] Now, in the twenty-first century, scholars and commentators of all stripes and creeds remain keenly focused on the ways mobility might still restore trust in the liberal democratic institutions and combat the alienation that can be so corrosive to the democratic experiment.[7]

A striking 2019 study by political scientists Christian Houle and Michael Miller explored the relationship between mobility and democracy through the experiences and perspectives of more than one hundred thousand people in thirty-three countries throughout Latin America and Africa.[8] Their findings are remarkable. In democratic countries, people who perceived themselves as being better off than their parents expressed greater support for democracy and were more opposed to authoritarianism or military rule. Across all countries, these individuals were "significantly more likely to believe in personal autonomy, to trust others, and to believe their society is fair."[9] By contrast, downward mobility made individuals less likely to support democratic values. These results held even when the authors controlled for factors such as the level of corruption in the government, the degree of poverty in the country, and whether the individual was rich or poor. The conclusion Houle and Miller reached is striking and lends empirical backing for what theorists had surmised for ages: social mobility is in fact deeply interwoven with democracy.

For most of its history, the United States was regarded as a vast wellspring of mobility—at least for those who were free to participate fully in society. This was the view of Tocqueville himself, who wrote that in this country, "fortune turns . . . with incredible rapidity and experience teaches that it is rare to see two generations collect its favors."[10] Recent studies of handwritten census records indicate that he likely had it right. In the mid-nineteenth century, the chance that children would end up in a different social class than their parents (intergenerational mobility) was greater in the United States than in Europe, in part because of higher rates of public schooling and rapid geographic expansion in the United States.[11]

In the decades that followed, however, mobility between generations in the United States fluctuated. Most experts now agree that by the late nineteenth century, mobility began to drop as a consequence of uneven economic development in the reconstructed South and the entrenched inequalities of the Gilded Age. This decline lasted until roughly the middle of the twentieth century, when the massive postwar investment in education and industrial development sparked a steady rise in rates of intergenerational mobility.[12] The tide soon turned again when the devastating economic shocks of the 1970s caused rates of mobility to fall for men, even as women—entering the labor force for the first time in substantial numbers—began to experience newly elevated rates of upward mobility.[13]

Today, economists contest many aspects of mobility, but at least two areas of broad consensus have emerged. The first is that the United States appears to have fallen behind many of its peers when it comes to "relative mobility," or the rate at which individuals move between rungs of the socioeconomic ladder relative to their parents.[14] That is, it is now harder for people in the United States to rise above the circumstances into which they were born than it is in other countries. This difference is especially apparent when one compares the mobility of the United States to that of countries such as Denmark and New Zealand that are now (according to the Varieties of Democracy Project) among the strongest and most resilient liberal democracies in the world.[15]

The second area of agreement is that the United States is now facing an alarming "stickiness at the ends" of the socioeconomic spectrum.[16] This means that even if families are mobile across the middle of the socioeconomic ladder, the poor are finding it far more difficult to escape from poverty than in the past, while the rich have become increasingly adept at creating advantages for themselves that consolidate their affluence across generations.[17] Brookings Institution scholar Richard Reeves has termed this latter phenomenon a "glass floor."[18] There are many likely causes for this ossification of the rich and poor at the extreme ends of the income spectrum, but one factor is surely the skyrocketing economic inequality that has plagued liberal democracies in recent decades, the United States in particular.

Such trends have rendered our world eerily similar to the one F. Scott Fitzgerald immortalized in *The Great Gatsby*, the tragic narrative of a poor boy from North Dakota who manages to rise spectacularly from poverty to the extravagant and rarified world of Long Island high society only to be killed amidst his opulence. The parallels of material excess and inequality are so apparent that the almost century-old novel has secured a place of honor in contemporary economic literature as the namesake of the "Great Gatsby Curve," a graph positing a close relationship between rising inequality and declining mobility. The curve itself is a topic of debate by economists, but it speaks to an intuitive connection, summed up by economist Isabel Sawhill's observation that "when the rungs of the income ladder get too far apart, it is harder to climb."[19] The curve captures an inescapable tragedy of the current American condition: at the same time that mobility has slowed, huge disparities in wealth and income have opened up in the economy. These divides are unrivaled in modern—and possibly all of—American history, and they are placing their own strain on the sustainability of democracies, draining faith in core institutions and frustrating the social cohesion that binds them.[20]

Still, one of the more striking facts of American economic life in the past century is that even when *actual* mobility has faltered, *faith* in mobility has endured. The American Dream, in other words, has held strong. Social scientists have long marveled that Americans managed to remain far more optimistic about their ability to get ahead than citizens in other countries, even as those countries begin to catch or even surpass the United States in rates of actual mobility.[21] They credited the persistence of the American Dream to America's long constitutional tradition of egalitarianism that is free from the entrenched vestiges of feudalism; a citizenry invigorated and shaped by immigrants who traveled to this country in search of a better life; and, importantly, the early and persistent prominence in American life of colleges and universities, which have always promised citizens new opportunities.[22]

One can understand how this perception of mobility—the steadfast dream of the possibility of a better life—is as important as the reality of mobility in shaping the aspirations and ideals of a citizenry, as well as the fate of a liberal democracy. Now, however, even the perception of mobility is showing signs of fading. In the face of ever-widening inequality, ever-deepening technological upheaval, and two periods of severe economic disruption in a span of fifteen years, there are the earliest signs that the American Dream as a realizable goal may be eroding in American consciousness, with severe social and political consequences. From World War II to the 1990s, it was common for most Americans to say they were confident their children would be "better off" than they were. But in the twenty-first century, these numbers have plummeted, from nearly 50 percent in 2001 to less than 30 percent in 2019.[23] Now that even this once unwavering faith in opportunity and mobility is no longer a guarantee, the consequences for the stability of liberal democracy are stark.

The Great Equalizers?

As it has evolved across the arc of American history, a university education has come to stand as one of the best guarantors of social mobility, at least for those students fortunate enough to gain entry.

The data are undeniable. One 2008 study found that a child in a family in the lowest income quintile was 3.8 times more likely to move into the highest income quintile during their lifetime with a college degree.[24] An American with a bachelor's degree in 2012 earned more than twice as much as an American with only a high school diploma, was more than twice as likely to be employed, and was three and a half times more likely to avoid poverty.[25] And the annual financial return on a bachelor's degree is now about 14 percent, far exceeding, in the words of one analysis, "the threshold for a good investment."[26]

The advantage provided by colleges and universities has soared in the past half century, a product of rapid technological change that has accelerated demand for highly skilled employees. Simply put, in terms of the knowledge and skills colleges and universities deliver, the specialized training they provide, and even the access to professional networks they unlock, a college degree has a propulsive and undeniable impact on individual opportunity. Universities have become indispensable way stations on the social ladder, among the core institutions that bear the immense responsibility of upholding not only the liberal ideal of individual flourishing and potential but also the democratic one of making opportunity ever more available.

Several years ago, Harvard economist Raj Chetty and colleagues undertook a sweeping study of more than 30 million college students between 1999 and 2013 to understand how well colleges and universities were moving students up the social ladder.[27] The researchers developed a metric they called a "mobility rate," which combined the fraction of students from the lowest income quintile at an institution with that institution's success at moving those students into the highest income quintile after graduation.

The standout institutions in Chetty's study were not, it turns out, the most selective schools, such as Harvard, Yale, Stanford, Duke, or MIT. Although these schools are exceptional in their capacity to launch students from the bottom income quintile to the top, the fraction of low-income students they enroll is low compared to some other institutions. Rather, the universities that proved most adept at enrolling high numbers of low-income students and moving those students up the social ladder at rates approaching the most selective schools were public universities like Cal State University, Los Angeles; the State University of New York at Stony Brook; and the University of Texas at El Paso. Chetty also found that the mobility provided by these colleges is, in his words, "scalable": their cost of educating a student is significantly lower than at many other universities.[28]

Perhaps the most remarkable observation in the study is that if every college in the United States had a mobility rate equivalent to the most mobile colleges, the country would achieve "perfect relative mobility, where children's outcomes were unrelated to their parents' incomes."[29] In other words, in a hypothetical world where each child were to attend college, and each college were to offer those students the combination of access and success *that the most mobile colleges already offer*, colleges could remove entirely the headwinds of social immobility in the country.

The power of higher education is so great that, at least in theory, colleges are capable of bringing about a world of unfettered opportunity.

In reality, of course, matters are more complex. For one thing, this model would require a substantial national commitment to raising the quality of education and student support at colleges and universities, so that these institutions can meet the bar set by the successfully mobile colleges. For another, in a country with vast inequalities in K–12 education and substantial disparities in the circumstances in which children are raised—including financial resources, engaged parents, safe and secure neighborhoods, nutritional sufficiency—not every child has an equal opportunity to be prepared for college. This is particularly true of the racial education gap in this country, where the lasting consequences of entrenched racism remain profound. Even so, studies such as Chetty's illuminate colleges' and universities' extraordinary capacity to serve as wellsprings of mobility, and as caretakers of the American Dream in the modern-day knowledge economy.

Given this capacity, the degree to which colleges and universities have come to embody just the opposite is especially distressing. They are now seen, as often as not, as ossified bastions of privilege and glaring symbols of inequality. The ways in which universities have contributed to, rather than resisted, the lure of privilege lies at the heart of recent critiques of meritocracy itself as an organizing principle for American democracy. Harvard philosopher Michael Sandel, for instance, locates colleges and universities at the center of his book *The Tyranny of Merit*. In his account, they have done "less to expand opportunity than to consolidate privilege" even as they have wrapped themselves in a cloak of meritocratic rhetoric.[30]

There is a painful truth in these critiques. Staggering disparities in higher education based on underlying socioeconomic circumstances are more than speculative. Nearly forty selective universities now enroll more students from the top 1 percent of incomes than from the bottom 60 percent of incomes.[31] The National Center for Education Statistics, meanwhile, reported that among a cohort of young people who were high school sophomores in 2002, only 14 percent of those from the bottom quarter of incomes had earned a four-year college degree (or higher) in 2012, compared to 60 percent for students from the top quarter.[32] Add to this the fact that 59 percent of children whose parents hold postgraduate degrees graduate from a four-year college, while only 17 percent of children of parents who never went to college do so. By some measures, then, *educational* immobility exerts an even firmer grip on American society than *socioeconomic* immobility, as highly educated parents pass their education on to their children at a greater rate than the rich pass on their socioeconomic status.[33]

Far from being the incubators of democratic mobility across generations, universities have come to represent, in the words of *The Economist*, a new "hereditary meritocracy."[34]

The rest of this chapter will explore how American universities—particularly our most elite institutions—have come to sabotage and deform, rather than to honor and defend, the ideal of equal opportunity. To be sure, the story of the American university is, in part, one of extraordinary investment, experimentation, and expansion. Fueled by transformative federal pieces of legislation (the Morrill Land-Grant College Acts of 1862 and 1890, the G.I. Bill of 1944, and the Higher Education Act of 1965), massive investment in higher education at the state level, and the efforts of university leaders who saw the democratic potential of their institutions, the share of American adults who held a college degree climbed from less than 1 percent of Americans in 1870 to 36 percent in 2019.[35] In 2018, nearly 70 percent of high school seniors enrolled in college immediately after graduating.[36] But the history of universities as vehicles of social mobility is unfortunately also marked by long stretches of self-serving retrenchment, exclusion, and gatekeeping in which neglect, prejudice, and disinvestment have prevented too many students from enjoying the immense benefits of a quality college education.

Sadly, we are in such a period now. The retreat of the federal government from its once robust and full-throated support of higher education alongside depleted state funding for public higher education has put colleges and universities in the position of needing to bear ever more of the burden of sustaining higher education's promise of upward mobility. These institutions have executed on this immense responsibility falteringly and imperfectly. Even as colleges and universities have mouthed a commitment to broad access, their own policies too often undercut it by keeping high-achieving, low-income students on the outside looking in, and contributing to an internal sorting process that has concentrated affluent students at the most selective and elite institutions and remitted low-income students to less competitive institutions where the investments in their educational experience are diminished. There are many casualties of this gaping divide, not least of which is faith among wide swaths of the public in the possibilities of liberal democracy for individual flourishing. For too many lower- and middle-income families, the nation's colleges and universities, which ought to be our greatest emblem of equal opportunity, are seen as the exclusive reserve of privileged and entrenched elites. But just as decisions made by our colleges and universities have contributed to this reality, there are choices they can now make to close the divide and begin reclaiming higher education's legacy as a ladder of mobility for all.

"Poor Schollers" in a Land of Colleges

The first college scholarship in North America was endowed at Harvard in 1643 by Lady Ann Mowlson (née Radcliffe), the shrewd widow of a British merchant and a devout Puritan. Her gift consisted of a £100 donation, the interest of which was to be used as a "perpetuall stipend for and towards the yea[rly] maintenance of some *poor scholler*."[37] Lady Mowlson had been persuaded to make this contribution to the welfare of needy students in the colonies by two early boosters for Harvard who had ventured back to England to drum up support for the seven-year-old college. Unfortunately, the gift was grossly mismanaged from the start. After its first recipient was expelled for stealing gunpowder and cash, Harvard effectively forgot about the Mowlson money until 1893, when some ambitious historians rediscovered it and Harvard revived the fund.[38]

Its uneven history notwithstanding, Lady Mowlson's gift is significant. Endowed just a few years after Harvard's founding as the first college in what would become the United States, it shows that American higher education was from its earliest days focused on ensuring that a student's means ought not to be a barrier to a college education.

Throughout the seventeenth and eighteenth centuries, local churches, community associations, and wealthy citizens nurtured the spirit of Lady Mowlson's generosity by funding scholarships for the poor students who enrolled each year at the handful of colleges scattered across British North America. By the early decades of the nineteenth century, however, this model of financing the education of needy students became increasingly strained, as the nation's first college boom got underway, with new colleges springing up across the landscape and new students thronging to attend them.[39]

It is estimated that in the first several decades of the nineteenth century, more than five hundred new colleges were founded, over two hundred of which survived into the 1870s.[40] The number of students also skyrocketed from just over a thousand in 1790 to sixty-three thousand in 1870.[41] Although college students still comprised only a miniscule fraction of the total college-aged population, the college movement was successful and widespread enough that the Presbyterian minister Absalom Peters was moved to call the United States of the mid-nineteenth century "a land of Colleges."[42]

There were many reasons for this onset of college fever. For rapidly growing religious denominations like the Baptists and Methodists, founding a bevy of colleges was an ideal method of training ministers and spreading the gospel. Colleges were points of intense local pride, too, beloved institutions that distinguished dispersed towns and regions in a rapidly expanding nation.[43] And, importantly, a college education had begun to emerge as a genuine vehicle for social mobility.

By 1840, a college education had become a sign of fitness for a host of careers, including the law, the ministry, engineering, and banking. Records also show that college graduates during this era were more likely to move from rural communities to bustling urban centers, to win political office, and to be listed in compendia of prominent Americans.[44] Although small and often underfunded, colleges offered real pathways to opportunity and tangible returns on investment. Citizens recognized this, too, as evidenced by the many students from modest backgrounds who flooded colleges during this period.

To meet the growing need for financial aid, new initiatives to finance the education of poor students—in addition to the informal system of private scholarships that had already been established—sprang forth. Some colleges established new "beneficiary funds" to support needy students, while others like Cooper Union in New York City and Berea College in Kentucky charged no tuition at all.[45] Newly formed associations like the American Education Society served as clearinghouses for charitable donations from people and organizations across the country.[46] And states, too, began to test programs and policies to support needy scholars. Massachusetts, for instance, passed a bank tax in 1814, proceeds of which were used to offset the tuition costs of poor students at Williams College, Bowdoin College, and Harvard.[47]

These various efforts were neither particularly systematic nor carefully coordinated, but they were effective. By 1860, more than 25 percent of New England college students came from families too poor to afford tuition, room, and board, and nearly 40 percent of students in the state of New York did not pay tuition.[48]

In an address delivered at Miami University in Ohio in 1835, eminent preacher Lyman Beecher was so moved by this collective drive to support higher education for all people regardless of background that he proclaimed that American colleges had become the "practical equalizers of society."[49] He had good reason to be optimistic, but he was surely overstating matters. As of yet, the nation's scattered collection of small colleges still only educated a fraction of students, and their emphasis on addressing economic inequality was piecemeal at best. Nor did they share any sort of cohesive vision for the role that higher education should play in the economic future of the nation, or for the precise forms of opportunity that colleges ought to provide to its citizens. The first attempt to realize such a vision on a national scale would come in 1862 with the passage of the Morrill Act.

Colleges for the People

On March 17, 1869, after years of grueling planning and more than a few setbacks, Iowa State Agricultural College welcomed its first class of 136 men and 37 women.[50] At a ceremony held that day on the college's Ames campus, former Iowa Lieutenant Governor Benjamin Gue commended the fledgling institution for helping to usher in a new era in American higher education. He proclaimed that the school would "supply a want long felt, for the benefit of that large and increasing army of students, who prefer to acquire a more thorough knowledge of the natural sciences, and useful arts." Moreover, he added, no one would be deprived of this education; the school's doors were open to all "anxious seekers for knowledge . . . regardless of sex, color, or condition."[51] Gue's praise of the practicality and accessibility of Iowa State reflected the optimism, enthusiasm, and democratic hope attached to the nation's first land-grant colleges established under the landmark Morrill Act of 1862.

Ushered through Congress during the middle of the Civil War, the Morrill Act was an audacious investment in the future of American education at a moment when the future of America itself was in severe doubt. The bill was the brainchild of Vermont congressman and self-taught son of a blacksmith Justin Smith Morrill, who had long dreamed of a national higher education system capable of strengthening the country's economy through scientific advances, of dispensing practical knowledge to students, and of being "accessible to all, but especially the sons of toil."[52] To achieve these lofty aims, the act granted states plots of federal land to use for the building of new colleges so long as they met a somewhat loose set of preconditions. In the twentieth century, the dozens of schools founded under the first Morrill Act would evolve into the world-renowned public institutions they are today and earn the moniker of "democracy's colleges."[53] In their early days, however, they fell somewhat short of the mark.

For all its sweeping vision, the Morrill Act did little in the way of providing a blueprint for how institutions founded under it should operate and toward what ends they should direct their efforts. The act specified only that, at Morrill schools, the "leading object shall be, without excluding other scientific and classical studies, and including military tactics, to teach such branches of learning as are related to agriculture and the mechanic arts . . . in order to promote the liberal and practical education of the industrial classes in the several pursuits and professions in life."[54] Morrill colleges were therefore expected to be a novel amalgamation of liberal arts colleges, agricultural research stations, engineering schools, and even potentially military training facilities. They had to balance myriad missions (even the group they were meant to serve, the "industrial classes," was undefined and interpreted broadly) that did little to clarify what kind of schools would be created in states that took the deal.

In the first few decades following the passage of the Morrill Act, states used the law's latitude to create a variety of schools, from devoted agricultural colleges with working farms to cutting-edge research institutions like Cornell University and Yale's Sheffield Scientific School to what one historian has termed "quasi-military schools."[55] In every state that accepted Morrill funds, contests erupted over what these institutions ought to be. Should they be devoted to a strictly agricultural education, as many farmers wanted? Should they commit themselves to a broad, liberal education that included a multitude of scientific subjects and only vocational education as an afterthought? Or should they pioneer original scientific discoveries?

The answers to these questions came to be bound up in whom the schools admitted and their aspirations for mobility. At Cornell University, New York State's land-grant school, founder Ezra Cornell's impulse to admit any eager student—including many with minimal formal education—often ran counter to the vision of Cornell's first president, Andrew Dickson White, of building a pioneering scientific research institution. For a time, the school was able to keep highly prepared students on a rigorous academic track while maintaining a separate vocational course of study for less prepared—and often poorer—students. After Ezra Cornell's death, White's vision of a premier research university ultimately prevailed, and the vocational track faded away almost entirely.[56]

Most early land-grant colleges followed paths similar to Cornell and thus did little to move the poorest students up the social ladder. Often, these institutions would adopt courses of study and academic standards tailored more toward well-to-do students than the more expansive education (often agricultural or vocational) that would have promoted true mobility. Without the academic preparation to successfully complete rigorous scientific courses and lacking the means to afford the cost of attendance, children from poorer families often found land-grant colleges closed to them.[57]

At Illinois Industrial University, for instance, even as more than 70 percent of students came from "agricultural, mechanical, or mercantile backgrounds" (the "industrial classes," broadly defined), a vast majority hailed from middle- to upper middle-class families, their parents the owners of highly lucrative farms and businesses. In fact, only 8 percent of the school's students were from families in the bottom 50 percent of the economic distribution.[58] And at Maine State College of Agriculture and Mechanical Arts, approximately 84 percent of graduates between 1872 and 1875 came from families of average to above-average means—hardly Morrill's "sons of toil."[59]

Their egalitarian rhetoric notwithstanding, the first waves of land-grant colleges did not immediately inaugurate a wholesale transformation of American higher education along more democratic lines. These schools were bold educational experiments, but they suffered from deep deficiencies.

This was especially true when it came to matters of race. Most northern and western land-grant colleges admitted African American students—even if only in tragically small numbers—and a network of fledgling Black colleges had emerged after the Civil War. But virtually all land-grant colleges in the Jim Crow–era South barred Black students from attending.[60]

In 1890, the US Congress sought to remedy this indefensible inequity by passing a second Morrill Act that aimed to provide some measure of racial equity in schools receiving federal funding. The law guaranteed that all Morrill schools would henceforth be eligible for annual appropriations—something not provided for in the 1862 act—so long as no "distinction of race or color is made in the admission of students."[61] States could sidestep this stipulation, however, if they established separate institutions specifically designed for African American students. Southern states uniformly chose this latter option, which made the Morrill Act of 1890 less a vehicle for the integration of higher education in the post-Reconstruction American South than a tool for expanding and supporting the existing network of Black colleges.[62]

The 1890 act conferred land-grant status on eleven existing Black colleges and helped to establish six additional ones, which today stand among the more than one hundred private and public historically Black colleges and universities (HBCUs) still in operation.[63] The 1890 land-grant institutions distinguished themselves for the breadth of their services. Many took upon themselves multiple roles as normal schools (to train teachers), as secondary schools (to remediate a deficit of K–12 schooling), and as agricultural training and research centers (to develop skilled farmers and a corps of Black scientists). In their early years, these colleges' ability to deliver on this last role was severely hindered by financial constraints, but they managed to serve as critical centers of primary and secondary education and, as important, teacher training.[64] In this respect, they played an absolutely vital role in putting in place the conditions for upward mobility for future generations of African Americans.

By 1900, Black colleges and universities—in one count—had graduated nearly two thousand students.[65] More than half of these graduates were teachers who played an essential role in expanding the educational attainment of young African Americans across the South. The racial gap in school attendance between whites and Blacks halved, and African American illiteracy rates sharply declined.[66] This, in turn, helped to expand professional opportunities and create the conditions for higher-level collegiate work for the generations served by these teachers. It was in this sense that W. E. B. Du Bois observed in a 1907 letter that Black colleges represented "the foundation of the school system and not its cap-stone."[67] Black land-grant colleges were indispensable in giving credence to assessments like Du Bois's and, like the institutions established by the 1862 act, in helping to set the stage for the next massive expansion of access to higher education that would occur in the early decades of the twentieth century.

To Teach Anybody—Anything—Anywhere

The dawn of the twentieth century marked a turning point in the story of American higher education. For the first time, college was securing itself as a critical pathway toward economic opportunity and occupational success for any person with talent and drive.

The number of students enrolled in colleges and universities skyrocketed from 63,000 in 1870 to more than 1,150,000 in 1944, the year the G.I. Bill became law.[68] As a share of the college-age population, enrollment grew fivefold in this period. Central to this shift was the spread of public K–12 schooling as a mainstay of American life, which generated a pipeline of students ready for a college education. And thanks to an economy increasingly reliant upon specialized knowledge and a higher education sector ever more defined by growth and differentiation (aided by the rise of technical schools for engineers, normal schools for teachers, and full-scale research universities capable of training students in applied science), the economic returns to a college education began to far outpace those of a high school degree.[69]

In 1937, *Life Magazine*—the quintessential publication of the aspirational American middle class—published a feature on colleges that called this period "the world's first great experiment in mass higher education." The piece described the myriad benefits of higher education in this era as constituting "the pith and kernel of what writers since Jefferson have called the American dream."[70]

Fueling the growth of higher education during these years was the nation's ever-expanding network of public universities, which by 1930 were enrolling four times as many students as private colleges.[71] Many of these schools had been founded under one of the Morrill Acts and had been receiving federal financial support since 1890, but they were now able to take flight thanks to rising state investments in higher education, which increased from $13 million per state in 1902 to $290 million by 1940.[72] This influx of state revenue enabled universities to resolve some of the fundamental tensions among academic excellence, scientific research, and broad access that had dogged Morrill institutions throughout the final decades of the nineteenth century—mostly, it turns out, by doing all three at once.[73]

In the early 1900s, schools like the University of Michigan and the University of Illinois emerged as fountainheads of cutting-edge research and insight. They built vibrant graduate and professional schools, recruited leading faculty from existing private research universities, created world-class libraries, and came together around new umbrella organizations like the Association of American Universities. They maintained high academic standards for their students and, importantly, still managed to keep tuition extremely low relative to private colleges: in 1933, the average annual tuition at public universities was $61 and $265 at private institutions.[74]

At the same time, America's public universities also developed new initiatives intended to bring the best ideas of the university (from macroeconomics to Elizabethan drama to the latest in agricultural technologies) to people in far-flung corners of the country who might otherwise not be able to attend their state's flagship university. The University of Wisconsin's Extension Division, for instance, offered credit and noncredit programs to students in isolated communities in an effort to fulfill the university's promise, in the words of one sympathizer, "to teach anybody—anything—anywhere."[75]

States also helped lead the way in maximizing the accessibility of higher education during this period through the creation of the public two-year junior college, the forerunner of today's community colleges. The first junior college was founded in Joliet, Illinois, in 1901, and by the start of World War II, more than two hundred public junior colleges were operating across the country.[76] These colleges served two primary purposes. For students eager to enter professions, they provided low-cost vocational education. And for young people who aspired to attend four-year universities but perhaps lacked the academic background to thrive in those institutions right out of high school, junior colleges were a critical educational waypoint.[77]

Thus, in the early twentieth century, America's public colleges and universities were proudly carrying the baton of democracy that had been seeded by the Morrill Acts. During the same period, however, the nation's oldest private colleges were doubling down on aristocracy.

Confronted with limitations of space and resources and a flood of new applicants, private colleges and universities opted to cap enrollment growth in an attempt to maintain control over their student bodies and retain the intimate experience of the residential college. As Dartmouth President Ernest Hopkins told undergraduates in 1922, "Too many men are going to college!"[78] What was needed, Hopkins said, was for elite private colleges to begin recruiting students of the highest intellectual merit, thereby cultivating "an aristocracy of brains, made up of men intellectually alert and intellectually eager."[79]

Such an attitude was a stark change from the private college admissions scene a few decades prior. For most of the nineteenth century, college had been a buyer's market, and admissions processes at elite private colleges were designed to let in as many students as possible. Harvard, for instance, publicly advertised in 1870 that 88 percent of that year's applicants had been admitted.[80] The process was simple: applicants took a series of entrance exams catered to the curricula of elite regional preparatory schools that served as feeders. Those who passed the exams were admitted—and most passed. Even those who didn't could still be admitted conditionally.

But this traditional system was quickly becoming outmoded. The expansion of public secondary schooling in the United States had sparked an explosion in college applications. Academic leaders eager to form a "natural aristocracy of talent" by identifying meritorious students from all parts of the country welcomed this surge of new prospects. But determining who should be admitted and why required retooling decades-old policies and procedures.

The first important step these colleges made was to abandon college-specific entrance examinations and adopt new standardized tests, such as the one first administered by the College Entrance Examination Board (CEEB) in 1901, a forerunner of the SAT. In most respects, the new examination model worked, but not always in the ways administrators expected or hoped. The examination was intended as a tool to identify more public school students and more students from other parts of the country. And, in fact, it did. Several of the Ivies saw modest increases in the number of public school students at their schools and an uptick in the geographic diversity of student bodies. Unexpected—and mostly unwelcome—was the fact that the examinations also led to a rapid increase in "socially undesirable" students from poor and immigrant backgrounds. Particularly alarming for some academic leaders was the substantial growth in the number of Jewish students who found themselves able to attend, for the first time, the nation's traditionally Protestant colleges.[81]

The numbers are striking. At Columbia in 1900, Jewish students comprised somewhere between 10 and 15 percent of the first-year class.[82] Eighteen years after adopting the CEEB exam, Jewish students made up well over 25 percent (and, by some estimates, as much as 40 percent) of the 1919 entering class.[83] Harvard, likewise, began using the College Board exams in 1905.[84] Between 1908 and 1919, the proportion of Jewish students more than doubled, from under 10 percent to 20 percent.[85] Other Ivies experienced similar gains. This sudden influx of Jewish students to academic institutions once reserved for the Protestant elite triggered furious reactions from alumni and a great deal of administrative hand-wringing, which in turn hastened another reinvention of elite college admissions in an effort to limit the Jewish influx.

Throughout the 1920s, these colleges abandoned exam-dependent admissions processes in favor of a holistic, character-based one that considered test scores as one factor among many, with applicants judged on their personal qualities and achievements (assessed through written materials, in-person interviews, and detailed family backgrounds) as well as their academic ability. The introduction of this new, more open-ended approach gave admissions offices tremendous latitude in shaping the character of a student body.

This process came to be known as "selective admissions," and it served a variety of ends. Sometimes, administrations deployed it as a blunt tool of bigotry to weed out Jewish and other "socially undesirable" students from applicant pools. (This even happened as late as 1942 at Johns Hopkins University when its president, Isaiah Bowman, initiated a quota on Jewish students.)[86] Indeed, after a public outcry forced President Abbott Lawrence Lowell of Harvard to retract an open quota he had tried to impose on Jewish students in the early 1920s, elite colleges used the discretion of selective admissions as cover to impose waves of quieter caps on Jews behind the scenes that persisted for decades. At other times and places, the character-based application identified truly talented students who might have otherwise gone unnoticed. Perhaps most often, however, this new application functioned as a means of cutting the difference between the meritocratic aspirations of universities, which claimed to want to admit talented students regardless of background, and a desire to shore up the support of the college's traditional constituents. One example of this phenomenon was the introduction of new preferences for the children of alumni, or "legacies." Princeton, Yale, and Harvard dramatically increased their enrollment of children of alumni during this era.[87]

The revolution that higher education underwent in the first half of the twentieth century set the stage—for better and worse—for many of the critical developments that would occur over the next eighty years. Public colleges continued to expand their reach and deliver on their potential with the support of states and the federal government. Private colleges, meanwhile, even as they grew in size and prestige, continued to struggle balancing democratic and meritocratic ideals with aristocratic traditions. These tensions would carry forward through the post–World War II period as colleges continued to grapple with questions of access, but now against the backdrop of transformative federal legislation.

The Entering Wedge

Although the Morrill Acts of 1862 and 1890 had spurred federal involvement in colleges and universities in the nineteenth century, the US government was mostly quiet on matters of higher education during the following half century. That all changed in 1944 with the passage of the Servicemen's Readjustment Act, or the G.I. Bill, the first in a series of landmark pieces of legislation enacted over the following three decades that redefined the federal government's role in expanding access to college. State governments and individual colleges and universities joined in, too, devising new mechanisms to deliver on the promise of making a college education available to all people. This was truly a golden age for college access.

The idea for the G.I. Bill was born in 1943 when the looming prospect of Allied victory in World War II triggered concerns at the highest levels of government over how to manage the demobilization of the US military. In a fireside chat broadcast on July 28, President Franklin Delano Roosevelt promised citizens that the federal government would take care of the nation's returning servicemen, assuaging the fears of millions who remembered all too clearly the government's failure to meet the basic needs of veterans following World War I. This time, Roosevelt assured listeners, American troops would not be "demobilized into an environment of inflation and unemployment, to a place on a bread line, or on a corner selling apples."[88] Privately, Roosevelt saw demobilization as an opportunity to do more than just correct the mistakes of the past. It was a chance to develop new social programs that would extend the promises of the New Deal into the postwar era, especially in higher education, a field in which he had long searched for an "entering wedge" that would allow him to amplify the federal role.

The legislation that made its way to Roosevelt's desk on June 22, 1944, was perhaps not as far-reaching as he had hoped, but it was still ambitious in scope, particularly for a bipartisan effort. It ensured that nearly all returning servicemen would be eligible for unemployment compensation, medical care, and low-interest mortgages and business loans. Most important for the history of higher education, it also guaranteed up to four years of subsidized education at any private or public college. Veterans were eligible for $500 annually toward tuition (a sum that exceeded the tuition at nearly every college in the country) as well as a monthly stipend.[89]

The G.I. Bill had its share of skeptics. Many were unconvinced that any significant number of returning servicemen would have an appetite for higher learning. As the *Saturday Evening Post* opined in August 1945, "the traditional four-year college course conflicts head-on with the ex-soldier's more ancient desire for short cuts to self-advancement and happiness—manifest in hasty marriages—to make up for precious years spent in military service."[90] Others, like University of Chicago President Robert Maynard Hutchins, feared that veterans would come to colleges in droves and turn dignified university campuses into "educational hobo jungles."[91]

Neither prediction was accurate. Between 1945 and 1956, more than 2.2 million vets swelled college campuses from Yale to the University of Texas—quite literally, in fact, since many colleges had to build new dormitories to house the throngs of new students.[92] And, contra the solemn fears of men like Hutchins about the vulgarizing effect these new students would have on campus culture, G.I. Bill recipients were frequently praised by administrators and faculty as being set apart for their diligence, candor, and intelligence.

The G.I. Bill was also a boon for mobility.

While the overall socioeconomic profile of G.I. Bill recipients tilted toward the upper ends of the income spectrum, the sheer number of recipients meant that many young men from working-class backgrounds benefited from it. In her history of the bill, *Soldiers to Citizens: The G.I. Bill and the Making of the Greatest*

Generation, political scientist Suzanne Mettler paints a vivid picture of the sons of farmers, coal miners, and railroad workers who received federal support, attended college, and went on to become engineers, teachers, and doctors.[93] A separate study of men raised in poor neighborhoods in Boston during the Great Depression found that those who served in the military and received education benefits from the G.I. Bill went on to experience greater job stability and economic security.[94] The doors that the G.I. Bill opened to millions of veterans did not, however, open nearly as wide for African Americans. Racist admissions practices, along with the difficulty of procuring adequate housing or employment as a result of redlining and segregation, severely curtailed the options for education and advancement.

The G.I. Bill ultimately proved to be precisely the "entering wedge" that Roosevelt had anticipated. It demonstrated unequivocally the federal government's capacity to make a college education available to a much broader swath of the population than had ever been possible previously.[95]

This capacity would be capitalized on further with the Higher Education Act of 1965, a piece of legislation designed with the explicit intent to make college affordable to more low- and middle-income families. A cornerstone of Lyndon B. Johnson's Great Society programs, it was also deeply personal. President Johnson signed the HEA into law on November 8, 1965, at Southwest Texas State Teachers College, his alma mater. In his remarks that day, Johnson retold his own rags-to-riches story, but he also spoke movingly of his experience teaching impoverished youth in rural Texas, for too many of whom the American Dream had remained only a dream. "I remember even yet," he intoned, "the pain of realizing and knowing then that college was closed to practically every one of those children because they were too poor."[96]

The Higher Education Act instituted a number of programs aimed at making college possible for all regardless of family background. These ranged from an enhanced national work-study program to a subsidized student loan program to teacher training. Among the most enduring innovations of the HEA was its creation of robust need-based education grants for low-income students. Called Educational Opportunity Grants, they were originally distributed to institutions to disperse among low-income students.[97] With the reauthorization of the HEA in 1972, however, these grants (renamed Pell Grants) were retooled to become direct payments to students based on need.

Pell Grants made college affordable for millions. For most of the 1970s, they carried a maximum authorization of $1,400, a sum that, at the time, was roughly equivalent to the average cost of annual tuition, room, and board at public universities, and was more than a third of the cost at private universities.[98] In 1977, nearly two million students received Pell Grants, a number that steadily rose until 2013, when there were more than nine million recipients, a consequence in part of both lower eligibility thresholds and more students enrolling in higher education as well as the fallout from the global financial crisis.[99] Rising tuition costs and federal neglect have made it so that Pell Grants are no longer the windfall for low-income students they once were, yet they nevertheless remain one of the most impactful and lasting forms of student aid ever devised by the federal government, and among the most significant legacies of the Higher Education Act.

The federal government was not the only actor during the postwar period making targeted efforts to expand college accessibility and affordability in the United States. Throughout the 1960s and '70s, states, alongside universities themselves, also began to experiment with new institutional designs and programs to ensure that as many students as possible could go to college.

California stood apart during this period for spearheading an effort to imagine a public higher education system dedicated to providing access to as many citizens as possible and to making a college education as affordable as possible. The 1960 Master Plan for Higher Education in California was created by a coalition of political and academic stakeholders from across the state, led by University of California Chancellor Clark Kerr. The plan brought the state's sprawling higher education system for the first time into a coherent structure divided into research universities, teaching universities, and community colleges.

This new structure enabled the state to coordinate policies to improve access and affordability. Among the most important provisions of the master plan were that California residents would pay no tuition for college and would be guaranteed admission to one of the state's colleges so long as they had graduated from high school. Initially, the top 12.5 percent of each graduating class were assured a place at one of the flagship University of California schools, and the top 33.3 percent were guaranteed spaces at any of the more numerous California State Universities.[100] All residents could attend one of California's expansive network of community colleges, where, if desired, they could take advantage of the system's generous transfer policies to move to the other tiers. Kerr described this system in explicitly democratic terms that captured the tensions between mass and selective education that had defined the previous half century: "It was Thomas Jefferson's vision of equality of opportunity for all and of service to all combined with contributions to the development of what Jefferson had called an 'aristocracy of talent.'"[101]

Although not all of its policies have stuck (public universities in California now charge tuition, for instance), the master plan still stands as a model for equitable higher education systems around the globe.[102] In 1990, thirty years after the plan was first designed and implemented, a team of reviewers from the Organisation for Economic Co-operation and Development (OECD) visited California to take stock of the long-term effects of the master plan and its influences on other institutions. They said simply that as a means of organizing an expansive and accessible higher education system, California's was "unsurpassed anywhere among OECD countries and probably in the world."[103]

While Clark Kerr was refashioning a sprawling public higher education system along egalitarian lines on the West Coast, another Clark on the East Coast was struggling to chip away at aristocratic privilege at one of America's oldest private colleges.

From 1965 to 1969, R. Inslee "Inky" Clark served as the progressive dean of admissions at Yale under President Kingman Brewster. During his brief tenure, Clark was responsible for making Yale coeducational and for expanding recruitment efforts to urban and rural high schools that had never had contact with Yale. He also fought a public—and ultimately losing—battle to walk back legacy preferences. Astoundingly, he managed, in a single year, to reduce the number of legacies in Yale's freshmen class from 24 percent to 12 percent.[104] This enraged alumni, among whom, in the words of one historian, a "cult of Clark hatred quickly developed."[105] That included William F. Buckley Jr., who griped that under Clark, "a Mexican-American from El Paso High with identical scores on the achievement test . . . has a better chance of being admitted to Yale than Jonathan Edwards the Sixteenth from Saint Paul's School."[106]

The intensity of the response all but ensured that Clark's battle against legacy preferences would be cut short. But other initia-

tives of his stuck. Among these was Yale's innovative and enduring policy of "need-blind" admissions.

Today, need-blind admissions encompasses an array of admissions practices, but when Yale became the first school in the country to formally adopt this policy in 1966, it provided the clear
assurance that no student would be denied admission to the college because of a lack of family financial wherewithal, and that
every admitted student would receive a financial aid package guar-
anteeing that the ability to pay would not hinder the ability to
attend.[107] According to President Brewster, this approach to admissions took the "pocketbook" out of the admissions equation,
such that low-income students could attend the university without worrying about how to finance their education, while those
from more privileged families could take "pride in the feeling that
[they] had made it on the merits rather than on the basis of something ambiguously called 'background.'"[108]

Most other elite universities followed Yale's lead in adopting
need-blind admissions policies in this era.[109] Not all of these transitions were easy. When Princeton went need-blind, for instance,
the fiscal stress nearly left fifty-one incoming freshmen that year
shortchanged on financial aid until some eleventh-hour fundrais-
ing and last-minute student attrition enabled the university to
close the gap.[110] But for the university's president, William G.
Bowen, such surprises were worth the headache in the quest to
achieve greater socioeconomic diversity. As he argued in a report
on Princeton's economic future, "We would not be serving the nation as we should if, in seeking to educate leaders for future generations, we were not to reach out for the best minds and the most
promising individuals wherever they may be found."[111]

At the end of the 1970s, these notable advances in admissions
and financial aid promised a new era of equity for American

higher education. But efforts hit a roadblock in the 1980s when the crushing realities of economic recession and a federal government increasingly suspicious of ostensible handouts precipitated reversals of many of the extraordinary gains in accessibility and affordability that colleges had made following World War II.

A Monster of Some Proportions

In 1981, colleges and universities that had been at the forefront of need-blind admissions during the previous decade faced a sudden reckoning. President Ronald Reagan had swept into office on a platform of shrinking the role of the federal government, including financial aid to students.[112] The cuts that were made—along with Reagan's rhetoric—created an uncertain budgetary landscape that led many schools to worry about their capacity to fulfill the financial commitments they had made to low-income applicants.[113] Beginning with Wesleyan in 1982, one university after another announced the reversal of their need-blind admissions policies.[114] It was the first sign of a troubling retreat. At the time, Bard College President Leon Botstein wrote in the *New York Times* that the rollback of need-blind admissions was "a declaration of defeat in the struggle for greater equality of access, with merit, to higher education."[115] These events, he worried, might mark "the start of a trend at private colleges and universities that will sharpen the class differences in our society."[116]

In hindsight, Botstein was right to be unnerved. The 1980s ushered in an era of widespread government retreat from college access in America, motivated by a view that postsecondary education is a private good that ought not to have a claim on public resources. The Pell Grant—that centerpiece of the federal embrace of access in the post–World War II era—was allowed to stagnate for years, covering an ever-shrinking fraction of the costs of attendance. In the 1970s, the maximum grant covered almost 70 percent of the average cost of attendance at a US college, a number that had fallen to under 25 percent by 2020.[117] And the rise of for-profit colleges in the 1990s and 2000s siphoned the federal dollars that remained toward costly institutions with little accountability for their educational and vocational outcomes.[118]

But some of the most damaging examples of government austerity can be found at the state level, where public universities ran into wave after wave of draconian budget cuts by state governments. From 1992 to 2010, the percentage of public research universities' budgets attributable to state funding was slashed nearly in half, starving the very schools that had been built to be "democracy's colleges."[119] These cuts were the product of a medley of forces: the fiscal pressures on state governments, the priority that states accord health care over educational funding (not surprising, in light of the relatively high rates of voter turnout by seniors in comparison to young adults), and the growing perception that a college education is primarily a private—as opposed to a public—good (and therefore its costs should be borne by its beneficiaries rather than society at large).

As a result of these cuts, the burden to shore up access and preserve mobility fell to colleges and universities themselves. The story of how institutions of higher education responded is a complicated one, with many peaks and valleys. On balance, however, it is a story of promise unfulfilled and one defined by what is perhaps the most significant trend in higher education over the past forty years: the steady and seemingly inexorable intensifying of competition among colleges and universities in a national and even global marketplace.

The modern era for colleges and universities has been one of increasingly fierce battles for everything from faculty recruitment to development dollars to reputation to—most significant for our purposes—the admission of meritorious students. If anything, it might be this chase for students where competition has wrought the most damaging consequences. It used to be the case that, to quote one leading admissions officer from the turn of the century, "most students stayed within two hundred miles of their hometown when looking at colleges."[120] Today, by contrast, the market for higher education is one in which students from around the country (and indeed the world) vie for limited spots at what they perceive to be the most desirable US colleges and universities, which promise to be sites of true opportunity, understanding, and engagement. And although this is not in itself a bad thing, it has contributed to the accretion of policies and practices across American colleges and universities that—even if unintentionally—have come to disadvantage poor and middle-income students and reward wealthy ones, thereby distorting and debasing our meritocratic ideals.

Perhaps no single event catalyzed this era of competition more than the rise of college rankings. *U.S. News & World Report* published its first annual ranking of 662 colleges and universities in 1983.[121] During its first few years, the list was reasonably stable and reflected the reputations of schools among college and university leaders. That changed in 1988 when *U.S. News* began tabulating its annual list algorithmically on the basis of various empirical measures, ranging from class sizes to standardized test scores to alumni giving.[122] Almost immediately, the old list was scrambled. Some institutions were propelled into the highest echelons of American higher education, while others once secure in the top tier tumbled into the second or third tier.[123] This new vulnerability, where a change to the weight of a single variable could dramatically alter a school's ranking, placed immense pressure on institutions to embrace policies that aligned with the criteria of the *U.S. News* list—and that all too often favored wealthier students.

In response, universities began to pursue admissions policies that amplified rankings. Take, for example, the efforts that universities make to manage their reported yield rates, the percentage of their offers of admission that are accepted by students. Because higher yield rates contribute to an institution's overall performance in the rankings, universities frequently engage in a series of practices that give them greater confidence that offers extended to student applicants will be accepted. One such practice is early decision, which allows students to apply early to their favorite college but then commits the student to the college if they are admitted. While early decision helps guarantee schools a higher "yield" of the students they admit and helps schools identify students who truly want to be there, it also has historically tended to advantage wealthier candidates, both because it favors those who are better informed about admissions policies and because it often binds students to a school before they can see a financial aid package.[124] By the turn of the century, nearly three hundred institutions were practicing early decision, fulfilling one dean's prediction decades prior that the policy would evolve into "a monster of some proportions."[125]

Another such policy is demonstrated interest. The term refers broadly to an applicant's enthusiasm for a given institution, which is typically measured by whether a prospective student has toured a campus or attended an information session. One study found that applicants who receive the greatest benefit from demonstrated interest are those who make the most expensive forms of contact, like visits to a campus.[126] In 2019, 40 percent of colleges and universities reported giving demonstrated interest either considerable or moderate weight in admissions, making it a more important factor than class rank and Advanced Placement test scores.[127]

Easily the most prominent example of an admissions policy change amplified by the gale force of rankings-based competition was the rise in stature and importance of standardized tests such as the SAT and ACT. Once *U.S. News & World Report* began to factor standardized test scores into its rankings algorithm beginning in 1988, schools came under immense pressure to ratchet up the average SAT scores of each incoming class. This transformed an instrument designed in the early twentieth century to measure innate academic talent into a critical lever in the arms race for institutional prestige.[128] It wasn't long before *U.S. News* rankings became so aligned with standardized test scores that one could sort American colleges and universities by average SAT or ACT scores and produce a close facsimile of the actual list.

It is undeniable that the current use of standardized testing in admissions practices hits low-income students the hardest. There is no shortage of studies showing that SAT scores are strongly correlated to family income.[129] Low-income students are less likely to hire private tutors, to enroll in commercial preparation courses, or to take a test more than once.[130] An analysis conducted in the wake of the Varsity Blues scandal of 2019 even found that students in wealthier areas are more likely to receive special accommodations for standardized tests, such as additional time or extended breaks.[131] The cumulative effect of these advantages for wealthy families is so large that scholars have described the modern testing regime as "an adaptive mechanism that upper-class families" have used "to secure their future social status."[132]

The culprit, however, may not be testing in and of itself. In fact, standardized tests are one of the few uniform measures of evaluation we have in a vast sea of subjective and haphazard criteria. The alternatives do not fare much better, as they, too, are deeply interwoven with family income: extracurricular opportunities, quality of high school curricula, and even grade point averages (GPAs) advantage the well-off.[133] My home country of Canada, for instance, where standardized tests are not used in undergraduate college admissions and the principal mechanism by which universities admit undergraduate students is high school GPA, has been afflicted by an epidemic of "credit mills"—private high schools that attract affluent families on the basis of their assurance that their children's performance will be evaluated through inflated grades that, in turn, assure high rates of admission to elite universities.[134]

As imperfect as standardized test scores are, I worry that jettisoning them outright from our admissions process is an overreaction to real—but rectifiable—issues in testing preparation and administration that will create other more serious challenges for those of us who believe in the meritocratic ideal. Abandonment will amplify the incentives for high schools, both public and private, to offer more liberal grading practices in an effort to assure parents that their students will not be injured in the admissions' lottery, with the net result of a "race to the bottom" in high school grading standards. Further, for those universities that have sought to discipline predictable pressures from well-heeled or influential parents by invoking test scores as an objective reason for admissions denials, the loss of standardized testing deepens the risk that they will be less able to resist those demands.

So what is to be done?

For all the criticism that standardized tests have borne—much of it justified—there is every indication that testing can be made more equitable if states, testing and ranking organizations, and universities work toward finding a solution. States like Michigan have shown that by requiring all high school juniors to take the ACT or SAT, it becomes possible to uncover thousands of low-income, college-ready students who otherwise would never have been identified.[135] The College Board has also taken meaningful steps to make the SAT itself fairer to low-income students, partnering with Khan Academy to roll out free test preparation and, in 2017, introducing an Environmental Context Dashboard (now called "Landscape") that provides college and university admissions staff with contextual information about test takers' high school, family, and neighborhood environments.[136] Yale credited the tool with making it possible for the university to welcome record numbers of Pell-eligible students (20 percent) and first-generation students (18 percent) to its class of 2022.[137]

Even *U.S. News & World Report* has recently begun to elevate these same principles in its rankings algorithm. In 2018, the publication altered its formula in an explicit effort to reward schools that promote social mobility by adding indicators for how many Pell-eligible students a school enrolls and how many graduate.[138] Although it is still too early to know by how much social mobility indicators will shift colleges' behavior, I can affirm that this shift has lent tangible support to the decisions we have made at Johns Hopkins—especially in the wake of an extraordinary $1.8 billion gift that was earmarked for student-based financial aid from alumnus and former mayor of New York City Michael R. Bloomberg—to commit to enrolling at least 20 percent of our class from Pell-eligible families.[139] Moreover, these changes have had a notable impact on the rankings themselves. In a single year, the new mobility indicators moved schools like the University of California, Riverside, and Howard University up thirty-nine and twenty-one spots, respectively, while causing a number of formerly top-ranked institutions to drop.[140]

This last point, in particular, underscores a core but underreported truth of the era of competition: the competitive impulse among colleges and universities does not inherently favor the amassing of affluence. This impulse can be steered toward either mobility or immobility; toward access or exclusivity; toward merit irrespective of background or the consolidation of privilege. It is, at least in part, a matter of design.

We have seen this sort of virtuous competition at work in higher education before. In the mid-2000s, media and political pressure over the price of higher education and the size of university endowments reached a fever pitch, with one US senator accusing universities of "hoarding" money while students were laden with debt.[141] This unleashed what observers at the time called an "arms race" in financial aid.[142] One after another, colleges and universities began pouring money into their financial aid policies, bidding against each other to attract middle- and low-income students with the best aid packages. From 2007 to 2009, "net tuition and fees"—the actual amount students pay on average after financial aid—at private colleges and universities fell more than 7 percent.[143] By 2011, nearly seventy institutions had implemented no-loan programs, including all of the Ivies and more than twenty flagship universities, meaning that, at least for students below a certain income level, financial aid to attend these schools would no longer be required to be repaid.[144] Granted, the *sticker price* at these universities continued to climb, a trend that served as a source of frustration for politicians and the public alike. But the *effective price* after financial aid fell and then stayed there—private universities, at least, were pushing money toward the lowest-income students in a sweeping, yearslong exercise in expanded access.[145]

One of the ironies of this entire episode is that while public alarm over endowments set it into motion, universities were only able to respond effectively by enlarging their endowments. A remarkable 48 percent of endowment income now goes to financial aid, far and away the biggest destination—a fact often neglected in calls for more taxation of university endowments.[146]

None of this is to say that universities' financial aid programs ought to be shielded from all criticism. Some observers have voiced concern about the appearance of a "barbell effect" in admissions, whereby universities cater to the neediest students (who receive full rides) and the wealthiest students (who pay their own way) while pricing middle-income students out of a college education.[147] Others note that the chase to win students through financial aid packages has led some universities to push grants to middle- or even higher-income students with the most desirable applications—effectively turning need-based aid into merit-based scholarships and diverting money from the lower-income students who need it most.[148] Still, the overarching lesson from this period is clear. If we elevate access and mobility as signs of an institution's quality, then the higher education sector will fight to realize those values. Change is possible through competition—not only in spite of it.

Inequality Machines

Despite the inroads colleges and universities have made with regards to financial aid, alarms continue to be raised over the ways in which the stark divides across democratic society are mirrored in (and even reinforced by) higher education. Indeed, from 1970 to 2018, the gain in the college completion rate of students in the highest income quartile (40 percent to 62 percent) has significantly outpaced that of students in the lowest income quartile (6 percent to 16 percent).[149] Affluent students are highly concentrated in well-resourced and selective universities, while low- and middle-income students have been pushed into under-resourced or for-profit colleges and laden with debt. Education experts have now taken to calling colleges and universities "inequality machine[s]."[150]

Prior to this era, the historic arc of higher education that began with Lady Mowlson's first scholarship in North America had been one in which—in fits and starts, irregularly and imperfectly—we sought, as a country, to expand the capacity of students of all backgrounds to receive an education that would actuate their potential. Something has clearly gone wrong. The engine of mobility that is the American college and university has slowed.

Part of the blame for this lies with the fraying of the government-university compact. Not since the 1970s has Congress passed a piece of visionary legislation to support colleges and universities on par with the Morrill Acts or the G.I. Bill or the Higher Education Act, one that is capable of reimagining the federal government's role in supporting the immense economic and personal possibilities of higher education for students of all backgrounds. There are many reasons for this retreat, not the least of which is a widespread perception that postsecondary education is a private, not a public, good and therefore ought no longer to have a claim on public resources.

I reject this categorically. Although it is undeniable that a university degree does, on average, confer real and durable income enhancements on graduates, there are also a host of benefits—or "positive externalities," in the parlance of the economists—from higher education that enrich society as a whole. Among them its ability to cultivate the sort of informed and active citizenship that lies at the heart of a vibrant democracy. In these terms, a nation that starves its colleges and universities is one that in turn starves not only its prosperity, its potential for discovery, its health and well-being, its creative and expressive proficiency, and its capacity for mobility but also, for the reasons set out in this chapter and this volume, its commitment to democratic rule.

I described the era starting in the 1980s as one—predominately—of governmental retreat from higher education. Since 2008, things have only worsened, especially for public universities. Following the Great Recession, state funding per student at the median public research university plummeted by more than 25 percent, rendering many public universities "public" in name only: at some, the percentage of their revenue coming from state funds fell to less than 10 percent.[151] To make up for these cuts, many schools made the unenviable but necessary decision to increase tuition. According to a 2020 report by the College Board, net in-state tuition at four-year public universities rose 24 percent between 2009 and 2015.[152] Observers now describe the years following the Great Recession as a "lost decade in higher education funding."[153]

COVID-19 constituted yet another shock for many colleges and universities. According to one September 2020 estimate, colleges and universities in the United States took a collective hit of more than $120 billion.[154] Rutgers University, one of the great American public universities and a seedbed of mobility for tens of thousands of students each year, provides a chilling example: by the summer of 2020, it faced $183 million in lost revenue and state budget cuts but received only $27 million directly from the Coronavirus Aid, Relief, and Economic Security (CARES) Act.[155] Contributing to (and reflecting) these pressures is the role of declining enrollment at many institutions. In fall 2020, undergraduate first-time enrollment in the United States fell more than 13 percent from the previous year, with underrepresented minorities experiencing the largest reductions.[156] As a consequence, fears abounded that the pandemic could force hundreds of colleges and universities to shutter their doors. With tens of millions of Americans on the unemployment rolls, studies already showed that low-income students were far more likely to withdraw from classes or delay their graduation because of the pandemic.[157] More than 50 percent of respondents in one survey of ten thousand college students reported no longer being able to afford tuition, and more than 7 percent said they were leaving college.[158]

The situation remains dire. The moment calls, in my view, for nothing less than the restoration of the historic compact between the federal government and the American university.

What might the restoration look like? This is, thankfully, a subject of spirited public debate. My own view is that it must begin with a vigorous reinvestment in direct funding for low- and middle-income undergraduate students in the grand tradition of Pell Grants. This might then be coupled with a far greater commitment to income-contingent loans—in which students' need to repay is limited by income—for graduate and professional students.[159]

The project also requires a broader reconceptualization of the federal role altogether, one that harnesses the competitive spirit that has come to define this era of higher education but that is directed toward new ends. One idea I favor is the creation of a new grant program in which the federal government commits money directly to cash-strapped state universities on the condition that states themselves make a matching investment. A feature of this proposal is that, unlike the traditional federal investment in financial aid directed to students, universities could use this money not only to keep their tuition low but also to invest in their educational programs to combat what has become a defining problem for American higher education and a drag for mobility: even as more and more students are attending college, they are not necessarily graduating.

As journalist Paul Tough wrote in the *New York Times Magazine* in 2014, "More than 40 percent of American students who start at four-year colleges haven't earned a degree after six years. If you include community-college students in the tabulation, the dropout rate is more than half, worse than any other country except Hungary."[160] This disparity falls the hardest on low-income students and those from marginalized backgrounds. According to an analysis by the Education Trust, the graduation rate for students who receive Pell Grants at nonprofit four-year colleges is 51 percent; for non-Pell students, it is 65 percent. Half of this disparity can be explained by the fact that "too many Pell students attend institutions where few students of any sort graduate, and too few attend institutions where most students graduate."[161] These students are being let down, in significant part, by the colleges they attend.

There are proven interventions that can have a real impact on completion rates, but they are challenging for cash-strapped colleges to stand up, let alone maintain, in the face of cycles of budget cuts. As Harvard economist David Deming has shown in proposing a similar grant program, the problem, at bottom, is in fact about money: there is a direct relationship between per student spending and degree completion.[162] With mobility in the United States flagging, this moment demands an infusion of resources in our colleges and universities.

This idea would also involve a state matching requirement to spur additional investment and innovation by state governments. We have every reason to believe a program like this will actually work. The first reauthorization of the Higher Education Act in 1972 included an under-sung initiative called State Student Incentive Grants (later known as the Leveraging Educational Assistance Partnership Program, or LEAP) that provided matching funds to states with financial aid programs for low-income college students. In just a few years, the number of states offering financial aid programs had more than doubled.[163] The initiative was eventually discontinued in 2011, having "accomplished its objective" of spurring every state to establish grant programs.[164] A revival of this basic idea of matching at scale, however, has the potential to spur a race to the top among states eager to secure the money to rebuild first-in-class public universities, and it could even represent a down payment by the nation on the promise of mobility reminiscent of the Morrill Acts and the "democracy colleges" they helped create 150 years ago.[165]

I prefer these approaches over calls for "zero tuition" for anyone enrolled in public universities and colleges. As numerous critics have pointed out, a policy of providing free college to everyone has the potential to be deeply regressive by benefiting mostly those students who hail from affluent families, both because those students receive little or no financial aid and because the cost of paying their tuition would be shared by all taxpayers, including low-income taxpayers without a college education. A study conducted by the Urban Institute estimated that 38 percent of the funding for a national free-tuition program would benefit students from families earning more than $120,000 per year, while only 22 percent would go to students from families earning less than $70,000.[166] This is money that is best directed to the students and institutions that need them most. I worry, too, that if the federal funds allocated to a no-tuition plan failed to keep pace with the actual cost of operating the school, then the plan could have the perverse effect of starving public universities of cash, which would then exacerbate the financial divides that already exist between these cash-strapped schools and their private peers. Public universities would be shackled to a tuition-free mandate, without the funds to support it.

Above all, what is needed is for the federal government once again to see itself as part of a grand common project with institutions of higher learning, one that recognizes the virtues of seeding the pastureland of colleges and universities in the country to generate widespread opportunity and mobility for future generations of citizens.

I sincerely hope that the government-university compact will regain its luster. But in the absence of a reinvigoration of government investment in access and mobility, it falls to other organizations, as well as colleges and universities themselves, to meet the challenges of inequity. There are promising signs that the logic of competition in the sector—in an era still defined by it—might be directed toward mobility once more. A new generation of dynamic and innovative organizations (the Posse Foundation, Quest Bridge, the American Talent Initiative, College Bound, Scholar Match, and the National Education Equity Lab, to name a few) has entered the picture, and these organizations are starting to help elite colleges and universities identify and recruit students of talent from first-generation or low-income backgrounds.

These efforts are already bearing fruit. From 2015 to 2017, according to an American Talent Initiative report, "20,696 more low- and middle-income students . . . enrolled at the 320 colleges and universities with the highest graduation rates."[167] Critically, philanthropists have started to step up as well, including, in 2020, through a series of historic investments in HBCUs.[168]

The financial aid efforts at my own university were given a historic boost by Michael Bloomberg's unprecedented gifts.[169] As someone born into a family of modest means, Mayor Bloomberg has always understood the importance of affording talented students the opportunity to participate fully in higher education. His generosity has enabled us to become a need-blind and no-loan institution, and to invest in an array of student supports designed not only to bring new students *to* but to also get them *through* and *beyond* the university. There is an undeniable energy in the political realm as well, with sweeping higher education proposals featuring prominently in presidential campaigns and public discourse in a way we haven't seen for decades. None of this means that the dilemma of immobility in higher education is on its way to being solved, or that it will solve itself. But we do see renewed momentum outside and inside American colleges and universities in support of their intrinsic democratic capacity for mobility.

Still, there are those who see in this moment a darker indictment of higher education and the project of opportunity. Critics of the meritocratic ideal like Michael Sandel and Daniel Markovits argue that universities' privileging of merit is a fiendish trap that has deepened the economic and political divides in society.[170] Even as they acknowledge that higher education is a good, that making college more accessible to those of modest means is a virtue, and that the training and credentialing of talent are important parts of a functioning democracy, they argue that the endless pursuit of merit and credentials has become wrenching for the winners and humiliating for the losers. In addition, they claim that the heavy emphasis our society has placed on education damages the mental health of those who go to college and the esteem of those who do not, and above all that the populist upheaval in democracies is due in no small part to those who feel an education-based meritocracy has left them behind.

There is truth in these critiques. It has been jarring to see how rapidly <u>a college degree has been transformed into one of the deepest fault lines in American politics.</u> And universities certainly bear an obligation to ensure that the college experience is not an emotionally withering one for students. But where Sandel, Markovits, and others see despair in the machinery of opportunity, I see hope. They point to the fact that just over 30 percent of adults now have a college degree as evidence that we have built a cathedral of educational elites. But among young people, nearly 70 percent are now going to college right after high school. As discussed, we must do a far better job of making sure that those who want a college education can access it, and that those who access it are able to graduate. Even if a college degree is a minority status, a totem of privilege, it need not be for much longer—that is, *if we commit to strengthening it.* This requires us to turn toward education, not away from it; to recommit to the potential of a human capital economy, not unravel it.

The path forward is for universities to commit our energy and urgency to expanding opportunity however we can. And on that point, I believe there is common cause between me and the critics of merit. With that in mind, I want to turn to one final matter that speaks directly to the question of mobility and the American university: ending the preference selective institutions give to children of alumni, otherwise known as legacy preferences.

Ending an Almost Exclusively American Custom

Legacy preference is immobility written as policy, preserving for children the same advantages enjoyed by their parents. It embodies in stark and indefensible terms inherited privilege in higher education and has compromised college and university admissions for decades. Moreover, it has drained the public trust in colleges and universities at a moment when the public is seething with rage at the seeming illusion of the meritocratic ideal and widening inequality. It is also a policy that is fully within the control of institutions to change at any moment.

The practice of giving admissions advantages to children of alumni is virtually alien to Canadian and European universities. Yet legacy preferences remain commonplace in the United States, where they constitute, in the words of journalist Daniel Golden, an "almost exclusively American custom."[171] Nearly seventy of the one hundred highest-ranked schools in the *U.S. News & World Report* list of national universities still engage in some form of the practice.[172] Remarkably, it has not yet buckled under the pressure of competition or rankings.

That such a naked form of hereditary advantage prevails in a country with a deeply ingrained commitment to the ideals of opportunity is striking. That it persists at institutions that otherwise exhibit such profound promise for socioeconomic mobility is tragic. My hope is that the competitive spirit—channeled, as it ought to be, toward accessibility and mobility—may yet end it.

As discussed above, legacy preferences were first introduced at the Ivies in the 1920s. After a series of meritocratic admissions reforms had started to push out these schools' traditional constituencies of prep schoolers and children of alumni in favor of public school students and, notably, Jewish students, anxious college administrators pivoted toward a holistic admissions process that frequently included some special provision for legacy students. This was a way to shore up alumni support and to reduce Jewish enrollment numbers while still preserving a sheen of meritocracy. At some institutions, the advantage given to legacy students became so pronounced that, by the 1960s, alumni children were virtually guaranteed admission to the country's most elite colleges.

Today, legacy status is no longer quite the guaranteed entry into elite institutions it once was, but the advantage it confers is still substantial, and evidence suggests that it is growing. One 2004 study estimated that legacy status afforded applicants to highly selective universities an admissions boost equivalent to an added 160 points (out of 1600) on the SAT.[173] A 2011 analysis of more than 200,000 applications to thirty highly selective institutions concluded that, controlling for other variables, legacy applicants were more than three times as likely to be admitted as their non-legacy peers.[174] And over the past decade, admission rates for legacy students have stayed constant at many selective universities, even as overall admission rates otherwise have declined, which has put the advantage legacy students receive each year on an upward trajectory.[175]

This boost does not even account for the leg-up legacy applicants already receive simply by virtue of having been born to college-educated parents. These students are more likely to grow up in stable and supportive homes, attend the best schools, receive tutoring, and participate in extracurriculars.[176] Legacy preferences guarantee that these students are doubly advantaged.

At most top-ranked national universities with legacy preferences, legacy students comprise anywhere from 10 to 20 percent of incoming classes. With numbers like these, legacy students can significantly influence the racial and socioeconomic composition of a class.[177] And we know that legacy students at the top-ranked universities in the country are not representative of American society. They are far more likely than their classmates to be wealthy and white, and so the existence of legacy preferences skews stu-

dent bodies at elite institutions away from low-income students—
sometimes with dramatic results.[178] At Harvard, for instance,
legacy students disproportionately have parents with incomes in
excess of $500,000 per year (40 percent of legacies vs. 15 percent
of non-legacies).[179] Similar stories could be told at many institutions across the country.

The bottom line is this: selective college admissions is a zero-
sum game. Every student who gets admitted to a highly selective
institution is taking a seat away from another student. Legacy
preferences ensure that more of those coveted spots go to the
young people most likely to have had a head start in life: wealthier, whiter, and with college-educated parents. That means fewer
seats for low-income applicants, for underrepresented minorities,
and for those who would be the first in their families to go to college. None of this is to undermine the accomplishments or merits of legacy applicants themselves, many of whom are exceptional
applicants. But affording such students a routine admissions advantage based solely on their parentage comes at a high cost.

In the past sixty years, there have been occasional swells of demand in and outside of academia to end legacy preferences, none
of which has met with much success. The reader will recall that
in the 1960s, Yale's idealistic dean of admissions, R. Inslee Clark,
tried to eliminate legacy preferences at the university, only to be
rebuffed by a chorus of furious alumni.[180] Later, members of Congress took up the banner. In the 1990s, Republican Senator Bob
Dole said the time had arrived to "take the next logical step on
the fairness front" and end "alumni perks [that] have absolutely
nothing to do with an individual's qualifications or merit."[181] In
2003, Democratic Senator Ted Kennedy floated a bill aimed at
discouraging legacy preferences, and a year later, then-President

George W. Bush, himself a beneficiary of legacy preferences, acknowledged that universities ought to give up the practice.[182] Nothing happened.

Despite these thwarted efforts, legacy preferences are not inexorable. In the past half century, a handful of universities have demonstrated unequivocally that legacy preferences not only can be eliminated, but also can be eliminated without any sacrifice in institutional quality or reputation. Oxford and Cambridge ended legacy preferences in the 1960s. The University of California, Berkeley, eliminated them in the 1990s. And extraordinary institutions like the Massachusetts Institute of Technology and Caltech never had them in the first place.

My own university offers a clear example of what can happen when a school eliminates legacy preference. Since 2014—when we ended the practice—we have seen remarkable results. The decision has created space for high-achieving students from diverse socioeconomic, geographic, and racial backgrounds to gain admission to Hopkins. In 2009, the year I arrived, our university had more legacy students in its freshman class (12.5 percent) than students who were eligible for Pell Grants (9 percent). In 2020, those numbers were reversed: 4.2 percent of first-year students had a legacy connection to the university (none of whom were given any legacy admissions preference), and 20.5 percent were Pell-eligible. Over the same period, the fraction of first-generation students in our incoming classes has more than doubled from 7 percent in 2009 to 16 percent in 2019 (figure 1). And all of these shifts have occurred alongside steady growth in the academic achievement of our incoming classes. Extinguishing legacy preferences was a foundational step for these shifts.

Defenders of the practice like to say that legacy preferences exist to nurture a sense of institutional loyalty across generations

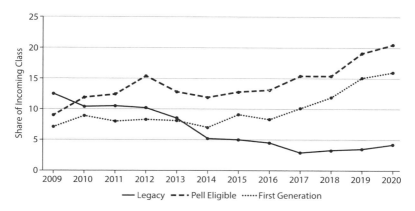

FIGURE 1. Share of legacy, Pell-eligible, and first-generation first-year students at Johns Hopkins, 2009–2020.

and, by extension, to develop relationships with alumni that will foster greater financial support to the university. One often hears that this is critical in building a multigenerational community. Community is a truly venerable goal; a sense of connection to each other, and our shared institutions, is the lifeblood of a thriving society. But this support need not be conditional on the future admission of our children. And a true community—a true American community—is one that brings together people from different socioeconomic and cultural backgrounds rather than the inherently insular community of wealthy legacies. In truth, many alumni long for the institutions to which they feel so deeply connected to be embodiments of merit for all talented students.

This has certainly been MIT's experience, and so far we have found it to be true at Hopkins, too. In 2012, one of MIT's admissions directors, Chris Peterson, took to the Internet to clear up once and for all the question of whether MIT practiced legacy preferences: They don't. He wrote that if the school even entertained the possibility of introducing legacy admissions, it would "face an alumni revolt."[183] At Hopkins, alumni participation has steadily grown since we ended legacy preferences in 2014, and when we went public with our policy in 2019, we saw broad alumni support.

I do not pretend that ending legacy preferences is itself adequate to reverse the scourge of immobility or assuage the frustration and anger directed at universities. Although legacy preferences, in direct and often painful ways, affect thousands of high-achieving students who lose spots in favor of their better-connected peers, the policy still affects a relatively small number of students, at a relatively selective tier of universities. Abolishing legacy preferences is a beginning, not an end, and it must be coupled with a broader mobility agenda for reinvestment in poor and middle-class students and struggling universities. Even then, there are entrenched structural inequities across our nation that will prevent us from achieving the goal that every child, no matter their background or circumstance, will be equipped to attend a selective university, inequities to which universities can only be—and yet must be—part of the solution. But these are hardly reasons for those colleges to leave an additional thumb on the scales in favor of the most privileged students. Ending legacy admissions represents a critical step in the direction of equity and mobility. Perhaps as important as the impact of legacy preferences on mobility itself is its impact on the perception of fairness—the very idea of opportunity. Legacy preferences are symbolic of the power of the privileged to entrench that privilege across generations in a way that is in direct opposition to the values of a university and the promise of democracy.

I began this chapter by arguing for the essential role social mobility plays in the liberal democratic project and how vital the collective belief in the prospect of mobility is to sustaining it. Democracies draw their credibility and their resilience from an implicit covenant that anyone with enough grit and talent can move beyond the confines of the circumstances into which they were born. As income inequality and stratification have grown more acute and intergenerational mobility has stalled, this central tenet of the American Dream has become increasingly fragile. Legacy preferences exacerbate this problem by eroding the credibility of colleges and universities and irreparably damaging the meritocratic ideal that is a centerpiece of democratic faith and that institutions of higher education ought to embody. They are, in a word, corrosive of the faith in mobility and therefore of the spirit that lights democracy itself.

No matter how many first-generation and low-income students they admit, how many scholarships they award, or how many more urban and rural high schools they engage, my view is that universities cannot truly stand for equal opportunity until they muster the courage to eliminate the most conspicuous vestiges of caste that still cling to them. Only then can they lay claim to their heritage as carriers of the American Dream, a dream that James Truslow Adams defined in words that sound in the mission of universities themselves: to "grow to fullest development" all people in "the hope of opening every avenue of opportunity" to them.

TWO

>>>><<<<

Free Minds

Educating Democratic Citizens

UNIVERSITIES ARE PLACES of boundless intellectual and moral energy. The challenge for faculty is how best to tap this reservoir of capability to make our world better. Nowhere is this challenge more compelling than in how we educate and inspire our students as citizens.

From the moment I earned my first appointment to the Faculty of Law at the University of Toronto, I understood that my principal responsibilities to my students related, first and foremost, to sharing the knowledge and understanding that I had acquired in my areas of academic specialization: economics, corporate law, and regulation. In time, though, I also came to understand that apart from these structured moments of teaching, the countless opportunities that the school offered for students to serve the public interest in clinical and other settings were just as instrumental to their growth and development.

First as a professor and then as a dean, I deliberately sought, alongside many colleagues, to expand the avenues for students to engage their communities: providing pro bono services across a broad range of organizations, increasing our poverty law and international human rights programs, and creating a program that offers law and justice-based courses and other experiences to high school students in several schools in Toronto. Since that time, I have also sought to imagine opportunities for students to use their knowledge and skills to support local community organizations. The benefits of these endeavors were obvious: through our students, the university could mobilize its intellectual and moral energies to benefit directly individuals and communities whose needs would otherwise be unmet, while simultaneously affording students the opportunities to better understand the duties, possibilities, and rewards of active citizenship.

Yet, as democracy has faltered, I confess to having had intermittent pangs of conscience as to whether these efforts sufficiently cultivated among our students a commitment to true democratic citizenship. I worry that colleges and universities have blithely assumed our students had an understanding of democratic citizenship that they did not in fact have. Perhaps we built these service programs not on a bedrock of democratic knowledge but on sand.

This was brought home several years ago at Johns Hopkins after a series of free speech incidents on American university campuses raised the concern that students evinced little appreciation for, or understanding of, the role and value of academic freedom in college life. Taking nothing for granted, we designed an orientation session for incoming first-year students that explored the critical role of freedom of thought and expression as core tenets of the university. The session introduced students to John Locke's and John Milton's cases for free speech, how these were linked to academic freedom, and why this principle was so essential for universities to honor. By design, we enlisted faculty members from across the ideological and disciplinary spectrum to explain why these values were so critical for their own research and writing.

After we held this session for the first time, we surveyed students to gauge their reaction. I was worried that the panel might be too rudimentary, or that we had missed the mark. The feedback we received was arresting. Student after student expressed appreciation for the panel. Many confessed that until that moment, they—who uniformly stood in the top 10 percent of their high school classes, who had SAT scores far above the national average, and who hailed from every state in the union—had never been exposed to the case for free speech in their high school studies. We were gobsmacked. This most foundational of American ideals, this cornerstone of citizenship, was somehow overlooked (or, more perplexingly, expunged) from our students' high school education.

In the years since, I have become more and more desolate about the civic literacy of students entering our universities. The fact is that our students, who show such remarkable sophistication and mastery across so many different fields upon entering university, are woefully undereducated in democracy's core precepts. Given the perilous state of our democracy, this is an astonishing state of affairs. It's also a problem about which universities cannot simply wring their hands, lamenting the state of the nation and beseeching someone else to solve. It's something they themselves have the capacity and responsibility to address.

Not Passed Down through the Gene Pool

The citizen is at the heart of the democratic project, but the capacities of good citizenship are not innate. These capabilities must be cultivated and instilled through a carefully prescribed education.

The idea of education for citizenship can be traced to ancient Athens, where the education of youth was aimed at developing virtuous citizens. This pedagogical ideal was captured in the concept of *paideia*, or the education of the whole person for goodness. Early in Athens's history, prominent families fostered young citizens through experiences ranging from exposure in theatres to the tragedies of Sophocles to outings in the courts and assembly to observe judicial and political deliberation firsthand.[1] Over time, this education became formalized as a rigorous instruction in history, military discipline, morality, and rhetoric. Such an education, wrote Plato, "inspires the recipient with passionate and ardent desire to become a perfect citizen, knowing both how to wield and how to submit to righteous rule."[2]

Modern writers have continued to echo this idea. In the eighteenth century, Montesquieu argued that "it is in republican government that the full power of education is needed."[3] At the dawn of the nineteenth century, Thomas Jefferson cautioned Americans that liberty would be "a short-lived possession, unless the mass of the people could be informed."[4] In the twentieth century, John Dewey echoed this refrain in explicitly reproductive terms, writing that "democracy has to be born anew every generation and education is its midwife."[5] More recently yet, former US Supreme Court Justice Sandra Day O'Connor, who in her retirement has assumed a leadership role on matters of civic education, revived Dewey's childbearing metaphor when she declared that "the practice of democracy is not passed down through the gene pool."[6]

Clearly, the idea that education is essential to the preservation of a democracy has been an enduring cornerstone of our shared history. This is truer of democracies than other forms of government because of the role that citizens play as the bearers of political power, responsible for both delegating their goals and values to representatives and then supervising that delegation through regular fair and free elections. While a variety of institutions—from families to voluntary associations to religious institutions—have the capacity to gird young people for these roles, the preeminent responsibility has resided in our K–12 schools and, to a lesser extent, our colleges and universities. When these places of learning do not fulfill this function, it is equivalent, in the words of Danielle Allen, Harvard political theorist and director of the Democratic Knowledge Project, to tossing out the "owner's manual" for democracy.[7]

Thanks to a recent renewal of scholarly interest in civic education following decades of neglect, we are now beginning to understand the full impact of this owner's manual.[8] We know, for instance, that civics courses help students from politically disengaged families to reach levels of engagement equal to those of their more politically socialized (and often wealthier) peers far faster than they otherwise would.[9] One study showed that when such students have high exposure to civics in school, they demonstrate levels of civic engagement that they wouldn't otherwise reach until age 30—if it all.[10] Research has also demonstrated that students who take courses combining lessons on political institutions and democratic history with open classroom environments that mirror the "rough and tumble of participatory democracy" experience marked improvements in political knowledge, are more likely to vote, and express a strengthened sense of political agency.[11]

These lessons learned do not disappear after graduation, either: one study examining the relationship between the acquisition of particular verbal skills necessary for citizenship—reading, writing, speaking, listening, and debating—and political participation showed that verbal aptitude corresponded with higher rates of voting and volunteering over time.[12] The implications of this research are clear—civic education is neither an illusion nor an exercise in futility. We can teach the art and science of democratic citizenship.

This has implications beyond the individual. A more robust national commitment to civic education may also translate to the stability and strength of its democracy writ large. Every few years, the International Association for the Evaluation of Educational Achievement administers the International Civic and Citizenship Education Study (ICCS), a survey of eighth and ninth graders around the world measuring many facets of civic education, including civic knowledge. (The United States does not participate in this study.) It happens that as of 2016 (the most recent iteration of the ICCS survey), the countries with the highest civic knowledge scores—with one notable exception—were also among those with the highest scores on the Varieties of Democracy Liberal Democracy Index.[13] In fact, the seven top-performing countries in civic knowledge include the four countries with the highest liberal democracy scores in the world: Norway, Sweden, Denmark, and Estonia (figure 2).

The outlier is Russia, which defies the pattern of other countries by demonstrating extraordinarily high levels of civic knowledge but abysmal democracy scores. One likely explanation for this is that for the past fifteen years, Russia has pressed an education

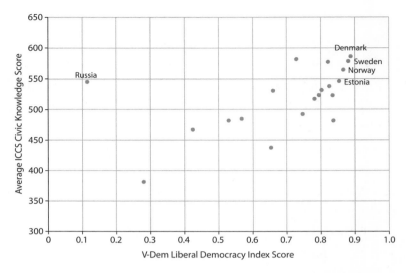

FIGURE 2. Average civic knowledge scores and Liberal Democracy Index scores by country, 2016. The chart includes all countries that met sample participation requirements and reported average civic knowledge scores in the 2016 International Civic and Citizenship Education Study (ICCS) and also received a 2016 Varieties of Democracy (V-Dem) Liberal Democracy Index score. The 2016 ICCS included twenty-four countries, but three countries did not meet sample participation requirements. Further, one country participated in the 2016 ICCS but did not receive a V-Dem score in 2016. Therefore Figure 2 includes twenty countries, five of which have been labeled. The correlation between V-Dem Liberal Democracy Index scores and average civic knowledge scores for the countries in Figure 2 is 0.51; when Russia is excluded, the correlation is 0.80.

Source: See Wolfram Schulz, John Ainley, Julian Graillon, Bruno Losito, and Gabriella Agrusti, *IEA International Civic and Citizenship Education Study 2016 Assessment Framework* (Amsterdam: International Association for the Evaluation of Educational Achievement, 2016); and Michael Coppedge et al., "V-Dem [Country–Year/Country–Date] Dataset v11," Varieties of Democracy Project, accessed March 25, 2021.

agenda focused on the formation of loyal patriots, designed to devalue rather than affirm the individual's role as antecedent and superior to that of the state.[14] In contrast, a country like Sweden, which has embraced a multiculturalist model of civic education that promotes democratic principles and the cultivation of individual identities, shows success in both civic literacy and national democracy scores.[15] Swedish students are far more likely than their Russian counterparts to believe that respecting the opinions of others is important to being a good citizen, to value public criticism of government, and to support gender equality.[16] These data are a reminder that the aims and values of civic education can have a demonstrable impact in shaping students' attitudes and behaviors beyond the specific knowledge transmitted.

This takes us to the very heart of current debates around civic education: What must citizens learn to be effective participants in liberal democracy?

Democratic citizenship rests on an irreducible set of foundational actions and duties that must be practiced for democratic self-government to thrive and endure. Effective democratic citizens reason and argue and tolerate and participate—they aspire to achieve the best version of their community and engage their fellow citizens and the political realm in that project. They are at once, in the words of political theorist Judith Shklar, "public meeting-goers," "joiners of voluntary organizations," and "political agents" eager to "discuss and deliberate with others about the policies that will affect them all."[17]

Basic skills like literacy and numeracy are necessary for this kind of citizen, but they are insufficient. A consensus has emerged that this multifaceted ideal of democratic citizenship is supported by four pillars: knowledge, skills, values, and aspirations.[18] Civic knowledge refers to a familiarity with the history and theory of democracy and its institutions, which ensures that one brings to public life a nuanced understanding of the past and the present. Civic skills entail, among other things, critical reasoning and bridging skills that enable citizens both to discern true from false and also to translate ideas into collective action. Civic values include a commitment to ideals of tolerance and equality that provide the standards against which citizens hold policies and policy makers to account. And, finally, civic aspiration denotes a disposition directed toward cooperation and collective action.

Through a rich and rigorous democratic civic education, citizens can acquire and cultivate these aptitudes and apply them in the world not only to preserve but also to renew and invigorate democracy. An education in democracy of the kind I am describing ought to stake out a position and take a viewpoint, too—inevitably, it will take a viewpoint. But that does not mean it must be either an exercise in reflexive, superficial patriotism or a wholesale critique of the entire democratic project.[19] Instead, it should cultivate in students a pride in the ideals of liberal democracy, a sober and clear-eyed recognition of its incompleteness and its failures, and a competence in the practices necessary to improve it.

Right now, there is every indication that too many citizens in the United States lack this foundation or commitment. The numbers are jarring. Faith in the democratic project has been deteriorating among Americans. Indeed, the fraction of citizens who report being dissatisfied with democracy now stands at a record high of 55 percent.[20] Since 1995, the share of young people who support the idea of a "strong leader" over "parliament and elections" has risen from less than one-third to nearly one-half.[21] And citizens are growing more suspicious of each other, too: tolerance for those of an opposing political party hit a twenty-year low in 2014 (a decline that shows no sign of abating), while our trust in each other has been dropping for forty years.[22]

Beyond these shifts in affinities and values, Americans are also less disposed to democratic involvement than previous generations. The number who deem it "very important" to stay informed about current affairs and public issues dropped from 56 percent to 37 percent between 1984 and 2014, with 20 percent saying that being informed is "not an obligation that a citizen owes to the country" (up from 6 percent in 1984).[23] Add to this the public's enduring ignorance of basic civic facts, with many studies showing stubbornly low levels of civic knowledge over the past several decades, and there is ample reason to believe we are witnessing deficiencies across the board in the most basic democratic competencies.[24]

The news is not all bad. Over the past few years, there has been an undeniable uptick in voter turnout and other forms of political action by young people. Between 2016 and 2020, youth turnout in national elections grew from around 45 percent to approximately 55 percent, a massive increase representing the highest turnout in this age group since 1972.[25] And sweeping protests on issues such as climate change and racial justice have been driven in no small measure by the newest generation of citizens. Still, it is far too early to conclude that this recent wave of protest and action heralds a reversal of the dispiriting decades-long trends across the full range of democratic competencies discussed above, all of which are essential ingredients of true democratic citizenship. We cannot afford to be complacent.

Habits of Reflection and Correct Action

A core component of the mission of our educational institutions must be to educate citizens in the theory and practice of democracy. Much of this burden has traditionally fallen on K–12 schools, and for many decades, they fulfilled their civic function admirably. As the common schools of the nineteenth century transitioned to the sprawling public school systems of today, K–12 education came to be seen as a central carrier of democratic knowledge and values. This was especially true in the early twentieth century, when standard course sequences in civics (which for several decades included courses in community civics, American government, and the topical "Problems of Democracy") became a mainstay of curricula and were seen to be one of the most effective ways to assimilate the waves of immigrants arriving on America's shores.[26] These courses came with their own pitfalls, as they had the potential to perpetuate invidious national myths even as they introduced students to the foundational ideas, values, and practices of democratic life.

In the late 1960s, growing disenchantment with the very idea of a unified civic culture and frustration with the sidelining of minority experiences and historical inequities led to the disappearance of many civics courses from K–12 curricula.[27] Civics education was further marginalized in the 1980s when falling scores in math and reading fueled a national commitment to test-taking for fundamentals. Funding for social studies and civics withered as these fields were deemed no longer essential and debates raged over what the content of these fields should be. As a consequence, weekly instruction time for such courses fell sharply, especially in already underfunded schools.[28] There is some evidence that the tide may have started to turn, with a number of states acting to restore civics to a place of greater prominence in the K–12 curriculum. But a majority of principals and other K–12 leaders across the country still say that their schools do not spend enough time teaching civics.[29]

In perfect honesty, it is hard at this moment to imagine civics being restored fully to the K–12 curriculum in a coherent and consistent way, given the hyperpartisanship that has called even the most settled civic norms into question.[30] Prominent civics scholar Meira Levinson has pointed out that "if we accept that teachers and school leaders are in fact tasked with teaching students certain values, it would seem to follow that they ought to stand up for those values when they're threatened." But, she adds, in this moment even the act of "determining that they are threatened is itself an exercise in partisan practical judgment."[31] The political rifts in the United States have made it more difficult than ever to achieve even a provisional consensus on what constitute basic democratic values.

The decades-long evaporation of civic education from primary and secondary schools has left a deep scar.[32] Students' scores on civic tests suffered a steep decline in the 1970s and have remained stagnant since.[33] Today, only about a quarter of K–12 students in the United States score as proficient in a test of civic knowledge, skills, and dispositions.[34] Even more disquieting are yawning gaps that have emerged in civic education across racial, ethnic, class, and geographic lines, which have produced a democratic landscape divided, in the words of one expert, between civic "oases" and civic "deserts."[35]

Higher education, meanwhile, has been walking its own fitful path.

Civic education at colleges and universities has taken a variety of forms over the past two hundred years. In 1818, the *Rockfish Gap Report* (a product of the University of Virginia's first Board of Commissioners and named for the watering hole where it was drafted) famously contended that higher education's duty with regards to citizenship training was to "develope the reasoning faculties of our youth, enlarge their minds cultivate their morals, & instil into them the precepts of virtue & order. . . . and generally to form them to habits of reflection, and correct action."[36] For most of the nineteenth century, colleges and universities fulfilled this mandate by developing students' moral faculties. Then, in the early twentieth century, they shifted to championing training in scientific reasoning as the basis of citizenship. After World War II, they created ambitious general education programs to instill in students the knowledge and values of a common cultural inheritance. Since the 1980s, colleges and universities have invested heavily in civic engagement initiatives focused principally on community service.

Each of these movements has privileged different aspects of citizenship, and none—perhaps with the exception of community service—has truly endured. It is difficult to measure the precise impact of these changes on our democratic capacity over the centuries. Nevertheless, as former Harvard President Derek Bok and others have pointed out, if colleges had been successfully requiting their role in training citizens, one would expect to see evidence that the dramatic expansion in college attendance in the twentieth century had led to gains in the democratic capacities of the citizenry.[37] If anything, there are signs of erosion on many of the key measures of democratic citizenship. Following the unfathomable insurrection on the US Capitol on January 6, 2021, leaders and organizations from across the political spectrum called for a renewal of and recommitment to bedrock civic ideals. If the preceding years had not already supplied enough evidence that American higher education could no longer be ambivalent about its neglect of civic education, the events at the Capitol made it agonizingly clear.

Colleges and universities are uniquely positioned for leadership on civic education. Most undergraduates are between the ages of 17 and 24, a period of development often referred to as the "impressionable years," in which young adults develop the civic skills, political convictions, and habits that will persist into adulthood.[38] As these take shape, they can be given depth and nuance in a classroom or campus setting. In fact, studies have consistently shown that well-designed courses and educational programs with a focus on political engagement can help college students develop greater political knowledge and motivation to participate in democratic life. This is particularly true for students who enter college with little political interest or socialization.[39]

Colleges and universities have the resources and expertise to inculcate enduring civic aptitudes—both for the undergraduates in their care and as a vital resource of expertise and data for K–12 school systems. In an intensely polarized political landscape where the prospects of achieving a national consensus on the ideal content of civics education in K–12 education are vanishingly small, our colleges and universities can serve as laboratories of experimentation for civic learning. Likewise, the heterogeneous nature of student populations at most colleges and universities has the potential to mediate and temper some of the vicious partisanship that is sometimes seen in state-level debates about K–12 civics. Today, with almost 70 percent of graduating high school seniors enrolling in college, we can ill afford not to make the education of citizens a priority.[40] To remit this duty will take more than aspirational rhetoric; it will require the resolve to make a robust democratic education a reality.

In this, we can take heart and inspiration from our history. The young republic in its earliest days looked to its universities as bearers of an education in democracy. Episodically, and particularly at moments of democratic threat, the country and its universities have returned to this endeavor. But now, more than two centuries later, we are still without a concrete and enduring program in democratic citizenship in our colleges and universities. Why have these efforts repeatedly faltered? And how can universities answer the latest call to civic purpose, without meeting the fate of those that came before? For that, we will need to peer back and track the ebb and flow of the history of universities as places of unending promise and repeated disappointment for civic education.

Fine Proportions of Character

After the Revolutionary War, leaders and thinkers across the newly established United States ruminated over how best to cultivate republican citizens. No effort embodied this concern more clearly than the quest among some of the country's most prominent leaders to establish a national university. In 1786, Benjamin Rush, one of the signers of the Declaration of Independence, called for the creation of a government-funded university designed to instruct youth in everything "connected with the advancement of republican knowledge and principles."[41] A year later, James Madison proposed (futilely, it should be noted) that a national university be included in the Constitution.[42]

The national university's most prominent advocate was George Washington, who in his first State of the Union in 1790 urged Congress to create a university that would teach its students "to distinguish between oppression and the necessary exercise of lawful authority."[43] Congress failed to act, but Washington clung to the notion that the United States needed an institution of higher learning to develop civic leaders and unite the nation. When he died in 1799, he bequeathed a handsome sum to building a university that would provide its students with "knowledge in the principles of Politics & good Government."[44] It didn't happen, and the national university idea mostly died with Washington (save for a momentary revival toward the end of the nineteenth century). Nevertheless, by 1800, this notion had helped to forge a broad consensus that college learning was integral to citizenship formation.

The medium through which republican citizens were to be cultivated in colleges was the curriculum. Most early nineteenth-century colleges adhered to what is known as the "classical curriculum," a prescribed sequence of courses that began with multiple years of recitations in Greek and Latin (with the occasional pilgrimage into history, English composition, and the natural sciences) and concluded with a moral philosophy capstone course, a wide-ranging seminar on philosophical and political ideas typically taught by a college president.[45] As a famous 1828 report from Yale's faculty defending this curriculum argued, this sequence aimed to develop in students "those liberal and comprehensive views, and those fine proportions of character" that would permit an individual to fulfill his—and it was always *his*—"duties to perform to his family, to his fellow citizens, to his country."[46] Through moral discipline and liberal learning, in short, the classical curriculum sought to forge republican citizens.

The purest expression of the connection between the classical curriculum and citizenship formation was the moral philosophy capstone. By the mid-nineteenth century, this course had been so widely adopted that it was, as one historian has put it, "as common a feature of the average American college as the president's house and the treasury deficit."[47] The course's civic purpose was to turn college boys into independent, moral citizens.[48] Timothy Dwight, Yale's beloved president from 1795 to 1817, used the course as an opportunity to pose and debate an array of political and philosophical questions with the school's seniors. According to notes taken by one Yale senior in 1814, these questions ran the gamut from "Is Party spirit beneficial?" to "Ought Capital Punishments ever to be inflicted?" to "Does the Mind always Think?"[49] Through ongoing dialogues between a president and students, the moral philosophy capstone gave students the opportunity to synthesize and apply the knowledge they had accumulated through-out their undergraduate career. At its best, this course served as a training ground for students to exercise moral agency and personal autonomy as they prepared to enter the republic as citizens.

In the latter half of the nineteenth century, however, the moral philosophy course, and the classical curriculum generally, began to fall away. Its disappearance was not the work of a day, but rather the accumulated effect of a tangle of forces that led to profound transformations in the nature of college education.

Driving this change was the ascendance of science as the dominant paradigm for intellectual inquiry and knowledge creation. The publication of Charles Darwin's *On the Origin of Species* in 1859 had fueled debates that consolidated and popularized a view of science as a tough-minded, dispassionate process by which novel facts were discovered and received truths were interrogated. Knowledge was no longer immutable, but something continually extended and refined through research and the scientific method. Under such conditions, it became ever more difficult to sustain a coherent curriculum grounded in an unchanging moral and spiritual reality.[50] In 1876, the same year that America's first research university, Johns Hopkins, opened its doors to students, famed Harvard psychologist William James published a withering editorial in *The Nation* that characterized the moral philosophy capstone—perhaps somewhat unfairly—as a fossil from a bygone era, whose "lifeless discussions and flabby formulas" left students "dampened and discouraged."[51]

Appeals to the authority of science were also instrumental in legitimating and distinguishing old academic disciplines like history alongside new ones like political science.[52] As these disciplines established themselves within a proliferating number of departments at universities, they began to subdivide into ever more specialized interests and areas of expertise, all of which had the potential to make an imprint upon the curriculum.[53] To accommodate the ever more specialized coursework introduced by new faculty and to satisfy growing student demand for vocational preparation, colleges and universities started to yield to the principle of student choice in the curriculum.

Thus the rigid structure of the classical curriculum gradually gave way to the liberating freedom of electives. At its most extreme, the elective curriculum allowed students to choose whatever courses they wanted throughout their education; in its more limited manifestations, a common curriculum in the first year or two of college opened up onto a buffet of specialized options in later years. The aggregate effect, however, was that colleges could no longer maintain a four-year-long fixed sequence of courses that affirmed the underlying unity and coherence of human knowledge. By the turn of the twentieth century, the classical curriculum was essentially an artifact of an earlier age and, with its demise, how colleges and universities educated for citizenship changed, too.

Securing the Scientific Attitude

Some recent commentators have argued that the rise of the elective curriculum marked the beginning of the end of postsecondary civic education.[54] The full story is more complicated. If anything, from the latter decades of the nineteenth century until the United States' entrance into World War I in 1917, colleges and universities seized their role in training democratic citizens with renewed vigor. Writing in 1910, education reformer David Snedden described this period as one in which colleges had finally "achieved results in conscious preparation for citizenship."[55] The form that citizenship training took, however, looked much different than it had during the heyday of the classical curriculum.

Whereas the old colleges directed their efforts toward discipline, uniformity, and character formation, the new universities celebrated science—sometimes broadly defined—as the keystone of citizenship education. Faculty and administrators insisted that the hard-won practical knowledge that students acquired in college, as well as the habits of the scientific mind they cultivated—like critical reasoning and dispassionate observation—were instrumental for good citizenship. As one turn-of-the-century scholar proudly put it, "the first requisite in training for citizenship is, in my opinion, the securing of the scientific attitude toward all social problems."[56]

While some of these invocations of science as the key to citizenship were mere lip service intended to underscore higher education's utility (leading a professor in 1913 to gripe about all the "frothy stuff about the glory and responsibility of citizenship" pouring out of universities), science applied to citizenship education was more than just savvy marketing. And the most meaningful expressions of this civic impulse were flourishing in the nascent social science and humanities disciplines.[57] Since their inception in the 1870s and 1880s, disciplines like history, sociology, economics, and political science had been reckoning with the question of how the specialized expertise they had come to represent might be directed toward the benefit of democracy.[58]

History and political science, in particular, assumed citizenship education as one of their primary charges, spurred in part by the corruption and excess of the Gilded Age and the profound social inequities that still haunted American democracy in the wake of the Civil War. In 1899, the American Historical Association argued that students at all levels of schooling needed to possess not only the "knowledge of the political machinery which they will be called upon to manage as citizens of a free state" but also "the broader knowledge, the more intelligent spirit, that comes from a study of other men and of other times."[59] And in 1913, the American Political Science Association asserted that departments of political science had three primary duties, the very first of which was "to train for citizenship."[60]

As faculty educated in these disciplines populated the ranks of colleges across the country, course catalogues swelled with new courses in government, history, and economics that armed students with knowledge about democracy and its institutions. Amherst began offering coursework in international law and public speaking, while Harvard introduced popular electives in constitutional government and social reform. Women's colleges, in particular, stood out for the exceptional rigor of their course sequences in the theory and history of democratic institutions, with one observer noting in 1896 that schools like Smith and Wellesley had "conspicuously succeeded" in offering a "genuine social or civic education."[61]

Unfortunately, the same factors that upended the classical curriculum and created the conditions for this abundance of new course offerings also limited their effectiveness, since these new courses were, for the most part, voluntary. Once students had the agency to choose their classes, it became increasingly difficult to maintain any semblance of a coherent educational program in politics or democracy. This casualty of the elective curriculum was not lost on critics of the period. In 1908, famed chronicler of American higher education Abraham Flexner criticized the university's failure:

[A youth] learns that he can vote at twenty-one; that all men are equal before the law. He absorbs the current ethical and political standards. But has higher education no positive duty here? Can it totally neglect this aspect of the boy's orientation? Under the elective system the college does neglect it. . . . In all that immediately pertains to his calling, the college proposes to equip at a high level, but in respect to his civic and human relations, it leaves him on the plane of accident, habit and prejudice.[62]

Flexner's concerns were not idle musings. They reflected a real pitfall of the elective curriculum—one supported by data.

Five years earlier, William A. Schaper, a political science professor at the University of Minnesota, had grown curious about how much political knowledge undergraduates outside of his own department actually had. With the support of the American Political Science Association, Schaper issued a five-question written examination that assessed a respondent's understanding of congressional representation, constitutional amendment and interpretation, and the structure of local and national government. More than 350 college students (112 engineering students and 238 non-engineers who had taken no classes in American history or government) at ten institutions across the country took the test. The engineers averaged an abysmal score of 26.7 out of 100, while the non-engineers achieved a merely disappointing 41.3.[63] In reporting these data, Schaper confessed that he had started "to fear that the want of information about the government and the utter want of comprehension of our political system may be the rule, not the exception among this much favored class of the rising generation."[64] As a way to reduce this deficit, he proposed new course requirements in colleges to ensure that "every candidate for a college degree be required to have attained a certain proficiency in American Government and American History."[65]

But this recommendation failed to take root. As the years passed, the social sciences and humanities beat a steady retreat from their civic aspirations by turning their focus inward, seeking to grow their disciplines through the training of future generations of scholars and a focus on academic research. Still, concerns over the absence of citizenship education within the elective system persisted. Only in the aftermath of the carnage of World War I would colleges and universities attempt to restore democratic education to the center of the curriculum.

The Essence of Good Citizenship

In the fall of 1918, just over a year after President Woodrow Wilson declared war on the German Empire, more than five hundred colleges and universities were transformed into de facto military training centers with the federal government's establishment of the Student Army Training Corps (SATC), which required enlisted students to wear uniforms on campus, to take courses from US Army personnel, and to conduct military exercises in parallel to normal academic life.[66] Although short-lived, this experiment profoundly affected college and university curricula.

Part of the army's goal was to persuade new soldiers in the righteousness and justice of the war. Beginning in July, the US War Department had started rolling out a new mandatory course for all enlisted students at participating colleges called "War Issues." Taught by nonmilitary faculty, the course was intended to introduce students to the political, economic, and philosophical underpinnings of the war. Although in practice War Issues likely didn't amount to much more than academically sanctioned drumbeating for war, it was, in the words of its director, the academic humanist Frank Aydelotte, "never conceived by us as a purely

propaganda course."[67] There were no official textbooks or syllabi, and faculty were given wide latitude to teach the course as
they saw fit. Student participation and discussion were actively
encouraged.

On November 11, mere weeks after the course was introduced
to colleges, the Armistice was signed, and the rationale for the
course crumpled. Still, almost three hundred institutions opted
to continue running War Issues for the remainder of the 1918–
1919 academic year to guide students through the peace process.[68] The devastation wrought by the war, the catastrophic loss
of life, and the uncertain future of democracy itself made this
course suddenly feel more necessary and urgent. However imperfectly, it had answered a felt need among colleges to renew and
reimagine higher education's civic purpose through required
courses. It loosened the elective system's hold (or, as one district
director of the course put it, helped to "burn up much of the
rubbish of elective courses") and created an opening for the re-
introduction of a core education in democracy back into colleges
and universities.[69]

Although it would not reach its apotheosis until World War
II, this was the first stirring of what came to be known as the *general education movement*, which gained steam in American colleges and universities during the interwar period. Broadly speaking, general education sought to deliver to undergraduates a broad
and synthetic introduction to the knowledge and skills believed
to be necessary for citizenship in a pluralistic, democratic society.

One of the few universities to seize the postwar moment to
establish a new general education curriculum was Columbia,
whose faculty had been instrumental in designing War Issues.
Eager to translate that course's potential to the complexities of

peacetime, Columbia's dean Herbert Hawkes encouraged the formation of a yearlong mandatory course for freshmen at the college that would help make them into "citizens who can participate in national affairs with clear judgment and intelligence."[70] It would achieve this, in the words of one of its faculty progenitors, by immersing students in "the insistent problems of today."[71]

From 1919 to 1929, the Contemporary Civilization sequence (as it was eventually called) became a centerpiece of the Columbia curriculum, pressing every incoming class of students into an engagement with the most urgent social, political, and economic issues of the day. As the course's popularity grew, however, so did its breadth. By 1937, administrators and faculty at Columbia had expanded Contemporary Civilization into a two-year sequence that encompassed all of Western intellectual history. On top of this, the college added another new two-year sequence in the humanities that came to encompass art history, music, and literature. These were valuable additions to be sure, but they represented a drift away from citizenship and toward a more comprehensive liberal education.

This movement away from civics was not uncommon among other general education programs during the interwar years. The general education sequences at new women's liberal arts colleges like Sarah Lawrence and Bennington—founded in 1928 and 1932, respectively—were designed, for instance, with the intention of nurturing individual passions and promoting community service. Meanwhile, the University of Chicago launched a general education program in 1931 called the "New Plan" that championed interdisciplinary learning; by the middle of the decade, President Hutchins was already trying to replace this program with a general education regime centered around the supposed great books of Western civilization, which would, in theory, cultivate students' intellect and spirits through engagement with canonical literature, citizenship education being at most a peripheral aim.[72]

World War II reignited the democratic flame of general education programs. As fragile democracies across Europe descended one after another into fascism and the United States was reluctantly forced to consider participation in another world war, American universities once again launched ambitious democratic general education programs. By 1950, nearly half of the colleges in the country had adopted a general education program, most with an explicit focus on citizenship formation.[73] An editorial published in 1946 in the first issue of the *Journal of General Education* summarized the predominant view: "General education seeks to instill attitudes and understandings which form the essence of good citizenship."[74]

Perhaps the most publicized general education effort of the World War II era occurred at Harvard in 1945 with the publication of a two hundred–page report titled *General Education in a Free Society*. Popularly known as the "Red Book," the report set out to determine how general education could be used to "both shape the future and secure the foundations of our free society."[75] The report's authors took the view that as much as democratic citizenship relies on freedom of thought and independent insight, it also demands, to an equal degree, a common set of understandings and capacities. They called for a reimagining of the curriculum that would balance the benefits of a specialized and scientific education with the coherence of the classical curriculum of the nineteenth century. These were noble aspirations, but the core of the solution they settled upon turned out to be roughly the same as the one Chicago had devised a decade earlier: every college student ought to read and digest the great works of Western thought.[76]

The following year, as the first waves of returning veterans swelled the ranks of campuses across the country, President Harry S. Truman convened a national commission to explore "the functions of higher education in our democracy and of the means by which they can best be performed."[77] One of the most ambitious and forward thinking documents on American higher education ever produced, the six-volume *Higher Education for American Democracy*, announces at its outset that the "first and most essential charge upon higher education is that at all levels and in all its fields of specialization, it shall be the carrier of democratic values, ideals, and process."[78]

Its proposals still feel timely. At a time when prejudice and want continued to bar vast numbers from higher education, it advocated for increased equity in the quality of college education and access for all regardless of race, gender, religion, or socioeconomic status. It also contemplated a dramatic expansion of the community college system in the United States, claiming for it a vital, unique place in the firmament of American higher education capable of vastly "improving the quality of [students'] lives as individuals and as citizens."[79]

Among the most urgent of the report's recommendations was that higher education had an imperative "to provide a unified general education for American youth."[80] Taking a more direct approach to democratic education than the Harvard Red Book, the report's authors imagined colleges and universities marshaling the vast expertise they housed to craft, for example, history courses that would "clarify the practice as well as the theory of democracy" alongside sociology courses that would, in the wake of the Holocaust, "translate statistics into human beings and orient the student to the social world with which he must cope."[81] Through such efforts, colleges and universities could be beacons of citizenship education in an era when the United States—and liberal democracy more generally—was emerging as a true international force.

Both the Harvard Red Book and the Truman Commission report garnered widespread national attention upon their publication: amazingly, the Red Book sold forty thousand copies, and the Truman report shaped other parts of federal higher education policy for more than a generation.[82] Yet their proposals for a general education program built on civic learning did not maintain their hold on the national imagination for long. As has been the pattern of civic education efforts in colleges and universities across our history, the events of subsequent decades would hamper their calls.

Lives of Involved and Committed Citizenship

With the war effort fading, the country's attention soon fixed on new priorities. Cold War anxieties intensified, and higher education found itself caught in a national race to technological and scientific dominance. Suddenly, the earlier focus—really, little more than a decade old—on teaching the art of democratic citizenship seemed quaint, and a distraction from the task at hand.

Meanwhile, the rise of the civil rights movement and the emergence of new interdisciplinary fields such as African American studies and women's studies upended the fragile consensus on which the general education movement was based—chief among them the notion that there is a preferred civilization (Western) and a preferred viewpoint on how to understand it (that of mostly white and male writers). This powerful and persuasive critique introduced new voices into the curriculum, but it made the maintenance of any sort of coherent core curriculum an increasingly tenuous and difficult endeavor. On the other side of the cultural wars was a growing movement of evangelical leaders who lamented that general education marked one more step along the way toward a fully secularized, heterodox education.[83]

Add to all this the resistance of faculty in many quarters to a structured civic curriculum. There was pushback over which classes should be taught and which ideas merited inclusion in the curriculum. General education courses did not always fit neatly into the disciplines in which the faculty plied their craft—and the movement sputtered. Civic education would not disappear from colleges and universities, but it would be pushed for a time to the periphery of academic life.

By the 1960s, the strongest expressions of civic aspiration at colleges and universities would be found outside the classroom. Student protests gripped campuses in response to racial injustice at home and the atrocities of the Vietnam War abroad. Dismayed by what they claimed was university complicity (at worst) and complacency (at best) to these injustices, students swarmed into streets and quads in an effort to direct institutions of higher learning away from what they saw as amoral leadership, corporatization, and a coziness with the military-industrial complex, and toward a renewed sense of civic purpose.

Sometimes these protests boiled over into unrest, and on a couple of occasions these demonstrations even forced the suspension of university activity. When Berkeley undergraduate and student leader Mario Savio stood on the steps of the university's administrative building in 1964, he implored his peers to "put your bodies upon the gears and upon the wheels, upon the levers, upon all the apparatus—and you've got to make it stop!"[84]

Eventually, this surge of activism and concern—certainly not confined to campuses but focused and clarified there—found its way back into the university classroom. The civic impulse of this moment helped to give rise to the service-learning movement, one of the most dominant and enduring forms of civic education in American colleges and universities to date.

The movement began in January 1984 when recent Harvard graduate Wayne Meisel set off south on foot from Colby College in Waterville, Maine. Five months, 600 miles, and at least seventy colleges later, Meisel arrived in Washington, DC. At every college he stopped at, he met with students to promote volunteerism and community service. He was determined to show the world that undergraduates of the 1980s were not the self-absorbed and petulant loafs portrayed in the 1978 box office smash *Animal House*.[85] Meisel saw a crisis of civic apathy in the United States, and he believed it was imperative that young people press back against the egoism and disengagement that had come to dominate modern life.[86]

Meisel's walk sparked a cascade of enthusiasm in colleges and universities for volunteerism and public service. One of the most lasting efforts to emerge in this period was Campus Compact, a coalition of colleges and universities formed in 1985 by the presidents of Brown, Georgetown, and Stanford and devoted to putting community service at the center of campus life.

By 1990, Campus Compact's mission began to expand beyond mere volunteering toward "service learning," which marries community service to academic work. With roots in the educational philosophies and practices of John Dewey and Jane Addams in the 1930s, service learning emerged in a piecemeal fashion throughout the 1960s and '70s via a loose network of practitioners eager to integrate faculty expertise and the rigors of college coursework with involvement in local communities.[87] Campus Compact's adoption of service learning helped bring the movement—and community service at colleges more generally—into the academic mainstream.[88]

By almost any measure, service learning has been more success-ful than any other postsecondary civic education initiative be-fore it. Since the early 1990s, hundreds of institutes, centers, and offices of service learning have been founded at colleges and uni-versities across the country.[89] This coincided with the rapid growth of Campus Compact's membership, from 102 colleges in 1986 to more than 600 in 1998. As of 2019, more than 1,000 colleges and universities are members.[90] In a 2003 survey, the American Association of Community Colleges reported that 71 percent of member institutions offered service-learning courses. And al-though the courses are elective for the most part, 53 percent of first-year college students and 60 percent of seniors in 2019 re-ported that some of their classes involved service learning.[91] Today, service learning is a centerpiece of civic and community engage-ment at colleges and universities.

But has service learning made students into better democratic citizens? The research is mixed.

One of the early claims of the movement's proponents was that service learning would cultivate in students "the informed judg-ment, imagination, and skills that lead to a greater capacity to con-tribute to the common good."[92] And, in fact, research shows that service-learning courses promote a range of democratic attitudes and skills. These include the capacity for critical self-reflection, an understanding and tolerance of others, and a motivation to partici-pate in service in the future.[93] Service learning also prompts stu-dents toward civic action: those who take service-learning courses in college are more likely to volunteer throughout their postcolle-giate lives and to demonstrate leadership within the communities of which they are a part.[94] As vital and important as these aptitudes are, however, they do not—on their own—constitute an education in the full suite of skills needed for democratic citizenship.[95]

To put this more bluntly, *our colleges and universities have been far more enthusiastic about teaching students to engage the communities around them than to engage the democratic systems through which they self-govern.* Each is an indispensable part of a comprehensive liberal arts education, but in recent decades, universities have embraced the former and shunned the latter.

This is part of a larger societal trend line. Beginning in the late 1980s, volunteerism skyrocketed among young people. Between 1989 and 2015, rates of volunteerism among young adults grew from 13.4 to 25.2 percent. Some of that spike has leveled off in the past several years owing to the much broader erosion of social cohesion in the United States, but young adults now consistently express a far *greater* sense of duty to volunteer than they did in the 1980s. However, these same surveys show that young adults also now have a *lower* sense of responsibility to serve on a jury or to stay informed about news and public events.[96] Political scientist Cliff Zukin and colleagues described this generational trend as the widening of the civic–political divide, with young people increasingly clustered on the civic, rather than the political, side.[97]

Universities may have unwittingly contributed to this divide by offering an education in democracy only incidentally, or as an afterthought—a limitation that many of the leaders of the higher education civic engagement movement now concede. In one paper, several acknowledged that the "movement has largely sidestepped the political dimension of civic engagement," and with a few exceptions, "institutional (and national) efforts do not explicitly link the work of engagement to our democracy."[98] By teaching students about engagement in local communities, service learning has done much good. But it is not designed to provide a focused training in political systems and democratic governance, to nurture affinity for democracy as a system of popular governance, to explain comprehensively why democratic values matter, or to give students the knowledge and agency necessary to engage or reshape democratic institutions. Service learning is and ought to be a pillar of democratic learning at our colleges and universities, but it simply cannot be the sole source of a civic education.

Marginal and Episodic

The history of civic education in colleges and universities is one defined, above all, by repeated bursts of civic resolve that have run aground or lost focus. The rise of science and elective curricula supplanted the classical curriculum; the general education movement ebbed in the 1960s because of a host of internal and external cultural forces; and, most recently, service learning, although enduring, has come to privilege the civic at the expense of the democratic. Sometimes these departures have been a consequence of shifting priorities; at other times, a given movement simply missed the mark of providing a genuinely democratic education. This is, of course, not to deny the thousands of talented faculty members on campuses across this country—my own included— who teach and cultivate an affinity for democracy in their students. But far too often, these classes touch only a small fraction of college students and are rarely tethered to any overarching institutional goal or broader program in democratic learning.

This neglect has occurred despite increasingly animated calls for reform by commentators on all sides of the political spectrum. The Truman Commission made this call in the 1940s. Throughout the 1970s and '80s, a steady drumbeat of reports and jeremiads continued apace. In 1999, Campus Compact convened university leaders across the country to discuss the democratic deficiencies at research universities, yielding a landmark declaration that implored universities to become "vital agents and architects for a flourishing democracy."[99] Thirteen years later, in 2012, an Obama administration task force on college learning and democracy's future issued a report that—with echoes of the Truman Commission—insisted yet again that universities "embrace civic learning and democratic engagement as an undisputed educational priority."[100]

These calls have not gone entirely unanswered. There are promising signs of a renewed commitment to democratic education at some colleges and universities. On the whole, however, it is fair to say that a democratic education touching all the pillars of good citizenship—knowledge, skills, values, and aspirations—has time and again failed to gain traction in American higher education. The idea is still very much an outlier, despite the broad recognition of liberal democracy's contemporary vulnerabilities.

There are several interconnected reasons for this. One is a lack of willpower on the part of university leadership to tackle this issue, a fatal vulnerability when one considers widespread faculty skepticism with, or opposition to, this idea. Meanwhile, broader divisions in society manifest themselves within the internal academic debates over the content of these courses—the Left and Right, for instance, have few canonical texts that aren't thorns in their political opponents' side. Such fissures make it all the more difficult to achieve a clear consensus as to what a comprehensive democratic education would look like on our campuses, rendering any attempt by a college or university to implement change politically treacherous. As a result, the work of civic education at colleges and universities remains, in the words of one higher education leader, a "marginal and episodic" feature on most campuses.[101] If colleges and universities are to discover more sustainable and effective means of delivering democratic knowledge, skills, and values to our students, we should begin by examining each of these causes more deeply.

First: *a lack of will on the part of leadership*. As the history of citizenship education at colleges and universities suggests, the momentum to implement and sustain a meaningful program in democratic education is perpetually at risk of being diverted by the emergence of new demands, more pressing needs, and prerogatives from some sectors that view civic training as devoid of rigor and intellectual content. Sometimes these come from within the academy (such as the forces pressing upon the fledgling social sciences in the early twentieth century) and sometimes from without (as, for instance, the race of nations to technological dominance in the Cold War).

Generating and sustaining willpower for civic education are not easy. Looking back across the long history of civic education, the moments at which this nation and its universities rallied most enthusiastically behind making higher education a carrier for democratic education was when democracy was emerging from periods of greatest stress, most notably the founding, the Civil War, World War I, and World War II. One need not agree with the proposed approaches to civic education to blossom in these moments to see in each the will needed to achieve a lasting result. It was a will born of immense sacrifice.

That sense of sacrifice is harder to come by today when citizens are asked to forego so little in terms of coin or toil to the sustenance of democracy. Indeed, the voluntary nature of military service has meant that recent wars barely touch the great mass of students from privileged backgrounds who are disproportionately overrepresented in the university.[102] So, perhaps it is not entirely surprising that many might feel less invested in the preservation of democracy's blessings and thus less desirous of committing to an education in democracy.

A second reason for democratic education's struggles relates to the *structure of the modern university*. The emergence of disciplines, the segmentation of the university into schools and departments, and the rise of curricular choice and distributed authority have all impeded efforts at creating a common curriculum in civics generally, let alone one in democratic citizenship. These forces have, of course, constituted the backbone of the contemporary university for decades, and they are largely responsible for the preeminence of universities as wellsprings of research and discovery over the past two centuries. But we need to recognize, too, that from the disintegration of the classical curriculum in the mid-nineteenth century to the unraveling of general education to service learning's emphasis on broad civic engagement rather than a more focused education in democracy, they have pulled at the seams of every major democratic education movement in the history of American higher education.

A final impediment to the sustainability of a democratic education at colleges and universities is the *contest of ideas*. By this I mean the unavoidable and ever-present dispute over what the content of a democratic curriculum ought to be. Few topics elicit such a diversity of viewpoints among faculty as civic education. Sometimes the nature of these pedagogical disagreements is simply about ensuring that certain disciplines are represented in the curriculum (that a knowledge of mathematics or statistics is just as important to good citizenship as an understanding of government, for example). These disputes can frustrate efforts to reach consensus on a design for a democratic education, as happened in the 1950s and '60s, when excessive tinkering led to what one scholar has called the "devolution of general education."[103] But debates about a democratic education can also spill over into ideological clashes that are as combustible as democracy itself.

The political Right has expressed deep distrust of the academy's ability to teach to democratic values. One conservative-leaning group published a report in 2017 claiming that, in the eyes of universities, "a good citizen is a radical activist."[104] By the same token, many within the academy have harbored skepticism about how the liberal democratic experiment has been conducted. Forged out of the experience of the 1960s and '70s—including the Vietnam War, Watergate, and the civil rights movement and magnified by subsequent experiences—there is a lack of confidence in the democratic project itself that can only translate into a lack of enthusiasm for teaching it.

The civics situation in colleges and universities may not be quite as politically fraught as it is at the K–12 level, where local and state officials have come to meddle in sometimes extreme ways in social studies curricula that magnify rather than attenuate our country's distressing polarization. But the deep wells of resistance to (and suspicion of) a democratic education in academia present a challenge in their own right. Facing all of this, it is only natural that university leaders might have concluded that it is simply easier to steer clear of introducing into the curriculum such a charged topic.

In his inaugural State of the Union address in 1790, George Washington sketched a vision of the American university as the vessel for a uniquely civic sort of education. Washington longed for a single national university to fulfill this vision, but he also wondered whether these ends could be achieved through the existing colleges and universities of the young republic—or, as he put it, "by affording aids to Seminaries of Learning already established." In his last will and testament, he lamented that "it has always been a source of serious regret with me" that the nation had not made meaningful progress on this vision.[105]

Centuries later, we are not much closer. At a moment when we should be relying upon a higher education in citizenry to help ensure democratic resiliency, it is absent. Liberal democracy is endangered at home and abroad, and the democratic capacities of the American people are dormant (at best) and in decline (at worst). Many primary and secondary schools are struggling to carry the burden. We need a renaissance in civic education at colleges and universities that vindicates Washington's vision, an infusion of democratic learning in these institutions that is at once adapted to the exigencies of this moment and responsive to the obstacles and forces that have doomed past efforts. We have allowed complacency, a lack of willpower, and partisan division to obscure an appreciation of what is at stake in teaching to democracy, and what universities are able to do to protect it.

Teaching Democratic Citizens

We can do something about this: our colleges and universities need to institute a Democracy Requirement into their curricula. Given the institutional diversity of this country's colleges and universities, no single approach could possibly be appropriate for a community college in Oklahoma, a flagship public research university in California, *and* a Jesuit liberal arts college in Pennsylvania. Every college and university has a student body, a mission, a mode of governance, and a culture that is distinctive to its identity and history—educating for democratic citizenship has never been and cannot be one-size-fits-all. Nevertheless, every college and university can plant a stake in the ground for democratic education with a requirement ensuring that students make contact with an education tailored toward questions of democracy at some point in their undergraduate career, and that they wrestle with the animating questions of democratic life, which include everything from how to structure political institutions to how to remedy the lasting wounds of centuries of racial injustice to the skills and the commitments required of democratic citizens.

One of the closest things to a universal law of academia is that change comes slowly. The times where colleges and universities have mustered the will and resources to oversee meaningful injections of civic learning into curricula are rare. In fact, as I have sketched in this chapter, most have occurred at moments of profound social rupture. And even if a new reform gains momentum, constant vigilance is necessary to overcome the temptations to distraction or dilution that so often beset civic learning initiatives.

This does not mean that the prospect of bringing democratic learning into the curriculum is hopeless, however. One recent success story is taking place at Stanford University. In early 2021, Stanford began piloting an undergraduate course titled "Citizenship in the 21st Century" as part of its new proposed core curriculum for first-years.[106] Designed through a faculty-led process, the course hearkens back to the years after World War I, when Stanford—in the mold of Columbia and other universities—ran a class titled "Problems of Citizenship" that aimed, in the words of one proponent, to form in students "those habits of mind and temper upon which, along with the knowledge of the right facts, the soundness of opinion depends."[107] That course—following the pattern of many citizenship-focused general education courses of the period—had been supplanted by a "Western Civilization" requirement in the 1930s.[108] This new class aims to return citizenship to the center of general education, by introducing students to ideas and duties of citizenship through a rich array of diverse texts (from indigenous writers to the framers of the US Constitution to the poets of the Harlem Renaissance) as well as "ethical and philosophical discussions" and "case studies."[109]

Another promising development can be found at the University of Virginia. In the fall of 2019, faculty at its College of Arts and Sciences voted by an overwhelming majority to approve a new curriculum.[110] Faculty votes rarely draw headlines, but this one was significant. It constituted the first major overhaul of the historic university's general education program in four decades. According to one of its architects, the program reflects an attempt to answer the question, "What, then, can give our university a common purpose in a highly pluralistic American liberal democracy such as ours?"[111]

The answer they arrived at is a required set of interdisciplinary "Engagements" courses. In the words of its architects, this general education program aspires to provide "a foundation for democratic citizenship" by nurturing specific civic competencies like critical and quantitative reasoning, a knowledge of political history, and the discussion of urgent social issues, among others. Divided into four broad categories—"Aesthetic Engagements," "Empirical and Scientific Engagement," "Engaging Differences," and "Ethical Engagement"—these courses are taught by a group of distinguished faculty called College Fellows who forego disciplinary teaching for two years in order to devote themselves fully to these small, intimate classes. This curriculum stands as a truly promising effort on the part of a flagship public university to follow through on its obligation to educate students in the capacities of citizenship in a way that builds upon the diverse fields of expertise of its faculty.

But not every attempt to reimagine a robust education in democratic citizenship has been as successful. In January 2019, President Mitch Daniels (no relation) of Purdue University told the university community that despite the widespread understanding that "a government by consent of the governed really needs informed citizens," low levels of civic literacy were a "national phenomenon."[112] So, he posed a challenge to his university community. He proposed that, in order to graduate, Purdue students should at least be required to pass an exam that tests civic knowledge.[113] Daniels admitted to still being open to "larger, grander approaches" to solving the problem of civic literacy, but he was happy to "settle for knowing" that Purdue students could show a fundamental understanding of the principles of self-governance.[114]

A working group of faculty answered Daniels's call, and in early 2020 they unveiled a multilayered "Test+" program that would have required students not only to pass an exam of the university's own creation but also to either earn three credit hours of relevant coursework, attend university-sponsored civic events for a certain number of hours, or complete a civics module designed by the university's Center for C-SPAN Scholarship and Engagement.[115] In spring 2020, the university's faculty senate voted down the proposal by a two-to-one margin. A year later, Purdue's Board of Trustees moved to institute the requirement anyway. When this book is published, the graduation requirement at Purdue will likely be policy, but its success will depend on garnering broad support from stakeholders across the campus, especially faculty and students.[116]

These three examples are vivid reminders of the absolutely critical role that faculty support plays in instituting a meaningful democracy requirement, as well as how difficult it can often be both to reach consensus on such a sensitive topic and to implement a program of change. Across history, civic education innovations at colleges and universities have succeeded best when leadership and faculty collaborated to reimagine the curriculum along more democratic lines. (The Contemporary Civilizations sequence at Columbia in the 1920s is but one example.) Given the political polarization embedded in every aspect of our lives, achieving a shared vision of goals and methods like that again may be impossible, but I continue to believe that open and honest conversations among faculty and leadership about what our students ought to know as citizens can still yield meaningful change.

As these examples show, a democracy requirement may take many different forms, but it should embody the fullest expression of civic learning. This is something we can do now in a way our predecessors could not, given the growing body of research on citizenship and civic education. The 2012 report *A Crucible Moment* from the National Task Force on Civic Learning and Democratic Engagement synthesized a framework for a truly robust education in democracy—similar to the one I proposed at the beginning of this chapter—that teaches *knowledge, skills, values,* and *collective action.*[117] To teach to these distinct capacities requires the recognition that studying historical texts from the archives of democracy is just as important as practicing the art of peaceful protest to enact change. Neither is inherently radical or reactionary—both are indisputably democratic. The education should have, as one of its core components, a rigorous exploration of the ways in which our American experiment has fulfilled its aspirations for equality across certain divides of race, ethnicity, or class, and, to the extent that it has not, the goals and instruments available to redress these failures. The key here would be to insist that any exploration of democracy's failures be firmly implanted on an understanding of its promise and a recognition of its inherent fragility.

Our touchstone for developing future civic initiatives should be the body of knowledge of how to teach to citizenship. But we also desperately need to make that body grow. Our understanding of citizenship and how to instill its virtues—while stronger today than ever—is still underdeveloped. On this much, there is a unison of views. The Association of American Colleges and Universities has stressed that "more evidence on civic learning is urgently needed."[118] The American Political Science Association, renewing a commitment to civic education that it first took up (and then departed from) nearly a century ago, says that although the field has made progress in figuring out how to design an effective civic education course, "major problems" remain, including that instructors rely mostly on "anecdotal evidence that whatever they tried, worked."[119] To that point, when educational experts surveyed thirty universities in Campus Compact, they found that only one was conducting a longitudinal study to assess the outcomes and efficacy of their civics classes.[120]

Fortunately, universities are precisely the institutions best situated to expand our understanding of democratic citizenship, how to teach it, and how to bring that understanding into the curriculum. As one example, Harvard University political theorist Danielle Allen launched the Democratic Knowledge Project, a research and action laboratory that is leaning into precisely this kind of work. In 2020, Allen also co-chaired a commission on democratic citizenship that called for the creation of a university-housed study of democratic engagement, and she contributed to a pioneering report on civic education that urged, among other things, for civics courses to incorporate the "best scholarship" in an array of academic fields.[121] Wake Forest University launched another initiative along these lines in 2001 through its "Democracy Fellows" program, in which thirty incoming students participated in a variety of intensive civic programming: they were enrolled in a freshman seminar focused on "the theory and the practice of deliberation" in a democracy; they collectively organized around and advocated for a social issue; and they even staged deliberations, first at the campus level and then at the community level.[122] Coming out of this program, students showed a greater interest in politics, voting, and "working with others in their communities to solve shared problems."[123] Researchers followed up with the original cohort of students in 2014 and discovered that they remained more involved in democratic life than their peers, more tolerant of others, and held a more textured understanding of citizenship.[124] Wake Forest has continued to nurture deliberation as a cornerstone of democratic education.

Building a new requirement into the curriculum—especially one that has the potential to be as controversial as a democracy requirement—is no mean task. The curriculum at any college or university lies at the intersection of a great many stakeholders—including faculty, students, and administrators—with a lot of divergent interests. The coursework students take must be responsive to students' needs and trajectories, accommodate the disciplinary expertise of faculty, and adhere to the broader aims of the administration as well as the structural and historical legacies of the institution. Even the best-laid plans for curricular reform can fall apart.[125] Meaningful and enduring reforms demand the sustained commitment of leadership and engagement at multiple levels of the institution.

I know these struggles firsthand. For all that my institution, Johns Hopkins, does on behalf of democracy as a research institution, and notwithstanding the stirring courses taught by individual faculty, an education in democracy has never, in truth, been a leading priority for us at an institutional level. This can be explained by many of the same historical forces that I have traced throughout this chapter: the demise of the classical curriculum, the rise of science, the specialization of disciplines and faculty, and the migration of civics to community service. The curriculum at Hopkins is built around rigorous, time-intensive majors; there are otherwise practically no required courses and many elective options; and faculty determine much of what is taught. These factors, for all their extraordinary effects, do not lend themselves to a focused education in democratic citizenship.

Over the years, we have worked diligently to build up an array of democracy-focused programming, research opportunities, and coursework. Through our Hopkins Votes initiative, we have seen sizable gains in voter turnout among our undergraduates. We have also founded the SNF Agora Institute through the generosity of the Stavros Niarchos Foundation. Staffed by a multidisciplinary cohort of faculty and external fellows, the institute is researching democracy's frailties and strengths, proposing practical solutions to these problems, and teaching courses to our students on what they uncover on urgent topics like polarization, disinformation, and populism. Not unlike its ancient Athenian namesake, the Agora is also a forum for dialogues between researchers, students, and community members about topics that bear directly on the state of democracy today. And perhaps most relevant for present purposes, it has infused our curriculum with a suite of new democracy-themed courses and programming throughout our university, and seeded connections among faculty and students across far-flung departments and campuses.

These efforts involve only a subset of our undergraduates, however. And, most often, that means they attract students who are highly politically literate when they enter the university. With key measures of citizenship flagging, that approach no longer feels adequate. When an education in democracy is optional, we should not be too surprised that the tenets of democracy itself seem, to many, also optional. And so, we at Johns Hopkins have started conversations about what instituting a democratic requirement at our own institution might mean. It is painfully clear that universities cannot simply assume their students will absorb the precepts of citizenship. As the arc of history has taught us again and again, democratic citizenship must be learned. Universities must do their part to teach it.

THREE

Hard Truths

Creating Knowledge and Checking Power

PRIOR TO MARCH 2020, the only other time Johns Hopkins University had shuttered its doors to students was in 1918, when a deadly flu swept through the nation, killing millions. One hundred and two years later, a global pandemic once again upended our community. At Hopkins, the spread of COVID-19 compelled us to take the excruciating steps of making classes remote for the remainder of the semester, winding down all but our most critical research operations, canceling events, and closing our libraries. Nor were we alone. Across the country, campuses went suddenly silent. But that didn't mean the debate, research, and discoveries that characterize university life disappeared—they had simply migrated, temporarily, from the quads to the cloud. We were not in retreat. In fact, universities across the world were throwing themselves into initiatives that would help humanity understand and combat this historic pandemic.

The collective university response in the early days of the pandemic was truly extraordinary. From the University of Arizona to the Massachusetts Institute of Technology, researchers were delving into the nature of COVID-19 and relaying insights nearly in real time. Georgetown University partnered with the Allen Institute for AI and other institutions to create the COVID-19 Open Research Dataset, an artificial intelligence–driven database containing tens of thousands of scientific papers on the coronavirus.[1] Stony Brook University researchers designed tools to identify regions most at risk from the virus.[2] Engineers at Iowa State University pioneered new fast-paced, at-home COVID-19 tests.[3] And scientists at Oxford University swiftly developed one of the first viable COVID-19 vaccines.[4]

Johns Hopkins was proud to play a part in the international response, too, releasing one of the first frameworks for ethical digital contact tracing, providing critical counsel to all levels of government on the public health management of the disease, and developing new medical treatment protocols for infected patients.[5] Our most public-facing effort, however, was the Coronavirus Resource Center.

The project began in January 2020 when one of our PhD students, Ensheng Dong, asked a question that did not yet have an answer. He was concerned about a new virus that was spreading through China, where his family lived, and began tracking its progress using available data. At the time, precious little was known about COVID-19. Fortunately, Ensheng's advisor, Dr. Lauren Gardner, is an expert in the spread of infectious diseases and was eager to help. Over the course of a long night, the two of them designed an interactive dashboard—with its now-iconic austere gray world map populated by red circles indicating spread—that used publicly available datasets to chart the trajectory of COVID-19.[6]

When the dashboard first launched, Dr. Gardner expected its audience would be confined mostly to a small coterie of academic colleagues. Yet as the virus jumped from country to country and continent to continent, the site quickly became a vital source of accurate, reliable information about COVID-19 accessed by individuals, governments, and media organizations around the world. The seemingly inexorable spread of the map's red circles gripped the world, putting to rest any hopes that the virus might be easily contained.

In time, the map grew into the Johns Hopkins Coronavirus Resource Center, which functioned as an online hub of up-to-the-moment information about testing, tracking, contact tracing, hospitalizations, and vaccines; a repository of analysis and insight for faculty to share their most bracing insights and discoveries; and a virtual convening space for experts, policy makers, and leaders from across the government and the academy to gather and pave a way forward. By the beginning of 2021, the site had been visited over a billion times.[7]

For me, the collective response and success of universities and the scientific community more broadly—along with the sudden celebrity status of government scientists like Dr. Anthony Fauci—was evidence that people around the world were starved for accurate, reliable information about the pandemic. Early polling supported this intuition, with one survey in April 2020 finding that 79 percent of Americans expressed trust in the medical advice and public health guidance coming out of research universities.[8] Perhaps, in this moment of shared crisis, we had finally found a way to break through the din of misinformation and hyper-partisanship that had so overwhelmed public life.

Of course, it was not that simple. In some countries (like Hungary), political leaders exploited the public health emergency to consolidate their power and accelerate their drift toward autocracy. In the United States, changing public health guidance on masks and gatherings—fueled by a federal government that was actively undermining the independent fact-finding and communication work of agencies—became weaponized in the service of partisan culture warfare.[9] None of this is to deny the enormous successes of this period. As I write this in early 2021, it is undeniable that science has been indispensable in guiding us through this historic crisis. But it is also evident that the pandemic response, like so many other facets of our public life, was engulfed in the same whirlpools of polarization as democracy itself, with *facts* a frequent casualty. The pandemic is an object lesson in the exceptional promise and the dire peril of expertise in our divided age. It is a lesson not lost on the academy.

A commitment to facts and truth is the terra firma of public discourse and reasoned decision-making in democratic life. Liberal democracies tend to be kaleidoscopic societies that encompass a vast array of competing approaches to life and claims to validity. Or, as the philosopher John Rawls put it, they contain "a plurality of conflicting reasonable comprehensive doctrines, religious, philosophical, and moral."[10] One consequence of this is that liberal democracies have no single central truth or dogma to govern them, and thus no easy recourse for reconciling all these claims into one coherent vision of society. Liberal democracies are invariably remitted to a world of debate and compromise in the public sphere.

But debate and compromise are not enough on their own to advance the common good. What links public policy to the public interest are facts. Ideally, legislators and judges rely upon facts to shape their decisions, just as citizens draw upon facts to form reasoned opinions that can be translated into voting behavior, dialogue, and political action. And when policies fail to deliver promised results, it is facts that allow us to establish discrepancies, to trace actions to actors, and, not least, to check elected officials and hold them to account. The political theorist and many-time White House aide William Galston describes the link between facts and this checking function in these terms: "Democracies cannot function without public trust, which depends on the public belief that officials are competent to ascertain relevant truth and committed to presenting it candidly."[11]

By contrast, authoritarian regimes reveal a willful and reliable antipathy toward facts in the pursuit of power. This was evident in Stalin's Russia, where the Holodomor—the mass starvation that took almost four million Ukrainian lives—was fueled by state-sponsored disinformation campaigns.[12] It was evident in the invidious Nazi claim that the reason for Germany's loss in World War I was a deliberately orchestrated "stab in the back" by Jews who worked to overthrow the monarchy in 1918–1919.[13] It is evident today in places like Viktor Orbán's Hungary, which has established its own research institutes to dispense warped narratives about the country's history. And it was distressingly evident in the outrageous lie propagated by President Donald Trump that the 2020 election was "stolen" from him by massive voter fraud coordinated by a cabal of Democrats and foreign influences.[14] In the words of the Polish poet and diplomat Czeslaw Milosz, authoritarians are always at the ready to "by-pass a fact when a concept comes into conflict with reality."[15]

Clearly, facts matter.

But what is a fact? Today, we understand facts to be fragments of information that are neutral, objective, and verifiable. This conception is of relatively recent vintage. It can be traced to sixteenth-century English jurisprudence, when courts began to distinguish "matters of law" from "matters of fact," assigning the latter to juries and asking them to determine the specific details of an alleged crime as observed by witnesses. Over time, this inchoate concept of the fact migrated to intellectual fields as far-ranging as natural philosophy, where scientists catalogued and studied "natural facts," and accounting, where bookkeepers maintained meticulous records of "usable facts," before traveling to a multitude of other emerging disciplines.[16] Although there never existed a universal consensus over what did or did not constitute a fact, the *idea* of facts as discrete pieces of satisfactory evidence that lead us toward truth took hold, giving rise to what historian Barbara Shapiro calls "a culture of fact."

We are the inheritors and the beneficiaries of that historical process. We recognize that observable, measurable, and articulable facts are foundational for sound decision-making and action by individuals and collectives. Yet even in a culture that broadly accords facts special evidentiary power, facts don't exist in a vacuum. They are always at the ready to be manipulated, weaponized, or politicized.

In a memorable exchange with Rudyard Kipling, Mark Twain famously explained why he found facts more valuable than fiction: "Get your facts first," he declared wryly, "and then you can distort 'em as you please."[17] Twain's remark does not deny the objectivity of hard facts but acknowledges that facts are simply the raw material undergirding opinions and understanding. "Even the barest facts," writes Sophia Rosenfeld, the author of *Democracy and Truth: A Short History*, "require interpretation, or assessments of their implications in light of other ideas or values."[18] The work of discovering, assessing, and interpreting them is difficult and painstaking, but it is absolutely essential if facts are to be inoculated from the distortions to which they are vulnerable. Accomplishing such a feat requires a class of individuals trained to perform precisely this task in every field of human knowledge. These are the experts.

Experts are at the heart of any fact-cultivating enterprise. From the biochemist studying the effects of certain chemicals on human physiology to the journalist who delivers the fruits of investigations to the public to the historian who illuminates the past to inform the present, the defining character of experts is that they unearth, validate, and secure facts and, ideally, deliver those insights to the broader public. No citizen can be an authority on every single issue, so we rely upon experts to uncover facts, reveal their context and meaning to the public, and correct errors and falsehoods that have wended their way into democratic discourse. Of course, for a given fact to have purchase in the democratic sphere, many other elements must be in place: a widespread acceptance of the methods used to produce facts, trust in the institutions that distribute them, an understanding that the facts are reliable and validated, and continuous affirmation and elaboration of those facts in open dialogue among citizens. Experts are integral to each of these functions, and their ability to give meaning to facts is integral to the healthy functioning of a liberal democracy.

Across our society, a great many institutions are home to experts. Among these are governments themselves, which gather, interpret, and publish everything from census data to geopolitical insights to environmental facts and which employ experts in a variety of fields to develop and implement policy and conduct the often intricate work of governance. These are perfectly legitimate functions, but in a free society the government alone cannot be entrusted with the responsibility to report facts, to ascertain truth, and to translate insight into action. And we have seen, too, in the past several years just how far some leaders will go to abuse the fact-gathering functions of government to perpetuate and consolidate power. Some twenty-first-century authoritarians have been labeled "informational autocrats" for their dependence upon the manipulation and management of facts to support a public veneer of competence and maintain popular credibility.[19]

And so, liberal democracies have come to depend on outside actors, armed with expertise, credibility, and norms, who can unearth facts and cultivate truth apart from the influence of the political sphere. Of these, the media is certainly the most celebrated, with its hallowed traditions of reporting and interpretation aimed at informing the broader democratic public of what is happening in their society. But the media is, rightly, constrained in important and necessary ways. For instance, it generally does not train and credential experts, surface new discoveries across virtually all fields of human knowledge, or rigorously assess the validity of that knowledge under robust theoretical frames.

Enter the university. The modern university is uniquely suited to this expert-generating function in the service of democracy. Much of this power resides in its governing principles and organizational structure, its adherence to norms of academic freedom, and the practice of tenure, which ensures that faculty are given a wide latitude to pursue research questions without fear of institutional reprisal or censorship, to challenge received wisdom, and to check errant power wherever it resides.

This foundational commitment does not mean that academic researchers are given carte blanche to pursue and publish wholly inaccurate claims. Universities are composed of schools and departments tied closely to scholarly disciplines that share norms and methodologies (including the protocols of hypothesis, experimentation, and peer review). These schools bear the responsibility not only of advancing the knowledge in particular fields, but also of training the next generation of experts and determining who can be considered an expert through the granting of degrees. And the disciplines they represent are given shape and structure by the vast network of scholarly societies (such as the American Society for Microbiology, the American Economic Association, and the Modern Language Association) and peer-reviewed journals that unite a guild of specialized experts in the shared project of defining the boundaries of a given discipline, creating norms of discourse to ascertain facts, and determining that claims made within this discourse are evaluated against the most stringent standards. Over the centuries, this intellectual ecosystem has continuously refined and practiced the best methods we have of ascertaining truth with extraordinary results.

The notion that institutions of higher education would come to bear such a responsibility would have been almost inconceivable to most Americans in 1800. For most of their history, American colleges saw themselves as being devoted exclusively to preserving knowledge, not creating it. The emergence of research universities in the 1870s profoundly altered that view. Universities rapidly established themselves as incubators of expertise across virtually all fields of human knowledge, and, in time, they pressed their knowledge outward in service of public policy and the healthy functioning of democracy. By World War II, the American university was drawn even closer to the democratic sphere when the federal government began supporting academic research at an unprecedented scale. This knowledge-based partnership between the university and the federal government—an extension of the compact that stretches back to the Morrill Act of 1862—became a wellspring of American prosperity and a model to the rest of the world. In the words of one of the great chroniclers of the research university, Jonathan Cole, universities have "evolved into creative machines unlike any other that we have known in our history—cranking out information and discoveries in a society increasingly dependent on knowledge as the source for its growth."[20]

Today, though, something has shifted: the once-stable framework of facts and reliable knowledge that has supported our liberal democracies is showing signs of fracture. The problems are well rehearsed. The staggering volume of information at our fingertips has made it more difficult for us to sift truth from untruth.[21] The splintering of media options and the logic of social networks has made it easier for people to encase themselves in echo chambers, with algorithms pulling them to extremes.[22] Withering attacks from political leaders have left facts as polarized as our politics, ridiculed as illegitimate or even outright suppressed when they become inconvenient. And the gatekeepers that once mediated these forces have been disrupted and discarded, with public trust in expert institutions collapsing to record lows—even before the world was hit with COVID-19.[23] One recent report has described these events as giving rise to a "truth decay" that, although not entirely without precedent in modern history, is worse in degree and form than previous moments.[24] The rapid rise and vast reach of conspiracy theories only underscore this fact. Even more disconcerting, these phenomena are a contagion without a ready antidote, weakening the heart of fact that supports and strengthens liberal democracy.

Against these forces, the responsibility of universities to step forward in defense of facts and expertise is greater than ever. It is incumbent upon us, as universities, to ask what their role has been in the denigration of fact and of faith in expertise. Are they discharging their role as custodians of fact in a way that is commensurate with the demands and conditions of the present? And is there more they can do in the years to come to bring facts closer to the open democratic life they serve? To answer these questions, we must start at the very beginning of this journey, at the moment when universities first came to take on their role as custodians of fact and curators of expertise.

Do Your Best Work in Your Own Way

In the first half of the nineteenth century, scientific research in the United States was still mostly confined to the scattered efforts of independent scientists. Unlike Europe, the United States had few journals to disseminate new findings and propel fields forward, few organized societies of researchers to define the norms and methods of disciplines, and, importantly, no institutional equivalent to the Royal Society in England or the École Polytechnique in France to pioneer new research. American scientists were rightly concerned with the lack of robust infrastructure for original scientific research in their home country. In 1846, Joseph Henry, the first secretary of the Smithsonian Institution, lamented that while the United States boasted many institutions that teach knowledge, there existed "not a single one which gives support to its increase."[25] At the time, Henry hoped to build the recently founded Smithsonian into just such an institution, and in the ensuing years it would accomplish a great deal for American science. By the dawn of the twentieth century, however, the institution that would ultimately serve as the principal locus of scientific discovery and training was the college.[26]

Few in the era would have predicted this outcome. Indeed, at midcentury, the prospects for higher education as a center of imaginative research in the United States looked dim. Colleges were widely regarded as—and largely functioned as—institutions devoted to the intellectual and moral formation of young people. They preserved and diffused knowledge; they didn't create it. And while colleges had been successful in bringing some scientific and vocational training into their curricula in the nineteenth century, there was a drive to incorporate ever more courses into the curriculum, which meant that the treatment of chemistry, engineering, and other topics was frequently fleeting and superficial.[27] In addition, the faculty who taught such courses often lacked the willingness, institutional resources, or time to conduct independent research on top of already demanding teaching responsibilities. As the *New York Quarterly* summed it up in 1853, "It is not enumerated . . . among the duties of any Professor in any College in our land, that he shall labor for the discovery of new truth."[28]

Given these limitations, American students eager to pursue careers in science and scholarship tended to seek advanced academic training elsewhere, with many choosing to expatriate themselves to study at European (primarily German) universities.[29] Over the course of the nineteenth century, an estimated ten thousand Americans (including such luminaries as Edward Everett and W. E. B. Du Bois) sought doctoral training abroad.[30] By contrast, American colleges awarded fewer than fifty PhD degrees between 1861 and 1876.[31]

The balance started to shift in 1876 with the creation of Johns Hopkins University. Founded with a posthumous gift from the Baltimore merchant Johns Hopkins consisting of B&O railroad stock worth approximately $3.5 million (with an additional $3.5 million going to the establishment of a hospital), "The Johns Hopkins University" began as an idea without a definition.[32] Hopkins himself had never attended college, and he made few efforts in his will to clarify to friends and colleagues what this institution bearing his name ought to be. That task fell to the university's first president, Daniel Coit Gilman, a former geography professor and librarian at Yale's Sheffield Scientific School who was serving as president of the University of California when he got the call to come to Baltimore.

Gilman had long dreamed of remaking American higher education in the image of the great European universities—particularly the German ones that had attracted so many American students in the decades prior—as a center of original thinking, research, and discovery. At Johns Hopkins, he finally met a project equal in scope to his considerable ambition and capability.[33]

There he built an institution that grafted adaptations of German academic traditions onto the familiar structures and forms of the American college. Hopkins retained the traditional American college for undergraduates but expanded its charge to include a graduate school for students to train as experts in particular fields of knowledge.[34] These advanced students would be taught by a faculty divided among discipline-specific departments who were specialists in fields ranging from chemistry to history to classics to mathematics.[35] In addition to their teaching responsibilities, the faculty were expected to conduct original research and were given the resources—libraries, laboratories, and, just as important, time—to do so.

The genius of combining an undergraduate college, a graduate school, and a research facility into one institution was that it created an educational ecosystem in which pioneering scholars and scientists could be trained in universities, venture new discoveries, bring those discoveries into the world, and infuse future generations with a deep appreciation for knowledge and inquiry.[36] This arrangement, in short, achieved a critical mass of teaching, credentialing, research, and publication, with each function feeding and strengthening the others. Although the German university had been its inspiration and the American college the foundation upon which it was built, Hopkins adapted and combined these forms in a singular way to create an institutional type unique in the modern world.

A cornerstone of this new arrangement was the independence of the university—and, critically, the research its faculty conducted—from external interference. In an era when more than 80 percent of all liberal arts colleges claimed a denominational affiliation (and tensions between an ascendant science and a defensive theology were high) and with the nation still reeling from the unprecedented political rupture of the Civil War and the Reconstruction era, the first trustees of Johns Hopkins were anxious that both the president and the institution be free from what they called "sectarian bias and political spirit."[37]

Gilman wholeheartedly agreed. Were the institution to be "limited to the maintenance of ecclesiastical differences or perverted to the promotion of political strife," he wrote, it would have ceded its central purpose of "the discovery and promulgation of the truth."[38] At the same time, Gilman was careful not to place the university in opposition to either the political or ecclesiastical realms. Instead, as he argued in his inaugural address, the university would "doubtless serve both church and state the better because it is free from the guardianship of either."[39] For the first faculty, implicit in this idea of academic autonomy was a promise that they would have the latitude to pursue their scholarly agenda freely, without fear of censorship or reprisal. Gilman summed it up simply when he gave Hopkins faculty the mandate to "do your best work in your own way."[40]

Creating the conditions for advanced scientific and humanistic research that was both impartial and unfettered by outside influences was a vital first step, but Hopkins at its founding also lacked a mechanism to push this research into the world. Gilman and others quickly recognized the value of the truism coined by Abraham Flexner that "publication and research are inseparable; what is accomplished if the work of a lifetime grows mouldy in the drawer of a desk?"[41] So, in 1878, Gilman established a small press at Hopkins to publish pamphlets, papers, periodicals, and, later, books by the school's faculty that would ensure the dissemination of new knowledge produced within the university.

The importance of this development is evident in the press's first publication, the *American Journal of Mathematics*, founded by Hopkins mathematics professor James Joseph Sylvester. As the first journal in the Western Hemisphere devoted entirely to research-level mathematics—far surpassing in scope and rigor early journals like the *Cambridge Miscellany* that largely appealed to a smattering of amateurs and undergraduates—the *American Journal of Mathematics* made it possible for a burgeoning mathematical research community to coalesce.[42] By the early 1910s, more than a dozen university presses had been established, responsible for publishing an array of journals and monographs annually, many of which were pivotal in forging the networks of scholars that would shape and define disciplines for decades to come.

In short order, the new research university model revolutionized not only American higher education but also the American research enterprise itself. In the years after the founding of Johns Hopkins University, dozens of universities followed suit, educating graduate students and hiring faculty capable of conducting independent research, many of them trained at Hopkins. By 1900,

American universities were producing between two hundred and three hundred PhDs annually (about five times as many as had been produced in total between 1861 and 1876), and these graduates were fanning out into all walks of life.[43]

By this time, universities had truly assumed their critical role as hives of scientific and scholarly activity. But in this new role, they quickly came into contact—and sometimes conflict—with a host of other entities, raising questions as to how their knowledge function would influence other democratic institutions and how those institutions would in turn influence them. In the decades that followed, the answers to these questions would both challenge and invigorate the core functions of the young research enterprise.

The Boundaries of the University

The collisions—both deliberate and unexpected—between the American research university and democratic life were especially evident at public universities, which were critical forerunners in devising novel ways of bringing academic expertise into greater contact with citizens and institutions.

No university put its resources to work for democracy more effectively or more expansively than the University of Wisconsin. The "Wisconsin Idea," as it came to be known, was a sprawling and ambitious agenda to bind the work of the university to the functioning of the government and the flourishing of its citizens. Its aspirations were encapsulated in the pithy motto that "the boundaries of the university are the boundaries of the state."[44]

Among the most innovative and lasting expressions of the Wisconsin Idea was the Legislative Reference Library, a small library in the state's capitol building (just a few blocks south of the University of Wisconsin's campus in Madison) established in 1901 to provide expert assistance to legislators in crafting bills.[45] Its original director, Charles McCarthy—who had received a PhD in history from the university—saw in this institution an opportunity to use academic expertise to correct what he believed was a disturbing imbalance between the state's legislature and its judiciary. Each year, a growing number of bills (many of which had been written by private companies or lobbying firms) were being challenged in court, all but transforming the judiciary into a de facto legislative body. McCarthy suspected one of the reasons for this was that Wisconsin's legislature suffered from a dearth of expertise in translating many of the most visionary and humane intentions of the Progressive Era into sound, actionable public policy.[46] To right this imbalance, McCarthy helped conscript dozens of professors from the University of Wisconsin to advise legislators and design policy, transforming the small library into a "bill factory" that was responsible for implementing the country's first viable state income tax and worker's compensation program, instituting new workplace safety standards, and reducing government corruption.[47]

By 1920, other states and even the federal government adapted the model that McCarthy had devised, developing similar bodies to channel academic expertise to policy makers.[48] These represented remarkable advances, forged in an era of reform, in the coordination between the academy and the work of democratic governance. But the role of academic experts in government was only just beginning to take shape, as the success of the Wisconsin Idea also birthed a new kind of public figure: the service intellectual.

Neither pundits nor politicians, service intellectuals were university professors who shared the fruits of their particular disciplinary expertise with government officials and agencies. This figure would rise to national prominence during the 1932 presidential election when Democratic candidate Franklin Delano Roosevelt recruited a trio of Columbia professors (two lawyers and an economist) to advise the future president on key policy issues.[49] The "brains trust"—as the *New York Times* initially named them before settling on the more palatable "brain trust"—fascinated the public and turned the participation of the professor in politics into a heated national debate.[50] Skeptics accused the group of being nothing more than a cadre of impractical academics that lacked any knowledge of life beyond the ivory tower and were liable to take a "dilettante approach to national problems."[51] But Roosevelt was steadfast. "The use of brains in the national government," he quipped, "seems to me a pretty good practice."[52] After he was elected, Roosevelt continued to rely on professors for their expertise—including in the crafting of the New Deal—and by the 1936 election cycle, professors had become such a mainstay at the highest echelons of the government that Roosevelt's opponents in the Republican Party formed a brain trust of their own to bolster Alfred Landon's presidential campaign.[53]

As these examples make clear, university faculty were playing increasingly prominent roles in democratic life. Inevitably, perhaps, this produced clashes between the content of research and the interests and expectations of outside interest groups. Often, when a given faculty member ran too far against the grain (be it because of an essay on the virtues of bimetallism or a lecture to union workers), he was likely to end up in hot water and, on many occasions, to be forced out of his position.

Take the case of Richard Ely at the University of Wisconsin. One of the most respected economists of his day, Ely had come to Wisconsin from Johns Hopkins in 1892.[54] Two years after his arrival, a local government official (and ex officio member of the university's board of regents) began to suspect that Ely had encouraged a labor strike.[55] This official subsequently took to the pages of *The Nation* to publicly charge the economist with not only provoking labor unrest but also spreading "utopian, impractical, or pernicious doctrines" throughout his published writings.[56] Ely was then brought before the university's board of regents to defend his life's work. Buoyed by his reputation as a first-rate scholar and the fact that his former students had achieved prominence at other universities, Ely ultimately won the day. In the aftermath of the case, the board issued one of the most forceful early claims for the independent research function of the university: "In all lines of academic investigation it is of the utmost importance that the investigator should be absolutely free to follow the indications of truth wherever they may lead."[57]

Not every such case ended like Ely's. (Even for Ely not all was well, with some historians suggesting that the ordeal had a chilling effect on his subsequent writing and research.)[58] Economist Edward A. Ross at Stanford, for instance, was summarily dismissed in 1900 when Jane Stanford took umbrage with his vocal advocacy for the Free Silver movement and ordered Stanford President David Starr Jordan to get rid of him.[59] Similar stories—like those of Edward Bemis at the University of Chicago and Scott Nearing at the University of Pennsylvania—accumulated throughout the early years of the twentieth century, and faculty across the country came to recognize the urgent need to clarify and solidify the still inchoate idea of "academic freedom."

In 1915, the recently formed American Association of University Professors (AAUP) met this charge when they published their "Declaration of Principles on Academic Freedom and Academic Tenure." This epochal document laid the groundwork for the modern understanding of academic freedom. It defined the university as an institution held in the public trust but buffered from the "tyranny of public opinion." Within the university, the scholar's proper sphere of activity was to teach the next generation of citizens, to pursue independent study, and to advise government officials. So long as faculty conducted their research in a spirit of "competent and patient and sincere inquiry," the report argued, they ought to be able to publish findings without fear of termination. Absent such guarantees, the university would eventually cease to be "an intellectual experiment station, where new ideas may germinate and where their fruit . . . may be allowed to ripen until finally, perchance, it may become a part of the accepted intellectual food of the nation or of the world."[60]

Despite its significance today, this statement made little immediate impact on actual practices in its time, owing in no small part to the patriotic fervor of World War I, which led to the curtailment of academic freedom across the country, often at the hands of many in the academy who had professed to be academic freedom's fiercest defenders.[61] Nevertheless, the declaration created an enduring framework from which would blossom so many of the defining qualities of faculty life in the modern university, from tenure to the right to publish controversial findings without fear of institutional reprisal. In the decades that followed the AAUP statement, these principles would come to be a polestar as academic research became increasingly enmeshed with the interests of democratic life and, along the way, subject to increasing democratic scrutiny.

Expanding the Frontiers of Knowledge

Throughout the 1920s and '30s, the work of the research university proceeded more or less along the lines that had been set at the dawn of the twentieth century. Even as its capacities for discovery expanded—in spite of the setbacks of the Great Depression—resources for research remained limited, and although the federal government's investments in science had increased during this period, there could hardly be said to have existed a coherent or consistent science policy.[62] During the same period, however, the basic research capacities of private industry accelerated rapidly with the founding or expansion of industrial research laboratories, Bell Labs chief among them. Staffed almost exclusively by university-trained researchers with PhDs, these laboratories were by 1940 even outpacing university research by some measures.[63]

That all changed with the outbreak of World War II in 1939. At the time, politicians and academic leaders alike worried that the United States was technologically and scientifically unprepared for war. The effort to ramp up scientific capacity in the interests of national defense was led by an extraordinary engineer and inventor, Vannevar Bush, who had been dean of engineering at MIT and had played a role on President Roosevelt's short-lived Science Advisory Board. Bush had a gift for politics and a strong grasp of the state of scientific research. As he saw it, the best path forward was the creation of a new organization to accelerate scientific discovery not only by funding government laboratories, but also by distributing federal money to scientists and scholars already employed at American universities. After securing a meeting with one of Roosevelt's closest aides who recognized the potential in Bush's idea, an appointment with the president was made. About ten minutes into that meeting, Roosevelt was persuaded, and Bush walked out of the Oval Office carrying a note that read simply "OK–FDR."[64]

From this encounter emerged the National Defense Research Committee (NDRC) in 1940. Bush organized the NDRC into a "pyramidal structure" that established more than 130 relationships between the federal government and research institutions (universities as well as several private corporations) to harness their facilities and scientific expertise in everything from entomology to epidemiology to mathematics to, most significantly, atomic physics.[65] These contracts were designed to advance national interests without impairing the autonomy of investigators that Bush felt was essential to good science. Under this regime, Harvard scientists could conduct invaluable research on sonar while engineers at the University of Pennsylvania calculated ballistics problems at the same time that researchers at the University of Michigan, Penn State, and Cornell University were finding ways to produce RDX (the chemical agent used in C-4 explosives) on a massive scale. With Bush as its director, the office (repackaged and expanded a year after its formation as the Office of Scientific Research and Development, or OSRD) proved immensely successful in accelerating scientific and technological innovation throughout the war effort. The *New York Times* described it in 1943 as a "super-brain" with "more than a hundred thousand trained brains working as one."[66]

In 1944, with Allied victory imminent and the OSRD's success undeniable, Roosevelt turned once again to Bush to inquire whether this unique alliance between the federal government and research institutions could be sustained during peacetime. His desire was to put the same model that had advanced the interests of national defense to work, as he put it in a letter, "for the improvement of the national health, the creation of new enterprises bringing new jobs, and the betterment of the national standard of living."[67] The war effort had enlisted science in defense of democratic institutions staring down fascism. Now, those same institutions, emerging from the devastation of war, would recruit science in service of society and the common good.

Bush answered the president's charge in 1945 with *Science—The Endless Frontier*, a bracing and visionary report whose title invoked that quintessential American symbol of discovery and progress—the frontier—and whose content emphasized the role of science in advancing human progress by building on the work of the OSRD for a new era of peace and prosperity. Bush proposed expanding the decentralized grant model of the OSRD into an enduring organization that would serve government interests without sacrificing researchers' autonomy, thus balancing "irreducible national functions against the free play of individual initiative."[68] Universities once again would be at the heart of this vision: not only were they already well resourced and staffed by many of the most talented minds in the world, but they also could "devote most of their research efforts to expanding the frontiers of knowledge" rather than to settling "practical problems."[69]

The agency that would eventually oversee this new endeavor would be the National Science Foundation (NSF), created in May 1950.[70] The NSF bore many of the markings of Bush's original vision. It was an independent agency with a keen focus on basic research, it advanced a model of research funds distributed widely to research institutions across the nation, and it instituted a competitive system of allocating those funds based on the merits of proposed research projects.[71] One of the innovations of this new research enterprise was that project proposals would be evaluated, in the main, not by legislators, political appointees, or other agents of the state, but by fellow scientists through a process of external peer review, in which scientific experts in relevant fields provided comments to individual proposals. Peer review had existed in various forms long prior to this, but its inclusion in this process preserved the rigor and ethos of science and helped to make peer review a defining feature of the success of the American research enterprise.[72] It bears mentioning, too, that there is something distinctly *democratic* about this practice, since it allows scientists to choose which projects merit funding rather than subjecting those decisions to the whims of a distant funding power.

Other government research agencies charted similar paths. Notable among these is the National Institutes of Health (NIH), which after World War II began to transition from a purely intramural government research facility to an outward facing patron of discovery that now devotes more than 80 percent of its budget to extramural research grants.[73] In time, this funding model expanded beyond the natural sciences to include the other areas of the academy, with the creation of the Social Science Research Program in 1957 and the establishment of the National Endowment for the Humanities in 1965.

Thus was born the government-university research compact, a singular partnership between the government and universities that has produced countless world-changing discoveries and innovations and has become the envy of the world.[74] Its formation represented a tectonic shift in the relationship between universities and democracy by establishing a system through which democratic institutions provided universities the resources to expand facilities, to invest in personnel and human capital, and to produce new research at an unparalleled scale. The capacities for basic scientific research forged at the end of the nineteenth century with the founding of Johns Hopkins were now being harnessed for the national welfare, all while advancing essential principles of scientific independence and academic freedom. This new compact embodied a broad consensus that scientific research, as it had come to be defined within the context of the university, was the gold standard of truth in a tumultuous and relativistic world.

At once objective and reliable, it was the fullest expression of the human potential for progress.

And although born of a moment when the need for research applications in health, technology, and defense were especially urgent, one of Vannevar Bush's most brilliant and audacious ideas was to commit the country to theoretical basic research. As Bush argued in *Science—The Endless Frontier*, basic research "leads to new knowledge. It provides scientific capital. It creates the fund from which the practical applications of knowledge must be drawn."[75] In the decade following Bush's report, "basic research" became part of our common parlance, with mentions of the term in the *New York Times* and congressional hearings multiplying fourfold.[76] Speculative and daring, basic research has yielded a never-ending series of breakthrough discoveries that have improved the human condition and transformed the world. It continues to do so today. Thanks to basic research on mRNA conducted in university labs for almost six decades, pharmaceutical firms such as Moderna and Pfizer were able to develop remarkably sophisticated vaccines for COVID-19 in a matter of months, altering the course of a global pandemic and saving countless lives. (Moderna, now nearly a household name, is even a portmanteau of "modified" plus "RNA.")[77] The genius and the legacy of the revolution Vannevar Bush spearheaded was the willingness to commit a nation emerging from the debris and destruction of war to an audacious and expansive investment in the future through basic research.

In a matter of years, the federal government had grown from a marginal player in academic research into the principal driver of discovery in the country. But as the research function of the university continued to expand, it also drew more government scrutiny of (and attacks upon) its work.

The Ethics and Logic of Inquiry

Among the most publicized and dramatic episodes for universities during the postwar years was the concerted effort to root out Communism on campuses. By the late 1940s, anti-Communist sentiment in the United States had reached a fever pitch. The first major postwar incursion into academic freedom occurred in 1948 at the University of Washington, shortly after a state-led Committee on Un-American Activities began lurking around the university. In an effort to get in front of the committee, the university's president, Raymond Allen, unilaterally terminated three professors for having been members of the Communist Party (though one, Ralph Gundlach, refused to reveal whether he had been a member or not), overruling the recommendations of a faculty-run tenure committee in the process.[78] In the years that followed, similar attacks on faculty multiplied across the country, fueled not only by similar state-level inquisitions but also by prominent national bodies like the House Un-American Activities Committee and Senator Joseph McCarthy's Permanent Subcommittee on Investigations. In most instances, efforts to expose Communists started with overzealous politicians, but—as in the Washington case—these all too often found willing accomplices in university administrators alongside rank-and-file faculty.[79] Even faculty who weren't fired in the McCarthy-era attacks—like sinologist Owen Lattimore at Johns Hopkins—faced intense and unrelenting attacks that tragically and irreparably damaged their lives and careers.[80]

These flagrant assaults on academic freedom had a number of consequences for the research function of the university, some of which were felt immediately and some of which lingered for years. At least one hundred university faculty and instructors were terminated or denied tenure in the 1950s owing to suspicions of Communist sympathies.[81] The University of California, Berkeley, saw its reputation "immeasurably damaged," in the words of one recent scholar of the period, when faculty revolted against its president's demand that they sign loyalty oaths, a wound that took years to heal—and it was only one of many institutions that enforced similar measures.[82] And there are signs that the trajectory of entire disciplines may have been sidetracked as professors drifted toward (and were rewarded for) politically palatable research projects.[83] This was a truly dark period in what continues to be a century-long struggle of the university to safeguard the integrity of its knowledge function from the caprices of political leaders or other external forces.

Despite these frictions, the escalation of the Cold War ensured that federal investment in university research proceeded apace, bringing American universities into closer contact with the federal government in more ways and at a greater scale than ever before. Throughout the 1950s, the US government ramped up research and development at an unprecedented rate. By 1965, the budget for the NSF alone had expanded to $416 million from just $225,000 at its founding fifteen years earlier.[84] It was during this period, too, that the American military began investing even more heavily in academic research—particularly in the social sciences.

The Korean War was a pivotal moment in this development. As the United States found itself drawn deeper into a fight across many theaters against what it conceived of as a global Communist threat, American military leadership recognized that having access to a knowledge base of human cultures and behavior might be just as crucial to national security as weapons research. Disciplines like anthropology, psychology, and sociology—along with several emergent area studies—held forth the promise of new tools and paradigms for winning hearts and minds (and the occasional battle) in the Cold War.

To harness this potential, the military began experimenting with new ways to recruit academics into military operations. After some early failures, they landed on Federal Contract Research Centers (FCRCs), semipermanent organizations funded almost entirely by the government but staffed by civilian academics and often located on university campuses.[85] While FCRCs had existed during World War II, their growth exploded in the 1950s. From 1951 to 1967, funding for these centers grew nearly tenfold.[86] FCRCs were designed to recruit knowledge workers into defense while forestalling fears that the United States was becoming, in President Dwight D. Eisenhower's words, a "garrison state."[87] For military leaders, FCRCs cut the difference between the grant-funding model of the NSF and NIH, which they worried was best suited for basic research and would thus fail to produce results tailored to operational needs, and simply hiring faculty outright, which they thought might dampen the spirit of freewheeling discovery, cross-disciplinary insight, and fierce critique that had come to define the academy and that the military was hoping to tap in the first place. Thus, in their idealized form, these entities sought to fulfill the mandates of defense while maintaining universities' "atmosphere of intellectual independence."[88]

Cold War–era social scientists were divided on the virtues of FCRCs. For some, they represented an opportunity to live out the highest ideals of the public-minded intellectual: staff could conduct independent academic research and see the fruits of their work applied immediately to problems of national—and even global—import in the service of democracy. For others, they posed serious ethical dilemmas, since researchers had few guarantees as to what uses the military would put their work. Public opposition to the Vietnam War effectively ended this model of social science research when campus activists, enraged by the militarization of American social science, trained their sights on university-affiliated FCRCs, forcing universities to cut ties. Nevertheless, as historians have been quick to point out, FCRCs, by virtue of their proximity to universities, were able to make important contributions to both research—albeit, some have argued, at the expense of theoretical development in the social sciences—and national defense.[89]

Even as the university-based FCRCs faded, universities continued to establish new and enduring partnerships with federal agencies like the Departments of Defense, State, and Energy. These relationships have led to groundbreaking work on challenges ranging from space exploration to national security to pandemic response to robotic prosthetics. They represent yet one more way in which universities have been drawn into closer contact with the promises and complexities of democratic life.

As universities found themselves roiled first by charges that they were too closely aligned with Communism and then by charges that they were too closely aligned with the fight against it, they became the target of intense scrutiny. Doubts about the integrity of academic knowledge only continued to grow in the years that followed.

Should We Be at War, Too?

With the rapid expansion of academic science in the 1940s and '50s, representatives from the other side of the academy, the humanities, began to voice concern that their areas of research and teaching (such as history, literature and language studies, philosophy, and classics) were being left behind. Even though enrollments in the humanities had been climbing steadily since World War II (between 1949 and 1970, the percentage of bachelor's degrees recipients in the humanities nearly doubled, from 9 percent to a historic high of 17 percent), financial support for humanistic research was still in short supply.[90] To correct what one influential report described as "an imbalance within academic institutions by the very fact of abundance in one field of study and dearth in another," Congress in 1965 established the National Endowment for the Humanities (NEH).[91] With a budget of $36 million, the new agency's resources paled in comparison to those of the NSF, but its growth was substantial. By the end of the 1970s, the NEH had an operating budget of $425 million.[92]

The birth of the NEH marked a period of growing strength and influence of the humanities. In the decades leading up to this moment, much of the frame around the humanities had been that these disciplines complemented rather than opposed the life sciences. But this vision of harmony was short-lived. Doubts within and outside of the university about science's claims to objectivity and unfettered progress led not only students to protest university ties to government but also scholars and critics across the humanities—and in certain pockets of the social sciences—to direct their well-honed practices of analysis and interpretation at the scientific enterprise (and the university) itself, scrutinizing its methods of producing and verifying knowledge, and chipping away at its purported purchase on truth.

In the humanities, this turn came to be encapsulated in the ascendance of "post-structuralism" in the late 1960s. The precipitating event for this shift was the international symposium "The Languages of Criticism and the Sciences of Man," convened at

Johns Hopkins in October 1966.[93] While the symposium counted among its participants the famed psychoanalyst Jacques Lacan and the literary theorist Roland Barthes, the event's true star was a precocious young philosopher named Jacques Derrida. His paper "Structure, Sign, and Play" came to define the symposium and earned him his reputation as—to quote one Hopkins professor present for the event—an "intellectual terrorist."[94] The essay was an agile and concerted attack on the then-vogue structuralist movement in the humanities and social sciences, which had, in the broadest terms, sought to uncover immutable patterns—or structures—undergirding human language and social reality.[95] Derrida argued instead in favor of the free play of language and meaning, unmoored from transcendental truth. Although the paper was, at the moment, simply one well-timed shot across the bow in a wider internecine debate within the academic humanities, its impact spread rapidly, breathing life into a powerful, theoretical force in the academic humanities that was deeply suspicious of absolute truth claims and Enlightenment models of reason, and eager to expose the supposed voids at their core.

Around the same time, a subset of American social scientists had also begun to bring their analytical tools to bear on the scientific enterprise. In 1962, Thomas Kuhn's massively popular book *The Structure of Scientific Revolutions* had reconsidered the history of science as a fundamentally social process that occurred within communities of practitioners.[96] Scientific progress, Kuhn argued, was not a steady march toward truth but a series of ruptures and reorganizations that were not always driven by reason and rationality. This thesis helped give rise to the fields of science studies and the sociology of scientific knowledge, which investigated the social dimensions of scientific discovery and practice.[97] These new areas of research—embodied in books like French anthropologist Bruno Latour's *Laboratory Life: The Construction of Scientific Facts*—were attuned to the human and political elements shaping scientific research and were intended to complicate the popular image of science as an unimpeachable source of authority by exposing its rituals, irrationalities, and blind spots. These two movements within the academy, which dovetailed with a sudden uptick in federal scrutiny of research spending (memorably embodied in Senator William Proxmire's monthly "Golden Fleece" awards in the 1970s and '80s), put science on its heels.[98] Counterreactions followed.

Tensions reached a boiling point in 1994 with the publication of mathematician Norman Levitt and biologist Paul Gross's book *Higher Superstition: The Academic Left and Its Quarrels*, a polemic directed against scholars whose work, in the authors' eyes, represented nothing less than "a rejection of the strongest heritage of the Enlightenment."[99] Thus began the "science wars." Scientists accused their colleagues in the humanities and social sciences of naive relativism and ideological fanaticism, while social scientists and humanists continued to chastise academic science for its seeming refusal to acknowledge its own entanglement in culture and politics. (The conflict at one point reached such a pitch that some science studies scholars even considered filing lawsuits against their critics.)[100] Throughout the latter half of the 1990s, partisans launched spirited (and sometimes mean-spirited) volleys in heated conference panels, in prominent journals (including the infamous "Sokal Hoax," in which a mathematician managed to publish a paper deliberately riddled with scientific errors in a prominent sociology journal), in public debates, and even in the pages of periodicals like the *New York Times* and *The Atlantic*.[101]

The science wars exposed deep divisions at the heart of the post–Cold War university, raising serious questions about the limitations and contingency of scientific inquiry, about what methods and knowledge it was legitimate to interrogate, and about the role politics and culture played in academic research. From one angle, movements like post-structuralism and fields like science studies were embodying the core ideal of the university to take nothing for granted and to subject everything (even the work of the university itself) to scrutiny. At the same time, scientists were right to be wary about the unsettling effects of having their disciplines critiqued by nonscientists, some of whom had ideological axes to grind. One can imagine a world in which the issues at the heart of the science wars resulted in a more dispassionate process of critical examination, interdisciplinary conversation, and self-correction than what actually occurred. Instead, the accusations and arguments that spilled out into the public sphere from within the academy gave new ammunition to a rising chorus of political critics of the university on both the right and left.

Some combatants in the science wars would later express contrition for the unforeseen consequences (and occasional misappropriations) of their critiques. Speaking at Stanford in 2003, Latour (one of the pioneers of science studies) reflected on the role of humanities scholars and social scientists in a post-9/11 world of perpetual warfare and dubious facts, where governments and the public alike were becoming increasingly suspicious of facticity and more prone to conspiratorial thinking. In such a milieu, the science wars took on a different hue: "Should we be at war, too, we, the scholars, the intellectuals? Is it really our duty to add fresh ruins to fields of ruins? Is it really the task of the humanities to add deconstruction to destruction?" His answer was a firm, if qualified, "No." In a world where everyone respected basic facts, Latour intoned, there had been room for scholars to interrogate the process of their discovery and circulation. But something had gone awry. As Latour admitted in his talk, among his neighbors, "I am now the one who naively believes in facts."[102]

Doubts about the reliability of academic research found additional fuel in another development of this period: the massive influx of money coming from private industry. For most of the twentieth century—notwithstanding some attempts by universities to cultivate industry relationships in the 1920s—support for university research from the private sector was negligible, and many corporations maintained vast in-house laboratories to conduct basic research with translational potential. This changed in the 1980s when the federal government, in an effort to stimulate a stagnant economy, introduced policy measures to encourage greater cooperation between universities and corporate partners.[103] The most notable of these was the Bayh-Dole Act of 1980, which enabled universities to patent and license the discoveries of federally funded research and unleashed a wave of university-centric innovation so profound that *The Economist* would later describe it as "possibly the most inspired piece of legislation to be enacted in America over the past-half century."[104]

The federal push to bring industry and academia closer together worked: two decades later, industry funding for university research had grown by a factor of ten.[105] By the end of the century, more than 90 percent of biomedical companies had a relationship with a university.[106] Observers at the time marveled at the "unprecedented size and scope" of the sudden industry presence in academia.[107]

As corporate investment in universities grew, so too did concerns about its effects on the integrity of research. The close alliance between private industry and the university was surely contributing to the development of new scientific advancements and life-saving products. But it was also introducing distortions into an academic research enterprise that was ill-prepared for this flood of money. Studies showed that industry-sponsored faculty in that era were more likely to report that commercial considerations had influenced their choice of research topic, and were "more likely to reach conclusions that were favorable to their sponsor."[108]

Meanwhile, the media began to report on a succession of high-profile episodes in which alleged conflicts of interest in academic research and clinical trials were connected to tragic consequences, which prompted several congressional hearings. One high-profile case involved the 1999 death of teenager Jesse Gelsinger as a result of an experimental academic gene therapy trial at the University of Pennsylvania. The *Washington Post* revealed that the lead scientist and the university held millions of dollars in stock in the company that had sponsored the research.[109] Gelsinger's father told reporters that although he had been inclined to trust the researchers implicitly, these revelations made him believe that he "had been duped by scientists who cared more about profits than safety."[110] Academic research was finding itself defined not by its promises to discover and to heal but by its vulnerabilities, biases, and blind spots.[111]

Unease spread throughout the research enterprise that academic institutions were not doing enough to manage the risks posed by the sudden influx of outside money.[112] And soon enough, stakeholders acted. Academic journals adopted disclosure rules that required authors to identify financial interests.[113] Universities strengthened their own internal policies to police conflicts, often at the prompting of federal agencies.[114] Professional societies issued their own guidelines, with two—the American Society of Gene Therapy and the American Society for Clinical Oncology— recommending zero-tolerance policies for financial interests in company-sponsored clinical trials.[115] Even Congress leapt into the fray, enacting laws that imposed more stringent rules about how agencies handled conflicts of interest and requiring medical companies to notify the government of payments or gifts they make to physicians and teaching hospitals.[116] With time, these measures quelled the tide of problems and quieted the criticism. But they were not extinguished. Occasional, isolated controversies involving the collision of industry largesse and academic expertise have continued to emerge, a lingering tension that still haunts public trust in the enterprise.

This brings us to the present day.

Across the history I have traced to this point are several distinct threads. The first and most foundational is the university's *discovery* role. From its inception, the American research university embodied the functions of research, training, discipline formation, and credentialing. In time, that role expanded dramatically through partnerships with the federal government and industry. As its reach expanded, the university struggled at critical junctures to preserve the *independence* of its research as it confronted threats and intrusions from within its walls and from without. These difficult moments, however, became the crucibles in which were established academic freedom and the practices of tenure and peer review. Finally, the university has throughout its history continually sought to *diffuse* the research of its faculty to the public and to democratic institutions. This began with the advent of university presses and the growth of academic journals, but in time it extended to innovative experiments like the Wisconsin Idea, which helped to inaugurate the service intellectual into American life and beyond.

These threads are interlaced and have not always followed steady paths. Still, with regard to two of them—independence and diffusion—the university has managed its way to a place of relative success.

On the former, the university has triaged its relationship with the federal government to the point where norms of independence have prevailed and we can claim a scientific research enterprise led mostly by scientists inside the government and out, with peer review as a hallmark of the system. This highly diffuse, scientist-led—even democratic—framework for science is not something to be taken for granted. Widely credited as one of the reasons for the nation's preeminence in innovation in the post–World War II years, it has made our system of science a model for the world, with nations seeking to build from the same blueprint within their own borders in the decades since. Additionally, our universities have found effective and pragmatic ways of constraining undue corporate influence on research. And as concerns have arisen over foreign influence on research, on the part of China and other nation-states, American universities have worked forthrightly with the federal government to address concerns in a responsible way that does not compromise the open and collaborative scholarly endeavor, ensuring the United States remains a welcoming destination for students and researchers from around the world.

As for the latter—diffusion—we appear to be in the midst of a new burst of public intellectualism in democratic life. Thanks to social media and proliferating news outlets, alongside investments by universities in platforms for faculty engagement, scholars have more ways to reach the public—and, in many cases, larger audiences—than ever before. (And technology has opened up opportunities to go further still.) Across the media landscape, university researchers are bringing their immense reservoirs of expertise to bear on vital social, scientific, and political questions in democracy. This new public intellectualism also comes with real risks. The fact that an errant tweet can irreparably damage one's professional credibility is cause for concern. It also creates the conditions for viral strains of misinformation to spread, or for misinterpretations of accurate information to take hold. Nevertheless, at a moment when deep, thoughtful research too often reaches the public too slowly to overtake the lies, this new frontier of scholarly communication is exceptionally promising as a way not only to inform but also to speak truth to power.

These are both ongoing projects, but it is fair to say that our norms and safeguards are robust. Even so, there is a threat to the knowledge function of the American research university, one that lurks at the very core of its claim to truth and its role as a discoverer of fact. In this moment, when facts themselves are more vital to democracy than ever but at the same time harder to come by as a result of the deluge of misinformation circulating through the public sphere, the capacity of the university research enterprise to make discoveries and produce reliable facts remains as essential to the democratic project as it ever has been.

Stage Another Oil Spill

In 2018, two writers from an organization with a history of climate change denialism published a report raising the alarm for what they claimed was an urgent crisis in science. "Improper research techniques, lack of accountability, disciplinary and political groupthink, and a scientific culture biased toward producing positive results," they argued, had made it virtually impossible to believe most scientific findings.[117] The proof of this rot, they claimed, was that a vast majority of scientific experiments could not be replicated.

At a launch party for the report on Capitol Hill, Republican Congressman Lamar Smith of Texas vigorously endorsed its diagnosis.[118] A year prior, Smith had introduced legislation barring the Environmental Protection Agency (EPA) from using science that is not publicly available in a manner that allows for substantial reproduction.[119] "The lack of reproducibility," he said, "is a warning that the scientific method is not being followed."[120] As many scientists were quick to point out, the rule Smith proposed would likely have the effect of barring a significant amount of climate science, since some of the research either relies on personal information from individuals (such as patient records) that cannot be made public or consists of sweeping analyses of Earth-altering events that by their nature defy replication. (As one scientist put it, the only way to reproduce a study of an oil spill is "to stage another oil spill.")[121] Prominent historian of science Naomi Oreskes called the proposal "a Trojan horse."[122]

Smith's bill was never enacted into law, but President Trump's EPA issued a similar set of regulations that were finalized in the waning days of his presidency. And while those regulations were later vacated by a federal judge, this episode remains a striking example of the ways in which questions about the reliability of science in the academy are now being weaponized against science in the democratic arena.[123] Addressing this threat requires us first to reckon honestly with the realities of scientific replication at this moment.

The idea that experiments conducted to discover scientific facts must be repeatable in order for those facts to be considered valid dates back at least to the eleventh century, when the Arab scholar Ibn al-Haytham insisted to readers in his *Book on Optics* that his experiments had been repeated without "variation or change" in their results.[124] Six hundred years later, such repeatability was formalized as a defining method of scientific practice. The polymathic scientist, theologian, and a founder of the Royal Society Robert Boyle, in his seventeenth-century essay "On Unsuccessful Experiments," advised his fellow scientists that it was "unsafe to rely too much upon single Experiments."[125] In the centuries since, the importance of experimental reproducibility has been reaffirmed time and again. It has come to stand as a foundation not only of the hard sciences but also of empirical work in the social sciences and humanities, a check on all-too-human tendencies toward enthusiasm, confirmation bias (the tendency of individuals to believe things to be true because they desire them to be), and hubris.

But replicating scientific experiments is a costly and time-consuming endeavor, with few immediate rewards for the replicator. As such, for most of the twentieth century, reproducibility was more often assumed than rigorously tested. Then, in 2005, Stanford physician-scientist John P. A. Ioannidis published a paper titled "Why Most Published Research Findings Are False." In it, Ioannidis made the provocative assertion that more than 50 percent of the conclusions drawn in scientific journal articles were untrue.[126] He grounded his claim on a variety of dubious practices that had cropped up in previous decades, from file-drawing (the tendency of researchers to bury negative results by tucking them away in a proverbial file drawer) to p-hacking (manipulating a study to achieve a so-called p value that makes scientific findings look more consequential than they actually are). Pointing to mounting evidence of these practices, and his own simulations of various study designs, Ioannidis argued it was reasonable to suspect that most reported findings in scientific literature would not hold up to sustained scrutiny.

The paper sent shockwaves throughout the scientific research community, compelling researchers from a variety of disciplines in the sciences and social sciences to launch initiatives to reproduce key studies in their own fields. The results have been dispiriting. A three-year-long effort to reproduce twenty-one studies in the social sciences published in either *Nature* or *Science* from 2010 to 2015 could only confirm the conclusions of thirteen (62 percent).[127] A similar effort in psychology organized by Brian Nosek at the University of Virginia sought to replicate one hundred studies in the field—only thirty-nine were successful.[128] Two economists at the Federal Reserve who attempted to replicate findings in highly ranked economics journals were unable to reproduce half of the conclusions—even with the assistance of the original authors.[129] And a few years ago, scientists at one biotechnology company were able to reproduce only six out of fifty-three "landmark" findings in cancer research.[130]

The precise implications of these results for the research enterprise as a whole are still being debated. From one perspective, the nearly instantaneous response throughout the scientific community, and the conversations it has prompted over how to respond, might fairly be seen as a snapshot of the scientific method in action at a grand scale, evidence of science's resiliency in the face of critique. But that does little to ease the immediate doubts these studies have introduced about the reliability of the academic research endeavor. Some of this unreliability involves outright misconduct or fraud, especially among scientists in countries such as China that are seeking to accelerate scientific output. Just as worrisome are growing concerns that the modes of scientific research and discourse designed to purge the academic endeavor of error, bias, and other distortions are collapsing. Disconcertingly, there is reason to believe the problem might be getting worse.

For one, the introduction of modern statistical software has made statistical manipulation easier than ever. For nearly a century, and especially in the past fifty years, it has been customary in empirical fields to attach a probability (or *p* value) to an evidence-based observation, which signals that the conclusion is not simply a product of chance.[131] The threshold for this is conventionally 5 percent, or $p < 0.05$, a value that was originally chosen in the 1920s because it was sufficiently robust and, importantly, calculable by hand.[132] In the decades since, this threshold has become the gold standard for facticity, and, as one scientist has written, a "passport to publication."[133] But *p* values no longer need to be calculated manually; we have sophisticated statistics software to perform that labor. And the ubiquity of this software, along with the reverence now accorded to *p* values less than 0.05, has coincided with a jump in the percentage of studies with *p* values that just so happen to fall *barely* below 0.05, suggesting that more and more researchers might be manipulating their data to fit their conclusions, rather than drawing their conclusions from the data.[134]

On top of this, the premium placed on rapid publication in an intense funding environment primes the research ecosystem for reproducibility issues. As one editor of a leading journal recently wrote, science is now at a point where "[n]o one is incentivized to be right. Instead, scientists are incentivized to be *productive*."[135] And, all too often, to be *first*.

All of which is to say that there is at least some cause for concern that problems are etched deep in the research endeavor, so much so that even *scientists'* faith in scientific fact has been damaged. In a 2016 survey of fifteen hundred scientists conducted by *Nature*, 52 percent said they believed that there was "a significant crisis" of reproducibility in science.[136] These doubts are not confined to the scientific community. News articles with headlines like "Is Science Broken?," "Scientists Who Cheat," and "How Science Goes Wrong" have become commonplace.[137] Studies show, too, that when citizens find out about reproducibility problems, it can lead to declines in their trust in the scientific enterprise.[138]

There are no simple answers to this crisis, which amounts to a malfunction in fact. One place to look, for starters, is within the disciplines themselves. Since the origins of the research university in the 1870s, academic disciplines have been the guardians of knowledge and method. As such, they have the strongest capacity for self-regulation and renewal.

We are already seeing hopeful developments on that front.

A number of fields have instituted concrete changes to how they undertake scientific research. One prominent, emerging practice is that of "preregistrations," where researchers submit the design of a potential study in advance of its undertaking to ensure that they are using data actually to test their hypotheses, rather than fish for enticing results. Open Science Framework, the most widely used database for preregistrations, reports that the number of preregistered experiments they host skyrocketed from thirty-eight in 2012 to more than eighteen thousand in 2018, and continues to grow.[139]

Some academic journals have begun to encourage the publication of experiments with unsuccessful or negative outcomes.[140] In 2017, the journal *PLOS One* published *A Decade of Missing Pieces*, a curated collection of negative findings from the previous ten years.[141] Other journals have announced they will start to publish work even if it has already been "scooped" by other researchers in an attempt to ease the most pernicious effects of the imperative to—as the saying goes—"publish or perish."[142] And at least one journal, at the prompting of researchers studying reproducibility, has participated in a "proof of concept" experiment in "journal-based replication," in which the journal itself contracts the replication of a study for articles it has accepted but not yet published.[143]

Separately, a renaissance in how we train future scientists and scholars is also underway, with calls surfacing in several disciplines not just for scientists to be better trained in quantitative methods, but also perhaps to reconsider the way they approach specialized research more broadly. At Johns Hopkins, faculty in the department of molecular microbiology and immunology, led by Bloomberg Distinguished Professor Arturo Casadevall and senior scientist Gundula Bosch, have designed an entirely new graduate curriculum known as "R3" that is trying to do exactly this. For years, Dr. Casadevall has been sounding the alarm about replication concerns in science. R3, which stands for Rigor, Responsibility, Reproducibility, is his answer.[144] The curriculum steers PhD education in the direction of broad, interdisciplinary training in areas such as logic, practical ethics, philosophy, and writing, in order to teach young scientists, in the words of Dr. Bosch, to "think critically, communicate better, and thus improve reproducibility."[145] The courses are available widely to students across the university—some enroll hundreds each year—and the curriculum is already spreading to other universities around the world.

There is also the question of whether the university as an institution should bear the principal responsibility of easing the tremors of irreproducibility. Departments and disciplines have mostly been shouldering this task thus far, which makes sense given that the contours of the reproducibility crisis vary so much by field. Nevertheless, in light of the extent to which irregularities in research can tangibly impair universities' contributions to public policy and erode public trust in academic knowledge, I think that university leaders have little choice but to engage this challenge. There are a number of possible avenues, none of which are mutually exclusive. Universities could invest in statistical training for faculty and researchers. They could ensure that the next generation of researchers is well trained to address this challenge and is sensitized to it throughout their graduate education. They could shape incentives in a way more conducive to the publication of negative results, which can be just as important to the realm of knowledge as splashier, positive ones. Or they could use their convening power to consider broader reforms in areas such as peer review and journal metrics. In short, universities could have considerable influence over this problem, and model practices that could reshape scientific norms across the sector.

Finally, any reform efforts may wither without a broader campaign to restore the research compact between academia and the government. Over the past two decades, research agencies such as the NIH have seen their budgets fall in constant dollars, a byproduct of austerity and neglect. The likelihood that a research grant proposal will be accepted by these agencies has fallen alongside it: in the case of the NIH, from well over 30 percent in years past, to about 20 percent today.[146] And the age at which scientists receive their first major grant has inched upward from 36 in 1980 to 43 in 2016, throwing up barriers in the path of an entire generation of talented young scientists as they seek to launch careers by initiating research projects of their own.[147] The scientific research enterprise has become, in the words of one influential article penned by science leaders, a "hypercompetitive atmosphere" of "perpetual disequilibrium," wherein an expanding scientific workforce vies for an increasingly scarce pool of federal dollars.[148] The situation is all the worse for scientists at public universities, which have faced massive budget cuts in the face of state fiscal pressure that have sent their research enterprise reeling further still.[149]

Again, a climate of scarcity is no friend to sound research practices and, at the very least, leaves little money available for the sorts of reforms that could make real headway on irreproducibility. If we starve the scientific enterprise, the incentives for poorly conducted science will persist. Devising credible and durable solutions to federal research support, so that funding is restored to a level that is equal to the magnitude of the nation's challenges, should be an urgent priority. For instance, Congress could credibly commit to federal research funding levels that are based on prespecified percentages of the gross domestic product, ensuring that investments in science and discovery grow with the economy and are protected from the vicissitudes of boom-bust funding cycles.[150]

All of these are critical reforms that will be necessary in addressing irreproducibility in science. But I want to spend the rest of this chapter turning to one broader idea that speaks directly to the reproducibility crisis while also speaking to, and even reimagining, the relationship between a democratic public and the university as a fact-generating, fact-communicating, and fact-checking institution: open science.

Show Your Work

In 2012, the *New York Times* profiled a group of researchers advocating for a new scientific paradigm that would leverage the potential of "friction-free collaboration over the internet"— through social networking sites, online databases, and open access research archives—to conduct and publish scientific research at an unprecedented pace and scale. The *Times* dubbed this nascent effort the "open science" movement.[151]

At the time, this movement was presented as a force with the potential to disrupt the staid, slow, and conservative practices of academic science—the Netflix to academia's Blockbuster Video. Nor was this an unreasonable comparison. That same year, the Royal Society released a report titled "Science as an Open Enterprise," acknowledging that "rapid and pervasive technological change has created new ways of acquiring, storing, manipulating and transmitting vast data volumes, as well as stimulating new habits of communication and collaboration amongst scientists. These changes challenge many existing norms of scientific behavior."[152] Even then, the academic research enterprise had all the hallmarks of a sector at the brink of technological disruption.

The signs of disruption have grown only more pronounced since. New online platforms have upended entrenched intermediaries as a flood of online, open access journals have burst onto the academic journal market, challenging a handful of established, for-profit players who keep most published articles behind subscription paywalls and control the majority of the academic research sector, often drawing profits each year on the order of 35 percent or more. Meanwhile, rogue websites have suddenly emerged to offer paid content for free, as happened in 2011, when a Kazakhstani neuroscientist named Alexandra Elbakyan launched Sci-Hub (think: Napster for science), a website that by one estimate offered free access to pirated versions of "two-thirds of all scholarly literature" in existence.[153] More legitimate (but still controversial) sites like ResearchGate and Academia.edu (both of which host millions of journal articles uploaded by users) have established themselves as players in this space, even as they have weathered significant litigation. Institutions, too, have begun to rebel against legacy content providers who are seen to be responding too slowly to change. The University of California system, for instance, which alone represents nearly 10 percent of all academic research activity in the United States, is one of a number of universities that are boycotting Elsevier, the largest academic publisher, over its failure to change the rules allowing users to access research.[154]

The open science movement is more than a reaction to technological upheaval, however; it aims to reconceive how research is conducted in the twenty-first century. Today, open science encompasses a number of interwoven strands. One is *open access*, or how easily citizens are able to obtain and understand the published research. Another is *open data*, or whether people have access to the materials used to support the claims made in articles. The final strand is *open source software*, or whether people have access to the software and tools necessary for understanding and interpreting those articles and data. These threads converge in a vision of a world where anyone can access and expand knowledge; where this catalyzes a rapid acceleration in the pace of discovery; where the testing and refinement of new ideas are fluid and ongoing rather than intermittent; where data are aggregated or fused together in ways that unlock patterns not seen before; where software and algorithms assist with the review and validation of scholarship in nearly real time; and where collaboration and the results of the scientific endeavor are inclusive and widespread not only within a single country but also throughout the world. As this list suggests, open science extends well beyond the natural sciences to the social sciences, the humanities, and indeed any field committed to uncovering truth.

For these reasons, many believe that one advantage a more open approach to science offers is that it might provide another antidote to the reproducibility problems discussed above. If scientific papers are shared as early and widely as possible, and if the data underlying those conclusions are made available in a manner that allows scrutiny by peers, then mistakes will be caught earlier—and more often—than happens now. The idea, sensible enough, is that openness has the potential to give rise to a rapid, iterative, and widely distributed mechanism for validating the accuracy of science outside the existing structures of the traditional peer review process.

There is reason to believe this could work. In the early 2010s, Swedish economist Anna Dreber had begun to grow uneasy at a spate of irreproducible studies in her field. She even worried whether her own research was producing false positives that couldn't be replicated.[155] In response, Dreber, an expert in risk, and her colleagues designed a series of prediction markets for the reproducibility of scientific studies (essentially an open version of peer review) that would test whether scientific research had the potential to self-correct.[156]

In Dreber's prediction markets, researchers in relevant fields were given a small pot of money to bid on a set of articles published in highly ranked academic journals.[157] Participants bought and sold shares in the studies based on their confidence that a given experiment was replicable, with the final price of each study reflecting the market's collective sense of the likelihood it could be reproduced. Strikingly, the markets predicted reproducibility with uncanny accuracy. In one market of twenty-one studies from across the social sciences, traders assigned the highest prices to the thirteen studies that were replicable, and the lowest prices to the eight studies that were not.[158] Another market devoted to experiments in psychology and composed of individuals with high levels of self-reported expertise in the field was 89 percent accurate.[159] As a group, the participants were able—to a remarkable degree—to divine the reproducibility of peer-reviewed studies: the crowd had outperformed peer review. Dreber's experiments point again to the tantalizing possibility that making scientific studies accessible early to scholars attentive to matters of rigor and accuracy could help science to solve its reproducibility problem.

The benefits of a more open approach to science also have implications far beyond the immediate problem of reproducibility that bear on universities' role as a bastion of fact in democracies.

In 2016, in the face of what it described as a "crisis of trust in news and basic information" and "in American democracy" itself, a panel of media luminaries convened by the Knight Commission wrote a sweeping report that urged "radical transparency" from news organizations.[160] New York University journalism professor Jay Rosen echoed this sentiment when he argued that journalists would no longer be able to get by on "an assertion of authority (trust us, we're pros at this)"—the new mantra must be "show your work."[161] The media responded swiftly. The *New York Times* and ProPublica now place the datasets behind their reporting online. PBS is creating video archives of interviews behind some of its reporting to let viewers see quotations in context.[162] The *Washington Post* launched a new series aimed at explaining the reporting process behind their stories.[163] And journalists are building online tools to help citizens distinguish legitimate from fake news sources in an express defense of democracy. Not all of these will work in reinforcing the standing of the media, which is facing a number of challenges on multiple fronts. But they collectively represent a purposeful effort by another fact-bound institution wrestling with an erosion of public trust, against a backdrop of democratic fragility, to reimagine how it does its work.

It is striking that relatively few universities have subjected themselves to similar soul-searching, at least at an institutional level, in light of their wavering credibility with a skeptical citizenry. Still, the historic disruption represented by open science—how technology has allowed us to connect our research with each other and citizens in ways that would have been unrecognizable even a generation ago—might be arriving at precisely the moment it is needed most. It offers a chance to reach across a widening chasm with a public skeptical of expertise and to meet the exigencies of democratic erosion. Neither openness nor technology is an easy fix or unalloyed good. But it is becoming clear that we can no longer sit on the sidelines. It is time for us, too, to "show our work."

Openness with Guardrails

With the arrival of COVID-19 in early 2020, the potential and peril of open science were put to the test on a previously unimaginable scale. It was clear from the beginning of the pandemic that universities would need to be central players in the fight against it, and they would need to act quickly.

University contributions in the battle against the pandemic have been extraordinary, from developing vaccines to communicating essential facts with the public to designing policy frameworks for legislators to building artificial intelligence–driven datasets capable of identifying critical information from within tens of thousands of academic articles. Driving these innovations was an open, collaborative approach to academic work that the urgency and scope of the pandemic necessitated. From the start, scientists were sharing the results of their research instantaneously on Twitter, Slack, and a number of collaborative scientific portals that are used to collect genomic sequences and anonymized clinical data.[164] Waves of articles and data about the virus were unleashed onto preprint servers: at one point in May 2020, nearly a third of COVID-19 papers were preprints, compared to just 3 percent of biomedical papers the year prior.[165] One data portal has used machine intelligence and sophisticated algorithms to mine tens of thousands of COVID-19 papers for insights into the virus.[166] And academic journals responded to the crisis by removing the firewalls that prevented access to COVID articles and cutting their turnaround time on submitted articles in half.[167] In some cases, journals published new papers within a matter of hours. One virologist described the speed and immediacy of this science as a "completely new culture of doing research."[168]

Throughout the pandemic, openness has become not only an aspiration but also a firmly established reality, accelerating the pace of exchange and discovery in ways that would have been virtually unimaginable several years ago. In the spirit of Anna Dreber's studies, it has also showed science's remarkable capacity to self-correct. To take one resonant example: early in the pandemic, when one study claimed a likeness between COVID and HIV and hinted that the virus might be man-made, dozens of scientists identified its flaws on social media and the preprint server, which led to a nearly immediate retraction. Rapid corrections to disinformation or flawed research have become a defining feature of the COVID landscape, revealing the remarkable agility and rigor of science during a global public health crisis.[169]

At other times, though, the experience of science during COVID has served as a cautionary tale. The confusion and controversy over the drug hydroxychloroquine illustrate this perfectly. In May 2020, the World Health Organization and other entities suspended trials into the effectiveness of hydroxychloroquine as a remedy for COVID after a study in *The Lancet*—one of the most prestigious medical journals—showed that the drug caused an increase in death and heart complications.[170] Not long after, the patient database that this study—and several others—relied upon came under attack for flaws and discrepancies in its data, which was compounded further when the company refused to let auditors assess its data.[171] *The Lancet* retracted the article, followed shortly by an announcement that the *New England Journal of Medicine* had retracted an article published using the same data.[172]

What is most distressing about this episode is that it indicates that the journals had rushed to publish the studies, that peer review had not caught the obvious problems with the data, and that, by the time the errors were identified, they had not only derailed the original clinical trials but complicated the beginning of new trials because of the onslaught of bad press. Just as damaging, this episode unleashed a torrent of attacks against the scientific enterprise. Social media accounts cited the controversy as evidence that "experts" and the World Health Organization were corrupt, supporters of President Trump—a known hydroxychloroquine advocate—lashed out at the studies as "fake news," and an op-ed in the *Wall Street Journal* condemned *The Lancet* for publishing what it described as "politicized science."[173] When clinical trials did finally resume, they demonstrated that hydroxychloroquine treatments neither caused harm nor offered any significant clinical benefit to hospitalized patients. But the damage to trust in science was already done.

We will not be able to grasp the full extent of COVID-19's impact on the scientific enterprise for some time to come. On the one hand, it has demonstrated scientists' ability to collaborate openly and fiercely across the lines of discipline and geography to fend off an existential danger. On the other, the rate at which new data are circulated in the public sphere has led to a number of disquieting setbacks that have further complicated and polarized the public's view of science.

Two critical lessons can be drawn from this pandemic. The first is that it is now almost undeniable that a more open approach to science, one that makes the barriers between scientists and between scientists and the public more permeable, presents a historic opportunity to renew the promises of knowledge creation and diffusion that have inhered in the modern university since 1876. This openness is both an accelerant of discovery and a salve for liberal democracy, helping to address the frailties of the reproducibility crisis and bringing science closer to the citizens it aims to serve. Second, COVID-19 has revealed a pressing need for the research enterprise and the institutions that house it to establish clear guardrails that will safeguard the legacy of academic fact creation and discovery—the knitted virtues of training, credentialing, rigor, and independence—that have defined that enterprise over the years and made it such an indelible asset to democracy.

There may have been a time when we could have assumed an open research environment would naturally incorporate these core virtues. But the ongoing experience of other industries upended by technological disruption should at least give some pause, especially now that this process is paired with a global pandemic. The social media revolution that fractured the intermediaries of traditional news media has ushered in an era of unrivaled connectivity, community, and conversation, but it has also unleashed forces of polarization, disinformation, and paranoia that have eaten away at liberal democracy. To this day, democracies are still struggling to build bulwarks to contain these forces. There's no particular reason to believe that academic knowledge is immune from these same sorts of dangers (and the inflamed reaction to pieces from *The Lancet* and *New England Journal of Medicine* seems like an ominous plume of what might be just over the horizon). Technological upheaval has arrived at the university's doors. The question now is whether we meet it and capture its fullest potential and minimize its risks, or allow it to overwhelm us.

What is needed is openness with guardrails. We intuitively understand openness, and the broader open science movement has identified key ways that universities could work toward greater transparency across the academic research enterprise. But what about the guardrails? That is a project where there is much thinking still to be done. The contours of such an endeavor would likely include the following:

- A reimagining of peer review both inside and outside the current journal-based system, ensuring that these core functions, indispensable to the validation and the success of science, are adapted to a more iterative and open era.

- New safeguards to ensure that openness does not inadvertently harm long-underrepresented groups who may benefit from blinded peer review and other existing policies.[174]

- Norms and structures to ensure that scientists—especially young scientists, who are at an early and often vulnerable stage in their careers—receive recognition for their work from peers and senior members of their fields in a more open landscape.

- An appreciation that some information, such as sensitive or proprietary data, is necessarily outside the reach of openness and may need to remain so.

- A reconsideration of how to communicate knowledge in an open world, to ensure university researchers and faculty are not merely transmitting their work to the world unbidden but conveying the meaning and context of that work clearly even as its pace and complexity accelerate.

Building a new knowledge ecosystem of this kind will be a monumental task that requires stores of deliberation and forethought. It will almost certainly be an exercise in institution-building akin to the one that led to the emergence of the great discovery function in the university a century and a half ago. We are starting to see the possible trajectories of this in initiatives underway at entities like the National Academy of Sciences, which has begun to detail incentive structures for open science; the University of California, which is exploring economically sustainable paths to make journals open access; and ASAPBio, an upstart group of reform-minded biologists who are pressing for novel experiments in peer review.

To bear fruit, open initiatives must be scaled and broadened, and they must include voices from across the entire academic community—from faculty to professional societies to students to libraries—as well as communities beyond that will be affected by these decisions. The incoming generation of scientists, who came of age in a world already remade by code and defined by iterative feedback, will have a particular role to play in shaping this new paradigm. Research universities, as institutions, must help lead the way. There are barriers to openness beyond the will of the university, but it surely can play a more active part in constructing a thoughtful and equitable openness. The university is a place where knowledge is shared beyond esoteric guilds of experts with the world, a role that was explicitly imagined in the service of democracy. It bears a special responsibility as a caretaker and producer of knowledge, and it should strive constantly to renew that system where needed. Only by claiming that mantle once more can we start to chart a truly open future.

FOUR

Purposeful Pluralism

Dialogue across Difference on Campus

Why don't my professors look like me?

Young. Black. Safe?

Injustice anywhere is a threat to justice everywhere.

THESE WERE JUST A FEW of the phrases displayed on signs held aloft by the dozens of students gathered at Keyser Quad on Johns Hopkins's Homewood campus in mid-November 2015. Organized by the Johns Hopkins Black Student Union, the protesters that day had convened to demand more support for Black students and greater representation for Black faculty, students, and staff. Similar protests had been organized on campuses across the country after months of uproar at the University of Missouri in Columbia following a series of deplorable racist incidents and escalating tensions on that campus. At Yale University, at Ithaca College, at Claremont McKenna College, and many others, students were rising up to demand change. They were having an impact, too. In fact, just days before the protest at Hopkins, the president of the University of Missouri system had resigned.

The anger, frustration, and anxiety of the Hopkins protestors was palpable—and entirely understandable. The events of the previous year had made it achingly clear that racial progress in the United States had stalled, a truth underscored by the tragic series of highly public deaths of Black men at the hands of police: Michael Brown in Ferguson, Eric Garner in New York City, and 25-year-old Freddie Gray in our hometown of Baltimore. Yet again, it was all too clear that our country had failed to realize the democratic ideals of equity and equality, and young people were calling universities to task as complicit in this failure.

I walked to Keyser Quad on that brisk November day first and foremost to listen. When I arrived, the students outlined a series of demands and enumerated the university's shortfalls at being a truly inclusive institution, pointing, as one piece of evidence, to the fact that our university's School of Arts and Sciences at the time counted only 5 Black faculty members out of 295 total faculty. To address these issues, they requested that I attend an open forum that they would hold. I agreed.

In the days preceding the forum, I considered what I wanted to say to our community. I had written a set of talking points highlighting commitments and actions from the university, but I thought it would be important, too, to know how my predecessors at Hopkins had responded in similar moments of reckoning. One trip to the archives later, I had laid out on my desk a history of episodes dating back to the 1960s in which students had called for more racial equity at Johns Hopkins. As my gaze darted back and forth between the words I planned to say at the forum and the responses of previous presidents, I became dismayed—they may as well have been identical. Time and again, university leadership had issued the same promises with too little progress to show for them. I simply couldn't return to our students repeating the refrains of the past. I threw out my prepared remarks and decided to start fresh.

On the evening of the forum, the auditorium overflowed with students, staff, alumni, and faculty. The ensuing two-hour discussion was at times tense and emotional, but it remained substantive throughout. A faculty moderator, selected by the students, set ground rules for the event and guided the conversation, ensuring that the audience could ask questions and that voices from all sides of the ideological spectrum were heard. When one student voiced concerns that reforms could lead to the institution of quotas, a chorus of boos and hisses started to build, but the students and moderator swiftly quieted the audience. I was able to share initiatives that were in the works to recruit more faculty and students to the university from underrepresented racial and ethnic groups, but similar plans had been introduced intermittently in the past without much in the way of sustained progress or momentum. And so, that night, we committed to a process that would help guarantee steady movement on these issues grounded in regular reports detailing faculty, staff, and graduate student diversity numbers. It was a road map toward a more diverse and inclusive institution that would involve faculty, staff, and students in its design. We still have a ways to go, but we are heading in the right direction, and a great deal of credit goes to the Black Student Union for pushing us to make good on our promise to be a more equitable institution.

This episode looms large in my memory because it embodied the best of a pluralistic academic community. From the initial protest on Keyser Quad to the public forum to the enduring and evolving policy changes, students engaged with university leadership and with one another in a way that represented the highest ideals of dialogue and debate across differences of perspective to enact meaningful change. Yet the experience also reinforced my sense that moments like this were all too rare. At a time when our democracy is ever more diverse and ever more polarized, our universities ought to be the world's models of how to talk to one another across the divides of identity and ideology. That they aren't—that universities have instead come to be seen as places of tension and fracturing—is a sign that we have failed to discharge one of our core contributions to liberal democracy.

The Fabric of our Pluralistic Democracy

The genius of liberal democracy lies, in no small part, in its capacity to value and give voice to the great diversity of the human experience. It accepts as a central premise the notion that there is no single overarching truth that should govern all affairs of humankind, and that we should, as much as possible, remit to the individual, not the state, the ability to decide what ends and goods are worthy of pursuit. This is why liberal democracy has historically placed such a high premium on tolerance. We may not agree with the choices that our fellow citizens may make, the values they cherish, or the gods they worship, but we understand that in order to live in a stable, pacific society, we have to muster the requisite respect for others' views to avoid a descent into endless strife and perpetual gridlock.

Herein lies one of liberal democracy's core dilemmas: to be sustainable, a democracy must find ways not only to channel the thrumming plurality of viewpoints, experiences, and dogmas in society, but also to fuse these perspectives into some approximation of a shared purpose, a public agenda, and a governable republic. For teeming multiethnic democracies like the United States, dialogue across difference is even more essential.

In 1848, as Europe was grappling with rapid democratization, the philosopher John Stuart Mill articulated the importance of conversation and debate to democracy. For Mill, experience alone, although essential to the development of one's attitudes and opinions, was ultimately inadequate to form proper judgments in a democratic society. These had to be molded, shaped, and interpreted in conversation with diverse others: "It is hardly possible to overstate the value . . . of placing human beings in contact with persons dissimilar to themselves, and with modes of thought and action unlike those with which they are familiar."[1]

The place where such encounters and exchanges occur is the public sphere. As the German sociologist Jürgen Habermas famously chronicled in *The Structural Transformation of the Public Sphere*, beginning in the seventeenth century, middle-class citizens gathered in salons (in France), table societies (in Germany), and coffeehouses (in England) to discuss ideas, art, and politics. These were spaces of "common humanity" in which, Habermas writes, "the authority of the better argument could assert itself against that of social hierarchy and in the end carry the day."[2] Such developments—along with the ascendance of print culture—set the stage for the modern public sphere, which has been integral to the health and longevity of liberal democracy as it has expanded to include ever more voices. Democracies require spaces for heterogeneous citizens to encounter one another and converse, argue, joke, and reason. They ensure, in the words of legal scholar Cass Sunstein, that "people will encounter materials on important issues, whether or not they have specifically chosen the encounter. When people see materials that they have not chosen, their interests and their views might change as a result. At the very least, they will know a bit more about what their fellow citizens are thinking."[3]

By most measures, such spaces are becoming increasingly scarce. Even as the United States has become a more diverse nation, our opportunities to make meaningful contact with people unlike ourselves, much less talk openly with them, has diminished considerably. Since the 1970s, research shows, Americans have sorted themselves into neighborhoods and social groups with similar cultural values, politics, religious affiliations, and income.[4] This steady process of self-segregation has accelerated the homogenization of the people we talk to, which has diminished the quality of our political life. An extensive study of American voters' social networks following the 2016 presidential election found, distressingly, that whereas more than a third of voters discussed politics with someone of the opposite party during the 2000 presidential campaign, only a fifth of voters could say the same in 2016.[5] In a separate examination of the discussion habits of citizens from a dozen countries, Americans were the least likely to discuss politics with someone with whom they disagree.[6]

Even more worrisome is the fact that when Americans do engage across difference, those interactions are increasingly defined by mistrust or even outright hostility. Indeed, the number of Americans who believe that "most people can be trusted" is at its lowest point in decades.[7] According to Pew, the share of Americans who hold a highly negative view of the other political party roughly tripled from 1994 to 2016.[8] The number of Americans who regard members of the other party as "selfish" or "close-minded" has also leapt to record highs.[9] In one of the more striking windows into the soul of a deeply riven nation, more than a quarter of Republicans in 2008 reported that they would be "somewhat upset" or "very upset" if one of their children married a Democrat, and about a fifth of Democrats said the same about their child marrying a Republican.[10] Five decades prior, those numbers stood at about 5 percent.[11] Such antipathy is even reinforcing where people live and how they feel about their neighbors. People now feel so negatively about those with competing views that the perceived desirability of a neighborhood can drop by as much as 20 percent when someone is told that members of the opposite political party live there.[12]

These trends are facilitated and exacerbated, of course, by the inescapable role of the Internet in modern life. Once heralded as the public sphere of the twenty-first century, online spaces have steadily been transformed into marketplaces of indignation and hotbeds of extreme beliefs. A few years ago, Yale University psychologist Molly Crockett analyzed big datasets from social media networks to study expressions of moral outrage on the Internet. Her analysis revealed that the sheer volume of immoral acts people learn about on social media combined with the low social costs to giving voice to heightened emotions has led to a massive increase in the volume and intensity of expressions of moral outrage online. Even though moral outrage sometimes has the potential to reinforce social norms and hold bad actors accountable, its online form all too often, in Crockett's words, "ricochets within echo chambers." She concludes, "There is a serious risk that moral outrage in the digital age will deepen social divides."[13] In sum, whether in our corporeal or online lives, Americans have drifted into ideological silos—and this has sapped us of the ability to engage with others beyond our bubbles and threatened the pluralist ideal undergirding liberal democracy.

Universities are one of the few remaining places where Americans of different backgrounds are guaranteed to encounter one another. This has long been true of higher education. Indeed, one of the great contributions of residential colleges and universities to American democracy has been the fact that they so often function as one of the first opportunities many young people have to leave their local communities and navigate their own identities in the presence of others unlike themselves. At first, these differences were limited mostly to geography and religion, but in time they have come to encompass class, race, gender, and even nation. The act of attending college has long been an experience at once discomfiting, developmentally meaningful, and fundamentally *pluralist*.

Across the centuries, colleges and universities have taken gradual steps to open their doors to groups excluded from other parts of American society. In many cases, they have even been ahead of their times, as with the daring nineteenth-century colleges that sought a path toward racial and gender parity decades before other institutions. As American colleges and universities in the twentieth century broadly embraced the imperative to recruit student bodies that more closely resembled the nation, they also created opportunities for students of diverse backgrounds and experiences to interact on campuses devoted to fierce debate about every issue imaginable. By the 1990s, data showed that college students were developing close relationships with peers across racial, economic, and ideological lines.[14] The psychologist Patricia Gurin, in an expert report filed in the affirmative action case *Gratz v. Bollinger*, cited evidence that these interactions were leading graduates, on average, to have "more diverse friends, neighbors and work associates" years after graduation. Colleges and universities, she suggested, had shown the potential to "disrupt an insidious cycle of lifetime segregation that threatens the fabric of our pluralistic democracy."[15]

Then, around the turn of the century, something shifted. Universities continued to make great strides in expanding the racial and ethnic diversity of incoming classes, but they no longer seemed to succeed in translating this additional diversity into a meaningful pluralism on campus. There were signs that students were drifting, more and more, into enclaves of familiarity. Of course, being with people like oneself is vital for individual and collective flourishing, but it cannot comprise the entirety of social interaction.[16] And universities have actually abetted these trends by removing policies in areas such as housing, dining, and coursework that had once served to draw students together. Worse, when interactions across difference do occur, they feel—for many—fragile and brittle, a consequence of the exclusion or silencing of those from different backgrounds or who hold different views.

This chapter sketches the emergence of the pluralist impulse in colleges and universities: how it came to flourish over the years, why it has flagged, and what can be done in response. Unlike the previous chapters of this book, which have focused on admissions, curricula, and research, this one turns to the less formal social interactions of campus life, to those moments of contact—sometimes spontaneous and serendipitous, sometimes structured and deliberate—across the unfamiliar that have occurred on campuses for two centuries. Such moments are notoriously difficult to tease out from the history of American higher education because they are so transient and fleeting and their impact so hard to measure, but the story is clear.

Over the course of the past two hundred years, universities have demonstrated a willingness and capacity to draw students together to engage others from diverse backgrounds, often for the first time in their lives. Of late, they have been passive in ensuring that those interactions across diversity actually occur once students arrive on campus, or that the ones that do are meaningful and productive.

They have adopted a hands-off approach toward campus interaction, mostly allowing students to sort out for themselves how to manage the complicated and sometimes even painful work of engaging with others who are different. They assume that students will simply chance upon encounters with people unlike themselves and cultivate independently the necessary skills to engage with one another across the gulfs of identity and ideology—an assumption drastically at odds with what we know of social psychology.

These issues are often debated in the context of high-profile controversies involving campus speakers. But those are a symptom, and not the illness. I mostly try to avoid relitigating them here, as such controversies have become so over-politicized that they ultimately tell us little about what universities ought to be doing differently in this moment. Instead, in this chapter, I want to look around and behind those debates to a conversation about where I believe universities actually have been most remiss. With regard to dialogue and speech in particular, we have resigned ourselves mostly to the role of referee, calling fouls on speech clashes when they arise.

But universities were not built to referee; they were built to educate. They should be hard-wiring into campuses spaces and programs that promote encounters, rather than standing to one side, or, worse, constructing barriers that keep people apart. They should be taking steps to model and teach discourse across that difference to students, rather than leaving it to students' own initiative. They should be reimagining their legacy as places of blending and vibrant discourse across all facets of identity and experience. They should be adopting, in other words, a *purposeful pluralism*.

As many have noted over the past several years, the experiment of realizing a truly multiethnic democracy in the United States (aside from the brief but powerful attempt during Reconstruction) only dates back to the civil rights movement, when the last great expansion of the franchise occurred. There is no blueprint for building and sustaining such a society. Our colleges and universities—once the exclusive province of white men from a narrow geographic region—are today among the most diverse institutions in our society. They ought to be on the vanguard of this grand, historic project, modeling what productive citizenship looks like in a world of difference, and yet they have lapsed in this responsibility.

There is cause for optimism, however. Colleges and universities have extraordinary resources to devote to the mission of cultivating a true pluralism: talented faculty, passionate students, and an ethos committed to dialogue and equality. This is a story of renewal, but it is one that requires us to start, once again, with what pluralism was at college before sketching a vision for what it can still be.

Scholastical Communion

Colleges of the eighteenth and early nineteenth centuries prized sameness over difference. According to one recent historian of the American college campus, the idea of a diverse student body "never entered the minds of early American college officials." If anything, "anti-diversity was the norm."[17] This was true at the level of admissions, since most students came from similar regional, racial, and economic backgrounds (with some modest exceptions for poor students, as I discussed in chapter 1). It was equally true of the college campus and the experiences it afforded, where homogeneity was the norm: students took the same classes, slept in the same building, and ate and prayed together. Colleges were not meant to be spaces of exploration or dynamism but of discipline, structure, and uniformity.

And yet, even then, college leaders recognized that there was something potent—special, even—about the way universities drew students together for serendipitous encounters at a formative moment in their lives. One of the earliest statements to this effect was recorded in 1671 by Harvard's governing board, which wrote of the "advantage to learning [that] accrues by the multitude of persons cohabiting for scholasticall communion, whereby to actuate the minds of one another."[18]

More than a century later, George Washington seized upon the democratic possibilities of this aspect of the residential campus in his idea for a national university in a 1795 letter to a friend. Washington wrote that an institution of higher learning with truly national aspirations must "assemble the youth of every part [of the nation] under such circumstances, as will, by the *freedom of intercourse* and *collision of sentiment*, give to their minds the direction of truth, philanthropy and mutual conciliation."[19] Washington believed that a university with a nationally representative student body could enable students to transcend what might sometimes seem to be irreconcilable differences of thought and background by living alongside one another, sharing honestly their beliefs and presuppositions, and challenging one another's ideas. In the process, they could begin to forge some shared sense of a democratic purpose out of a young, far-flung republic still in the process of stitching itself together. In this was the seed of a pluralistic college society.

As I discussed in chapter 2, Washington's national university never materialized, but in the early decades of the nineteenth century colleges did become more geographically diverse. In New England, for instance, the fraction of out-of-state students at institutions other than Harvard and Yale rose from 53 percent to 72 percent between 1800 and 1860. At Harvard and Yale, the shifts were even more dramatic, with out-of-state students growing from 18 percent to 53 percent at the former and 32 percent to 71 percent at the latter.[20] Yet even as colleges grew more diverse, the realities of student experience in the eighteenth and early nineteenth centuries did not always match Washington's lofty ideal of interaction.

Among the most characteristic features of campus life in the early republic were not expansive fellowship and vigorous debate but fistfights, riots, stabbings, and property destruction. Many of these spasms of violence were directed toward faculty and college leaders, whether it was students at the University of North Carolina who whipped the president in 1799 after a popular student had been expelled or those at the University of Virginia in 1825 who capped off a night of drinking by physically assaulting one professor and tossing a bottle of urine through the window of another.[21] Students fought each other, too. At Harvard, the nineteenth-century scholar George Ticknor described the "rude frolicking among the undergraduates, such as was not very rare when the college officers had left the tables."[22] Sometimes eruptions were a form of protest against suboptimal living conditions or abusive treatment by faculty; at others they were—to quote the poet Samuel Taylor Coleridge—acts of "motiveless malignity," disturbing expressions of a then-widespread masculine culture of brawling and alcohol (a potent combination) that found fertile soil on isolated campuses.[23]

Not all students resorted to violence. Some forged pathways that came closer to approximating Washington's vision of the free and open exchange of ideas. These were often the students—chronicled by campus life historian Helen Horowitz—for whom college was a place not for revelry and rebellion but labor, study, and self-improvement.[24] Many found refuge in another defining feature of campus life in this period: the college literary society.

Student born and student run, literary societies first began appearing on campuses in the early 1700s as egalitarian places for students to hone their rhetorical and compositional skills alongside their peers, free from the oversight and strictures of the faculty. These societies proliferated in the first half of the nineteenth century, becoming so prevalent that it was common to quip that no newly founded college was worth its salt if it didn't have at least two functioning literary societies before it opened its doors.

Called by one historian "little republics," literary societies—with grand Hellenic names like the Philomathean Society, Linonians, or the Clariosophics—were elaborate organizations.[25] They maintained libraries, developed governance structures independent of the college, elected members to be "professors" who delivered regular lectures on assigned subjects, and staged debates. At bottom, they were a space for students to socialize with one another on the battleground of ideas. As the constitution of one early literary society at Dartmouth stated, its mission was "encouraging free, and unreserved observation and forming a lasting and honorable fellowship."[26]

This aspect of the societies came into relief in the debates, which provided students a crucial space to cut their argumentative teeth and to test their views on important issues without—crucially—resorting to violence.[27] Students did not take these debates lightly. They were, in the recollections of one participant, "very earnest and called forth talent and research."[28] Over time, the topics these societies covered grew more contentious. Prior to the Revolutionary War, they tilted toward moral and philosophical conundrums; later, as students became thrilled by the possibilities of independence, they drifted in the direction of more urgent social and political questions.[29] By the onset of the Civil War, many literary societies were consumed by the same questions of slavery, sovereignty, and the fate of the Union that were rending the nation, straining the limits of decorum and debate.[30]

Yale is a good example of how the looming war tested the pluralist limits—in geographic and ideological terms—of literary societies. In 1819, sectional rivalry within Yale's Linonian Society (spurred by the election of a Northerner to the society's presidency) had precipitated an exodus of Southern students who formed their own literary society, Calliope. Although the societies were divided roughly along geographic lines following the split, the Calliopes still counted a few Northerners among their membership, while the Linonians retained some Southern members. Then, in 1851, this truce frayed entirely. That fall—a year after the passage of the Fugitive Slave Law—the remaining Southern members of the Linonians shifted their membership to Calliope.[31] The *Yale Literary Magazine* reported—ominously—that this act "has drawn more definitely the sectional differences of the students."[32]

What ultimately precipitated the decline of literary societies was not the Civil War, however, but the emergence of another kind of student society: the fraternity. Unlike the mostly egalitarian literary societies, fraternities promised secrecy and exclusivity, which made them desirable for students eager to make important social connections in college. Fraternities also solved an administrative headache of housing students, as they bought and maintained permanent residences near campus that colleges didn't have to pay for. Between 1876 and 1920, the number of fraternities with their own residences shot up from 1 to 774.[33] The college literary society couldn't compete.

Nevertheless, throughout their brief hegemony in college life, literary societies were an important venue in which students could freely encounter one another as equals and grapple peacefully with difficult ideas alongside their peers. Their prevalence was an early demonstration of the potential for colleges to cultivate communities defined by the vigorous exchange of a diversity of ideas. Yet for much of the nineteenth century, the demography of student bodies at most colleges remained more or less homogenous, with few colleges reflecting the composition of the nation, save for growing regional diversity. The tides began to shift, slowly, in the latter half of the nineteenth century toward more representative student bodies.

Collision of Views

Following the Civil War, radical Republicans and newly enfranchised Black citizens were eager to create a truly integrated American nation. They were initially successful, too: as many as two thousand Black citizens held political office during Reconstruction.[34] This desire to create more representative institutions extended to colleges, too, and inspired several noble, if tragically short-lived, efforts to transform college campuses into genuine laboratories for the formation of vibrant pluralistic communities.

In the South, a handful of institutions emerged as models of integrated higher education. One was Berea College in Kentucky, which, following the lead of Oberlin College (the first college in the United States to admit students regardless of race or sex), announced itself as "opposed to Sectarianism, Slaveholding, Caste, and every other wrong institution or practice."[35] Berea welcomed its first class of 187 collegians in 1866, more than half of whom were Black.[36] Although the school experienced its share of what one white alumnus described as a "friction, and of a most perplexing kind" between Black and white students (though we might wonder if this friction was as perplexing to his Black peers), Berea students attended church together, played on the same sports teams, took the same classes, and sparred with one another in debates.[37]

The University of South Carolina (formerly South Carolina College) took similar steps in 1873 when its trustees declared the university to be "the common property of all our citizens without distinction of race."[38] In order to accommodate new students (which included white students, formerly enslaved Black students, and Black men and women who had been free before the Civil War but unable to access higher education), the school eliminated all tuition and housing fees. One Black undergraduate marveled at the atmosphere of collegiality and mutual respect that prevailed on campus. Living and studying at the University of South Carolina was, he concluded, "the finest argument in favor of 'equality before the law.'"[39]

Ultimately, the waning of Reconstruction and the rise of Jim Crow forced both Berea and the University of South Carolina, among other residential institutions with similar aspirations, to abandon their pluralistic ambitions and become segregated institutions. Nevertheless, these trailblazing experiments in interracial and coeducation stand as vital reminders of the pluralistic and egalitarian societies that colleges, at their most ambitious and visionary, could be.

In the North, another push for a more diverse student body was afoot at Harvard. President Charles W. Eliot, who took office in 1869, was eager to transform Harvard from a historically provincial college whose constituency was mostly affluent young men from New England into a university of "national resort."[40] Achieving this status required a student body remade in the image of the nation. Eliot's blinkered opinions of coeducational and interracial education are well documented, but he strived to make

Harvard a place open to young men from "different nations, States, schools, families, sects, parties, and condition of life."[41]

Eliot had some success. A year after he took office, 56 percent of the graduating class were born in Massachusetts, only one student was Jewish, there were no reported Catholic students and a single international student (from Bavaria).[42] By 1909 (forty years later and near the end of Eliot's term), the fraction of graduating students from Massachusetts had dropped to 43 percent—6 percent of the class was Jewish, 8 percent was Catholic, and there were two avowed atheists along with representatives from ten different countries.[43] Political views, admittedly, were less well represented, with 309 Republicans and 40 Democrats (along with a handful of Mugwumps, Independents, and Socialists). Clearly, though, the demography of the nation's oldest college had shifted.

There was also a pedagogical dimension to Eliot's vision. Eliot saw a marked benefit in having people of different backgrounds encounter one another on campus. Echoing Washington from almost a century prior, Eliot believed in the potential of a diverse student body to yield a vital "collision of views" that, in his words, "promotes thought on great themes, converts passion into resolution, cultivates forbearance and mutual respect, and teaches young men to admire candor, moral courage, and independence of thought."[44]

Eliot's democratic fervor was not always accompanied by actions to transform rhetoric into policy. Reluctant to intervene too directly in the construction of undergraduate social life, Eliot believed that students ought to be "free to do their own social sorting."[45] What resulted was a steady stratification of social arrangements on campus, with wealthier students migrating to upscale private housing off-campus (the so-called Gold Coast) while poorer students (who were also more likely to be racial, ethnic, or religious minorities) lived in dormitories. Eliot championed dorms as being "occupied in a completely democratic manner as regards the schools from which the occupants have come and the parts of the country from which they have come," but he wasn't able to break up the Gold Coast.[46]

That task fell to Eliot's successor, Abbott Lawrence Lowell. At his inauguration, Lowell declared that Harvard had fallen short of "its national mission of throwing together youths of promise of every kind from every part of the country."[47] To achieve this end, he developed the Harvard House Plan. The plan entailed building seven new residence halls (completed in 1930), each of which was a highly structured little society that every year admitted a different cross section of students to avoid homogeneity. This plan did not go far enough in providing a forum for engagement across difference, however, since Lowell's well-documented bigotry meant that his vision of pluralistic encounter was severely circumscribed. Nevertheless, it was a demonstration of the long path the nation's oldest college (followed soon thereafter by Yale and Princeton) was taking toward realizing a more diverse and engaged community on their campuses.

The period between the end of the Civil War and the early decades of the twentieth century was one of remarkable transformation not only in the shape and structures of American colleges and universities but also in the composition of student bodies, animated by a growing conviction that pluralistic encounters (along multiple axes of identity and ideology) were a necessary part of the college experience. Yet as new groups of students enrolled in college, they continued to confront virulent prejudice and hostility, tragic obstacles to the "freedom of intercourse" that George Washington had envisioned. To meet these new conditions, students from marginalized groups adapted by reviving social organizations like the literary society as a means of preserving group identity.

It Alone Can Do This Thing

Many of the new students drawn to American higher education at the end of the nineteenth century were the children of immigrants (often from Catholic or Jewish families) then arriving in waves on America's shores. Between 1907 and 1920, the number of Catholic students enrolled at non-Catholic institutions grew from more than seven thousand to forty thousand.[48] Jewish students represented as much as 20 to 40 percent of the student body at many elite colleges in the 1910s and 20s. Meanwhile, Black Americans continued to press their claims to access universities from which they had been historically excluded. By 1910, institutions that were not historically Black colleges and universities (HBCUs) were admitting more than four times as many African American students as they had three decades prior, although these students still represented less than 1 percent of the total student body at these schools.[49]

Attending predominantly white, Protestant campuses, these students often encountered communities inherently suspicious of them, if not outright antagonistic and sometimes even violent. How, under such conditions, could they find ways to profit from the "collision of views" with diverse others while still preserving their cultural identity and finding support and kinship as members of deeply marginalized groups on campus and off? Their solution was to forge societies organized around identity that enabled them to create enduring communities on campuses as well as to move more fluidly and confidently between worlds.

Among the earliest of these identity-based groups were the Newman Clubs, formed by Catholic students beginning in the

1880s. The first was formed at the University of Wisconsin in 1883 after a Catholic student complained to a local Catholic family with whom he was having dinner that one of his professors had disparaged the Church during class. What he needed, he argued, was a place where Catholic students could talk freely about the ideas that were important to them and seek support in the face of discrimination. A place, he said, for "self defense."[50] The club they founded (originally named the Melvin Club for their dinner hosts that evening) took the form of a literary society with a distinctly Catholic focus: it created a space for Catholic students both to socialize freely with one another as well as to engage with and debate doctrine, theology, and ethics, topics that may not have been entirely welcome within the formal curriculum. In time, these clubs (rechristened as Newman Clubs after the famed British Catholic intellectual John Henry Newman) spread across the country, many—with the support of the Catholic Church—even building their own halls for meetings.

Just over two decades later, a similar movement took root among Jewish collegians. In 1906, the first Menorah Society was founded at Harvard. By 1919, eighty chapters had been established. Like the Newman Clubs, Menorah Societies also patterned themselves after the literary societies of the nineteenth century, encouraging the study of Jewish history and literature, organizing lectures, and even staging plays by Jewish writers.[51] A periodical, the *Menorah Journal,* served as the medium for Menorah Society members and nonmembers to share their views on Jewish topics and to record their experiences of college life.[52] The famed literary critic Lionel Trilling recalled the journal with fondness: "Content and meaning must be given [Judaism] in a form as fine, as dignified, as effective as possible. I think that the only thing in Jewish life that could have done that for me was *The Menorah*

Journal. There are thousands of young men for whom it can do the same thing, and it alone can do this thing."[53]

Black students during this period, meanwhile, frequently faced more dire circumstances than their Catholic and Jewish peers. When they arrived on predominantly white campuses, they experienced profound institutional neglect, whether in the form of having direct confrontations with racist students and faculty, being prohibited from living on campus, being denied entry into social circles (for instance, working at white fraternities that would never admit them as members), or being barred from many facilities that white students took for granted. Their numbers were so small at most campuses that fellowship was often hard to come by. As a result, Black students struggled to feel at home on campuses, and attrition was often high.[54]

By 1904, the Black student population at Cornell University had been growing steadily for several years.[55] But when none of the six Black students who arrived on campus that fall returned the following year, it was clear to the Black students who remained that action needed to be taken.[56] In response, a group of Black upperclassmen formed Alpha Phi Alpha, the first Black fraternity in the United States. Although it resembled in some ways the white fraternities that lined the main boulevard of Cornell's campus, Alpha Phi Alpha owed its identity more to the long history of African American benevolent organizations and secret societies. It was a source of support for Black students coming into the college and of aid to Black high schoolers and community members. Like the eight other African American fraternities and sororities founded in its wake (the "Divine Nine" as they are now called, several of which were first established at HBCUs), Alpha Phi Alpha became an instrumental institution for generations of Black students at Cornell and dedicated itself to the uplift, education, and perpetuation of an African American student community on a traditionally white campus.[57]

In each of these cases, college students from marginalized groups formed social and intellectual organizations on campus as a way to reinforce their sense of cultural identity and cohesion in the midst of white, Protestant university campuses. It would be a mistake to see these groups as being antithetical to pluralistic encounters. If anything, they were a necessary precondition to pluralism—a means of ensuring a continuity of presence for underrepresented populations on campuses that enabled diverse communities in higher education to blossom and flourish. As important as the collision of views and encounters with difference were and have continued to be, the growth of Menorah Societies, Newman Clubs, and Black fraternities—among other similar organizations—were evidence of the truth that for students from marginalized populations, such groups were equally necessary for them to thrive on increasingly diverse campuses. They also anticipated the complex group dynamics that would shape post–World War II campuses.

I Don't Think They Thought It Out

The second half of the twentieth century was a period of unprecedented diversification at colleges and universities, much of it the work of university administrators who, like Eliot and others in the nineteenth century, recognized the urgency and democratic significance of forming representative student bodies. The period was also one of tension and, eventually, conflagration.

Change came slowly at first. Following the passage of the G.I. Bill in 1944, the Veterans Administration was careful to allocate an equal share of readjustment benefits and educational assistance to

Black and white veterans. Yet segregation and unequal access to colleges and universities blunted Black veterans' ability to reap the full benefits of the bill.[58] Universities bore direct responsibility for this state of affairs. As historian John R. Thelin wrote about this period, "racial integration . . . was an effort almost always dismissed by governing boards as a nuisance to institutional advancement."[59]

The dam started to break at the nation's most selective universities alongside the cresting civil rights movement. As education scholars Anthony S. Chen and Lisa M. Stulberg have chronicled, in the early 1960s, ambitious higher education leaders began beating the drum for greater diversity in their admissions, even at the cost of their own livelihoods. They conceived diversity similarly to how Eliot had nearly a century earlier. To quote the president of Amherst in 1961, they were eager to recruit students "of all races, of all faiths, and even no faith."[60]

The passage of the Civil Rights Act of 1964 removed explicit discriminatory admissions practices at colleges and universities that received federal funding, which began the process of desegregation at public universities.[61] University leaders—especially at institutions without explicitly discriminatory policies but that had neglected African American students—were inspired by the movement to enroll students who were more reflective of the nation. This was also a moment when tensions across the country were at a fever pitch, following the high-profile assassinations of civil rights leaders and the swelling opposition to the Vietnam War.[62] How universities navigated these tensions tested their pluralist mettle and profoundly shaped their histories. The experiences of two universities (Cornell and the University of Pennsylvania) offer a stark contrast in approach.

James A. Perkins assumed the presidency of Cornell University in 1963. His tenure began with a virtually unparalleled effort to recruit African American students and ended in an armed standoff. A progressive liberal from Philadelphia whose resume included a PhD in political science from Princeton and an impressive list of government and philanthropic leadership positions, Perkins came to Cornell committed to putting the resources of the university to work to advance pragmatically the cause of justice. Among his efforts was the Committee on Special Education Projects (COSEP), whose charge was to develop programs that would "make a larger contribution to the education of qualified students who have been disadvantaged by their cultural, economic and educational environments."[63]

COSEP was remarkably successful by most measures. Its activities took the form of recruiting African American students from inner cities and the rural South, offering them substantial financial aid packages, and helping shepherd them through Cornell. In purely numerical terms, COSEP increased the number of Black students at Cornell from 8 to more than two hundred in just four years.[64] The money allocated to financial aid at the university increased as well, growing from a mere $13,000 in 1964 to a total of more than $1 million by 1970.[65] But while COSEP significantly multiplied the number of Black students at Cornell, the campus was unprepared for the tensions that engulfed the student body. As one Cornell student described the campus atmosphere: "I think [the administration] wanted us to have a multicultural experience, but I don't think that they thought it out in terms of personalities and people's backgrounds . . . normal conflicts [were] exacerbated by people's ignorance about other cultures."[66]

In 1969, things came to a boil, the end result of years of escalating tensions between groups on campus, the increasingly radical politics of some students, an administration often frustratingly passive in the face of outrage, and a series of unambiguously racist acts, including a burning cross in front of the university's residence for Black women.[67] Together, these factors moved members of Cornell's Afro-American Society (AAS) to seize control of the university's student union, Willard Straight Hall, which they successfully did on the morning of April 19. Later, after a group of white students tried to force them out, the occupiers armed themselves with rifles and barricaded themselves in the building until the university acquiesced to a series of sweeping changes on the campus. After a tense twenty-four-hour standoff, the occupation ended peacefully, but the university community was unsettled by the specter of violence. President Perkins resigned shortly thereafter.

Similar clashes occurred at universities across the country, revealing the stark and uncomfortable truth that sometimes even earnest and considered efforts to construct truly representative and inclusive campuses could not inoculate a university from the struggles, prejudices, and violence of an era. Not all campuses experienced such dramatic standoffs, however.

Like Cornell, the University of Pennsylvania in the 1960s was also a university undergoing rapid diversification. By 1968, the school was enrolling more Black students than any other Ivy League university.[68] (Cornell came in a close second.) As with other campuses, Penn saw its share of post-'68 protests, but without the violence and rupture. What made the difference?

The answer appears to lie in structures that Penn put in place to accommodate student disagreement and conflict. In 1968, the university had formed the Commission on Open Expression and Demonstration on Campus, a faculty-student committee chaired by Penn Law professor Robert Mundheim charged with outlining the parameters of protest and debate on campus: where such actions could occur, what was or was not permissible, and what sorts of discussions ought to precede protest. Although the *Daily Pennsylvanian* complained that once "stripped of its circumlocutive prolixity the report says very little that is revolutionary and much that is objectionable," the commission's recommendations were not only officially adopted as university policy but appear to have been widely embraced by students, faculty, and administrators alike, including activist groups on campus.[69] In response to the report, one student activist applauded the university, saying, "We're glad the university has dropped the parental approach and has stopped acting like they were faced with either sophisticated revolutionaries or naughty children, instead of a bunch of intelligent adults."[70]

So, when students staged a sit-in at College Hall in February 1969 to protest the university's proposed construction of a new Science Center that threatened to displace Philadelphia residents, there was a framework within which to navigate the various sides of the debate. Although the sit-in was the longest in the university's history (six days), it adhered to the Mundheim report's call that at a university there existed "the freedom to experiment, to present and to examine alternative data and theories; the freedom to hear, to express, and to debate various views; and the freedom to voice criticism of existing practices and values."[71]

Over the course of the six days, university trustees talked to protestors, faculty spoke to one another, and students argued with administrators (and one other); statements were read aloud, criticized, and shared; and votes were taken and tallied. In the end, everyone came to an agreement they could abide. In the words of one student, "Nothing was destroyed, but we built a hell of a lot."[72] The event thus marked, in the words of one historian, a pioneering "liberal-pluralist student/faculty movement" that resulted in "a more peaceful process of change than was the case on many other campuses."[73] Or, as a Penn faculty member characterized the sit-in, "a strange war in which all sides won."[74]

Speculation, Experimentation, Creation

Although still reeling from the violence, turmoil, and transformations of 1968, colleges and universities in the 1970s redoubled their pursuit to recruit a more racially diverse student body. Race-conscious admissions policies became standard practice at colleges and universities across the country during this period. Some institutions merely gave a slight preferential tilt to an applicant's race, while others established explicit racial quota systems. The effectiveness of these measures was striking. By 1975, the number of Black undergraduates nearly tripled, rising from 370,000 in 1967 to nearly 950,000.[75] But affirmative action faced sharp criticism from many corners, and high-profile lawsuits soon followed.

Debate over the merits of affirmative action came to a head a couple of years later when the US Supreme Court heard *University of California Regents v. Bakke*.[76] At the heart of the case was Allan Bakke, a white man twice denied admission to the medical school at the University of California, Davis, who blamed his rejection on the school's racial quota system. In its decision, the court deemed racial quotas unconstitutional but nevertheless affirmed the value of race-conscious admissions.[77] Justice Lawrence F. Powell wrote that "the atmosphere of 'speculation, experiment and creation'— so essential to the quality of higher education—is widely believed to be promoted by a diverse student body."[78] In this, the decision allowed for race to continue to be a factor in admissions by affirming—echoing university leaders from across generations— the distinctive educational benefits of diversity (whether racial, religious, geographic, or ideological) on campuses.[79]

Even without quota systems, colleges and universities continued to make strides throughout the 1980s in creating more diverse campuses as well as in promoting student interaction. A
groundbreaking study from William G. Bowen and Derek Bok
(former presidents of Princeton and Harvard, respectively) confirmed this empirically. Surveying thousands of students at more
than two dozen universities in the United States who first entered
college in 1989, Bok and Bowen found that 90 percent reported
knowing well at least two peers from different parts of the country, and more than half said they knew well at least two peers from
families much poorer than their own, with a similar number saying they knew well students whose politics differed significantly
from their own.[80] What's more, a greater percentage of whites
knew well two or more Black students at schools with higher
levels of Black enrollment than those with lower levels. A separate study by sociologists Peter Espenshade and Alexandra Watson Radford confirmed these results. Surveying students from the
entering cohorts of 1983, 1993, and 1997 at eight selective colleges, they found that just over 60 percent of all students reported
socializing often with students of a different race, while half of
students said that they counted a student of a different race among
their five closest friends.[81] Both studies found definitively that the
more diverse a campus, the more likely students of different racial backgrounds were to interact with one another.

This is not to say that the work of inclusion was easy, friction-
less, or complete. Take the University of California, Berkeley. Over
the course of the 1980s, the share of white undergraduates at California's flagship public university dropped from 66 percent to
45 percent, making it among the first major research universities
with a student body that lacked a single ethnic or racial majority.[82] This did not suddenly result in racial harmony, however, as

students from underrepresented communities still faced prejudice, whether in direct confrontations or in racist messages spray-painted on buildings across campus.[83] And many students acknowledged frankly the difficulty of bridging differences to form new friendships. As one sophomore at the time explained, "It's kind of awkward to go up to someone who's not your race, and maybe doesn't speak your language, and say, 'Hey, would you like to associate with me on a day-to-day basis?'"[84] Across the country, other colleges followed a similar trajectory.

These changes were painful and halting, but they were also evidence that universities were evolving into sites of pluralist interaction that truly reflected the nation, places where students learned and practiced the difficult art of reaching out and building across difference. The period saw a similar pattern play out with gender, where schools started to admit women in far greater numbers, aided by administrators willing to rebuff hostile alumni afraid that the presence of female students would sap historically male-only institutions of their masculine heritage; by students who coordinated rallies and wrote scathing editorials; and, eventually, by Congress's passage of Title IX, which in 1972 gave colleges seven years to transition to "being an institution which admits students of both sexes."[85] Women faced discrimination, tokenism, and an immense pressure to excel, not to mention the unnerving experience of always being "watched."[86] When Yale announced in 1968 that it would be admitting women for fall 1969, nearly 4,000 women applied, 576 of whom (or 12.5 percent of the student body) enrolled.[87] Their presence helped to transform not only the demography of the campus but also the attitudes and beliefs of its students. A *Life Magazine* feature on coed dorms at Oberlin included positive reflections from both men and women at the college on the benefits of coed living arrangements. Tellingly, one male freshman told the magazine he started "taking [his women classmates] more for granted as people, something I'd never done before."[88] Such a remark is a testament to how important women's presence on traditionally male campuses was to combating pervasive sexism and also an unambiguous sign of how much work remained.

In countless dorm-room conversations, leisurely walks to class, work-study jobs, seminar room debates, extracurricular activities, late-night study sessions, and sporting events, students of different backgrounds, ethnicities, and genders—and eventually, in increasing numbers, nationalities—were encountering and meaningfully interacting with one another.[89] Whether they were aware of it or not, they were honing the skills to navigate pluralistic societies. This period bore all the markings of pluralism in bloom.

Almost Like a Dating Website

The 1980s and '90s had seemed to place colleges and universities on a trajectory to pluralistic flourishing on campus that educators and leaders a century earlier could hardly have anticipated. Yet in the two decades since, there is a sense that something has shifted. The pluralist endeavor on campuses seems to have lost much of its purchase.

This is not to say that universities have given up on diversity. Incoming classes at selective universities are, in most respects, more diverse than ever. Once students arrive on campus, however, engagement across differences of identity and ideology has stalled. Indeed, students seem to be drifting apart, and when they do come together across difference, their interactions can seem brittle and fearful. As diversity experts might put it: *structural* diversity (numeracy of different groups) is no longer leading to *interactional* diversity. We have made our campuses more diverse, but we are not reaping the benefits of pluralism and exchange across this difference.

I would posit several reasons for this. One is that our colleges and universities aren't immune from the broader trends afflicting discourse in America. The polarization and distrust infecting our society affect our students no less than the rest of the country, and in many cases, much more.

Beyond that, though, is the unavoidable fact that as communities become more diverse, the *potential* of pluralism grows, but so do its *complexities* and *challenges*. For a good portion of the history of the United States, universities were mostly homogenous places. Even in the eighteenth and nineteenth centuries, discourse on campus was challenging, depending on what region students were from or what religion they practiced. Now, in the twenty-first century, we are starting to approximate a level of diversity on campus that truly looks like the world. Achieving a pluralist community across this tapestry of difference is inevitably going to be all the more difficult. This is what we see happening in our own democracy. As we struggle to realize the promises of multi-ethnic democracy, eruptions of anger, resentment, fear, and violence by those who feel they are being displaced ripple throughout our society. As universities continue to walk the path of making our campuses more racially and ethnically diverse, and see increased representation from first-generation students and others, it is imperative that we ensure these voices enter the conversation of the academy. History and science teach us that this task requires purpose and intent. It will not happen on its own.

Universities have not adapted fast enough to the newly diversified campus. If anything, they have actually dismantled structures on campus that had once pulled students together across difference. And when it comes to speech, they have been generally content to adopt a passive approach, entering the picture when needed to adjudicate disputes, but otherwise allowing students to sort out for themselves how to manage the complicated and sometimes even painful work of engaging with others who are different. Universities should be at the vanguard of designing ways to bring students together across this new diversity—discourse is etched into their mitochondria. Still: universities have gone to great and important lengths to restructure their admissions processes to promote diversity, yet they have done vanishingly little to adapt newly diverse campuses to pluralist ends.

The remainder of this chapter describes what I believe is the scope of the pluralism challenge on campuses and what we can do about it. Let's start with the question of interaction across difference. In recent years, we have begun to see on our campuses a drift away from the collision of views that Eliot and others championed and more self-segregation of groups. Of course, we need to be careful about sweeping claims of balkanization. The 1990s—a time when interactional diversity on campuses was high—were replete with headlines declaiming the segregation of American universities like "Separate Ethnic Worlds Grow on Campus" and "College Dorms Reflect Trend of Self-Segregation."[90] A raft of similar headlines could easily be culled from major publications over the past several years.

Still, there are signs that something is different now. Experts say the problem has shifted, and worsened, in no small part because universities have become increasingly complicit. Speaking to *The Atlantic* in 2016, Temple University professor Sara Goldrick-Rab said, "Not only are the poor kids and the rich kids going to different schools, but they're being segregated in their living spaces . . . and there are institutional policies that contribute to this."[91]

Nowhere is this more evident than in housing policy. From the rise of residential fraternities in the nineteenth century to Eliot's and Lowell's battles with the "Gold Coast" at Harvard and beyond, housing has been one of the epicenters of campus pluralism. For a time, one of the defining features of the campus experience for newly arriving students was the "assignment"—either random or decided upon by university staff—of a first-year roommate. Considerations of how to assign roommates had been a part of the student personnel literature since the 1930s and dovetailed, at some institutions, with the integration of on-campus residences.[92] Many universities had long assigned students to rooms in residence halls; others came to the practice in the 1980s or later with the express aim of encouraging greater interaction as campuses became more diverse.[93] By the 1990s, meeting their assigned roommate was a rite of passage for newly arriving students at colleges across the United States.

In no small part because of the experimental conditions created by the random assignment of roommates, a deep body of research emerged showing that when a student rooms with someone different than them, it exposes them to new perspectives that shift how they see or approach the world. Students assigned a roommate of a different race show less racial bias, express a greater appreciation for diversity, and interact more often and more comfortably with members of other races.[94] Roommates affect students' politics, too: first-year students' political ideology "tends to move toward the ideology of their roommates," and if their roommates discuss politics and current events, students are more likely to be politically active later in life.[95] And this even holds for wealth, where rooming with a peer from a low-income background increases the likelihood that a student will engage in volunteer activities after they graduate.[96] (The opposite effect also seems to hold: students assigned a student from a high-income background are less likely to support higher taxes on the wealthy!) What is clear is that roommates are a surprisingly rich source of pluralist education, expanding students' horizons in ways that resonate across their schooling and even their lives.

Beginning around the 2010s, however, universities started adopting a hands-off posture toward housing by allowing incoming students to choose their own roommates. These decisions were a consequence of demands from parents and students for more choice in roommate selection as well as the emergence of social media platforms that made it far easier for students to pair off on their own. Students flocked to online communities on Facebook and other platforms in the hopes of locking in a first-year roommate to their liking before they arrived on campus, while universities partnered with new online apps like RoomSync and Roomsurf to streamline the process. (One student described this matchmaking process as "almost like a dating website.")[97] When left to their own devices, students began choosing roommates from backgrounds similar to their own. Administrators found that students from more privileged background, in particular, were pairing off with each other.[98] One informal survey showed that approximately 70 percent of universities in 2012 permitted incoming freshmen to select their own roommates.[99] At the University of Virginia, about 65 percent of incoming students matched with roommates on their own in 2018. At Duke and Vanderbilt, almost half of the class chose their own roommates before they put an end to the practice in 2018 and 2020, respectively.[100]

The changes did not end there. Around the same time that they were shifting their roommate policies, universities were also cultivating—with echoes of the elite private housing of Gilded Age campuses—a new generation of sometimes lavish student housing options that have served to divide rich students from poor students, effectively replicating the homogeneity of the past. Sometimes, universities have built these structures specifically to attract wealthier students. (Public universities have even responded to budget cuts by, ironically, investing in luxury amenities to entice out-of-state students, who are not eligible for discounted in-state tuition.) Other times, out of a desperation to find space for expanding student bodies, universities have partnered with—or ceded the problem entirely to—corporate developers to construct extravagant new residence halls. The result is a modern campus where wealthier students often live and socialize amongst themselves in luxury complexes out of reach for their poorer classmates, many of whom are also from underrepresented populations.[101] As one professor put it, "We're re-creating socially stratified communities on campus instead of giving students opportunities to live among people from different walks of life."[102]

I should caution that assigned campus housing affects some groups differently than others. One recent study of interactional diversity among randomly assigned roommates showed, for instance, that "Asian, Black and multiracial students . . . perceived a substantially less welcoming campus environment than their same-race peers who chose their roommates."[103] Hence any move back toward assigned housing must be accompanied by an acute attentiveness to any concerns that may arise, a willingness to move students when problems emerge, and a host of wrap-around programming and services related to student diversity and engagement. That is, the answer is for the university to become *more engaged and purposeful*, not to wash its hands of the problem and leave students to sort it out.

This is also why attacks on affinity groups established for women, LGBTQ students, or racial and ethnic minorities as drivers of segregation are profoundly misplaced. As has been true for decades, students need not only "bridging" opportunities to forge links with students different from themselves, to use a frame made famous by Robert Putnam, but also "bonding" opportunities to connect with other in-group members.[104] This was true of the Newman Clubs and the Menorah Societies of yesteryear, and it remains true of the array of affinity groups that populate our campuses today, from Hillel to LGBTQ groups to Black student unions and so many more. These spaces provide affirmation and repose alongside peers who share backgrounds and experiences, which then act as trampolines that launch students back into the hurly-burly world of diverse campus life. In-group affiliation is not only inevitable but also fiercely valuable—that is, as long as these spaces don't become isolated enclaves that limit students' social experiences in college.

Much of this discussion so far has been about housing, but the trend toward more campus options, and more campus sorting, has not stopped there. The same phenomenon has played out in dining options, in social opportunities (like student clubs), and even in the classroom, where the dilution of core requirements has hastened the retreat of a curriculum that once had thrust students with different interests and perspectives into a single classroom, mixing budding philosophers, economists, historians, and scientists in debate and conversation.[105]

This latter phenomenon has been the case at Johns Hopkins. Beginning in 2017, when we revisited our undergraduate curriculum, we discovered that the erosion of distribution requirements across majors, along with the accumulation of disciplinary requirements within majors, meant that many students were now rarely leaving the confines of their own majors. A faculty report pointed out that students majoring in psychology, for example, could choose to satisfy more than 90 percent of their distribution and writing requirements through courses within their major, while many engineering disciplines had been *requiring* students to take more than 80 percent of their credit hours within the major just to graduate. Our faculty rightly criticized this drift toward curricular silos and proposed a redesign of the undergraduate curriculum to steer students toward a deeper blend of classroom experiences. They have proposed replacing the errant distribution requirements with a new set of foundational abilities that students would be required to develop. One of those would be the deeply pluralist capacity, by now familiar to readers of this chapter, to "engage effectively as citizens in a diverse world" and "articulate and examine their own beliefs, practices and values while being open to and respectful of the beliefs, practices and values of others."[106] Achieving these goals requires reimagining aspects of campus life that extend from the classroom to the residence hall and beyond.

Without Fear of Restraint or Penalty

There is more to pluralism than just the serendipity of encounters with difference. Just as important is the question of the quality of those encounters. When students do come into contact with new ideas and new people, are they equipped to navigate those interactions productively?

At this point, it is conventional to say that American campuses are in the midst of a speech crisis. While this view is not confined to the Right, it has taken a particular hold in the conservative imagination. Undergirding this is the claim that American university campuses do not merely lean toward the political Left, but are in fact sites of orchestrated liberal indoctrination that silence ideological dissent. Such skepticism of the academy has been simmering since William F. Buckley Jr. called on readers of *National Review* to send evidence of "classroom indoctrination" in 1956.[107] After Allan Bloom's *The Closing of the American Mind* became an unexpected bestseller more than three decades ago, this line of attack has become ever more strident, with books like Ben Shapiro's *Brainwashed: How Universities Indoctrinate America's Youth* in 2004 and David Horowitz's *The Professors: The 101 Most Dangerous Academics in America* in 2006—aided by a steady stream of op-eds in prominent news outlets—convincing millions that American universities are hotbeds of dangerous progressivism. According to one recent poll, two-thirds of Republicans say they have only some or very little confidence in higher education. When asked why they hold such diminished views of universities, far and away the two most frequent answers were that universities were "too liberal" and that they were "not allowing students to think for themselves."[108]

The reality on our campuses is far less sensational, it but raises important questions nevertheless.

First: indoctrination by faculty. Since 1958, when Paul Lazarsfeld and Wagnar Thielens published *The Academic Mind*, their thorough and dispassionate study of the political leanings of social scientists in the wake of the McCarthy trials, there has been a consistent and growing body of empirical evidence showing that the political views of faculty (throughout the humanities and social sciences, at least) tilt consistently left.[109] Over the decades, this ideological gap has grown considerably (despite a brief spike in self-identifying conservative professors in the 1980s).[110] One survey of tens of thousands of professors showed a persistent gap in the ratio of liberal to conservative faculty that has widened over time, from 2 to 1 in 1989 to 6 to 1 in 2014.[111] A separate analysis of faculty voter registration found that in the fields of history, economics, law, communications, and psychology, there were 11.5 Democrats to every 1 Republican.[112] Sociologist Neil Gross, author of one the most rigorous academic studies of this phenomenon in the past decade, concluded that the American academy "contains a larger proportion of people who describe themselves as liberal than just about any other major occupation."[113]

We should approach these data carefully. For one, party affiliation says only so much about actual political beliefs. Moreover, evidence that ideological leanings actually affect classroom behavior is elusive at best. While some data show that conservative students are more likely to avoid speaking up in social sciences and humanities classes out of fear of receiving a bad grade, there are also studies demonstrating that those fears are unjustified: faculty do not award conservative students worse grades than their liberal classmates.[114] And although students on average become slightly more liberal while in college, they do so at the same rates as people the same age who do not attend college.[115] As educators, university faculty and administrators should take seriously any suggestion that student voices are being shut down in the classroom. That being said, evidence of mass liberal indoctrination is grossly overstated, and focus on the topic is somewhat misguided.

We should be asking instead why so many disciplines suffer from a dearth of conservative faculty in the first place and what the consequences of that imbalance are. Throughout my career, I have seen many brilliant conservative scholars flee the academy for think tanks, where they feel their ideas will be more readily welcomed.[116] This brain drain cannot be healthy for the university. If the professoriate continues to congregate on the political Left, it shortchanges conservative and liberal students alike.

Conservative students need to feel that their campus is one that invites their views in the endless refinement of ideas through reason, both outside of the classroom as well as within it. They need to see faculty nourishing the kinds of open debate about a great variety of ideas that either do not or cannot flourish at other institutions across our society. And they need mentors who can model the virtues of intellectual discourse and engagement rather than provocation and confrontation, and support and guide them through college and beyond—including, perhaps, into graduate school in fields not usually populated by right-leaning thinkers.[117] For students whose sympathies lie with the political Left, the presence of conservatives—particularly conservative faculty—is an instruction in how to engage ideas different than one's own, to test one's own assumptions accordingly, and perhaps above all to see those who hold different views as participants in a conversation, a shared endeavor, rather than as strangers or, worse, enemies.

Several universities across the country have begun to seek solutions to this disparity. One anecdote at the University of Colorado Boulder is particularly revealing. Since 2013, the university has invited a "visiting scholar in conservative thought" to its campus.[118] On a campus where only about 8 percent of the faculty and 20 percent of the students identified as conservative, these invited scholars were initially viewed with deep skepticism. With time, however, that suspicion seems to have subsided. Several years ago, one student left a note for that term's visiting scholar, a philosophy professor and evangelical Catholic: "I have come to believe that one of the duties of citizenship is to listen to points of view unlike one's own. Liberal Democrat that I am, you made the job a pleasure. You also taught me that kindness, courtesy, and humility would at least get an audience to listen to you in a way that criticism never can."[119] To inspire such sentiments in students is itself a powerful argument for the need to maintain intellectual diversity on our campuses.

Beyond the matter of faculty is how students themselves approach issues of speech and free expression on campus. Critics on the right now warn regularly of a "free-speech crisis" and a "silencing of dissent" on campuses, citing "student mobbists" who shout down and threaten speakers (and other students) with whom they disagree.[120] Stories crowd cable news broadcasts of speakers disinvited or disrupted, of faculty and staff fearing for their jobs, and of a pervasive "cancel culture" that has anyone whose political views are not in lockstep with the Left walking on eggshells. Late in his term, President Donald Trump's Department of Justice echoed these claims, insisting that the "very core of university life—open debate among scholars and students—is under attack."[121]

But if we peer behind the anecdotes and invective, the evidence of student antipathy toward free speech is more nuanced. Facts on the ground suggest that the silencing of conservative students in campus spaces beyond the classroom is less prevalent than often reported, while speaker disinvitations in the United States number in the range of one or two dozen at most per year, a small fraction of the speaking engagements that occur annually without fanfare.[122] Some have posited that the recent arrival of Gen Z students on campus may be transforming campus culture in a more restrictive direction. In a 2020 survey by the Knight Foundation, 63 percent of college students reported that "the climate on their campus prevents some people from saying what they believe because others might find them offensive," ten percentage points more than said the same in 2016.[123] The theory goes that this newest generation of students who came of age in the shadow of multiple national crises and in the crucible of social media have sharply higher rates of anxiety, and they may be exhibiting a particular sensitivity to speech. But persuasive evidence of a major change on campus is elusive. Available data do seem to show an uptick in intolerance for controversial speakers and a decline in support of an open learning environment, although it seems too early to tell if this is a trend or merely a blip. One back-and-forth about the available evidence between leading advocates on both sides of the campus speech debates ultimately led to a grudging detente, with the two acknowledging that "the little data we have [on Gen-Z] may mark the beginning of a trend" in attitudes toward speech but "doesn't show big shifts."[124]

As a university leader who has watched these debates unfold over more than three decades, I share this view. Claims of a speech crisis on campus are, in my view, exaggerated, and tend to be the product of isolated and high-profile cases of outside speakers that have been blown out of proportion. Still, an unmistakable pulse of dogmatism has surfaced on campus. Light, though perceptible, it appears in what I see as a growing impatience with opposing views, a reluctance to listen, and a resistance to compromise.

Some of this can likely be attributed to the profound changes underway on our campuses. As student bodies have become more representative, campuses are giving fuller expression to the complexity of human identity. With new voices joining the conversation, dialogue shifts and the rules of the road change, which presents a host of new challenges that we must all learn to navigate. Pluralism among a few different voices can be difficult; pluralism among a great diversity of voices can be all the more complicated and has the potential to fracture. The unremitting task of the university is to make room for these voices, to bring people into the conversation, and to uphold the liberal values of discourse and exchange in democratic societies. The reality, of course, is often more fraught. Our communities are constantly negotiating and renegotiating the lines separating permissible speech from impermissible speech. This often plays out in public disputes over who gets to have a platform on campus.

I was confronted with these conflicts almost from the moment I arrived at Johns Hopkins in 2009. Within months of starting the job, a student organization invited to campus Tucker Max, the crude satirist, provocateur, and author of the *New York Times* bestseller *I Hope They Serve Beer in Hell*. At the time, Max was a particularly controversial figure, and I was pressured to cancel his speech.[125] Since we did not know what Max intended to say, I worried that withdrawing the invitation would constitute the most draconian form of speech regulation, a restriction on speech before it is made. To my mind, it was preferable to let Max speak than to censor either him or the student group who invited him. The event was protested but went ahead without incident.

In the following months, a series of similar controversies erupted. We resolved each as best we could, but we realized that we couldn't keep proceeding in an ad hoc manner. In our case, we needed a set of principles to guide decisions about speech on campus. After a campus-wide consultative process led by Joel Grossman, a colleague from our Department of Political Science, the university's board of trustees adopted a formal statement on academic freedom.[126] The statement focused in part on academic freedom as it applied to scholarship and research, but it also addressed another facet of academic freedom: the freedom of students to learn, affirming the "right to speak and create, to question and dissent, to participate in debate on and off campus, and to invite others to do the same, all without fear of restraint or penalty."[127]

Our statement was one of several released by universities during this period. As speech-related controversies flared on campuses, a multitude of other universities undertook their own measures to make their commitments to free speech explicit. They were fortified by the call of University of Chicago President Robert Zimmer, who in a *Wall Street Journal* op-ed declared unequivocally the imperative for free speech in the modern academy, focusing explicitly on the relationship between these principles and true education.[128] The University of Chicago has traditionally been among the most vocal defenders of free speech, and its statement of principles (the "Chicago Principles") has either been adopted by or inspired the creation of similar principles at more than seventy-six different universities in the United States.[129] Though the path has been neither straightforward nor easy, American universities have at least sought through these statements to honor their historic commitment to open discourse, which is the ethos of the academy and the lifeblood of liberal democracy. Statements of principle are a beginning, however, and not an end. By themselves, they cannot address the broader work of building a sustainable and engaged pluralistic community.

A Purposeful Pluralism

Democracy is an unfinished project that continues to unfurl and expand around us. On our campuses, greater representation from racial minorities, first-generation students, and low-income students means that new voices and perspectives are continually being brought into the ongoing conversation that has characterized academic life for centuries. As I have suggested throughout this chapter, diversification introduces new frictions and points of conflict in that conversation, and to ensure those new voices are heard demands deliberation and purpose. We have not evolved to match this particular moment. As places defined by discourse and shared discovery, we should be at the front lines of the experiment to promote contact and dialogue across difference. Instead, I worry we have been passive.

Over the years, colleges have approached their role on the questions of speech and discourse as something akin to a referee officiating a sporting event. Too often, when speech disputes arise on campus, universities step in to resolve the conflict, adjudicating flare-ups after they've occurred, only to then step back and largely remove themselves from the fray of student speech on campus, allowing it to play out as it might until another dispute occurs. But this reactive posture, coming in to manage disputes after the fact, is not one for which universities were designed, nor one for which they are especially well equipped. Universities are built first and foremost to educate, not to adjudicate. It shouldn't be surprising that few inside or outside of the academy have regarded this approach to the tumult of free speech on campus as especially effective in recent years, for it skips precisely the role universities are best suited to assume: the instructive one, in which they focus their energies on modeling for students how to consider and respond to perspectives or statements that are unfamiliar or uncomfortable and, in so doing, how to be responsible citizen-participants in that marketplace of ideas.

"Diversity is being invited to the party. Inclusion is being asked to dance," writes social commentator Vernā Myers.[130] Universities have been so focused on the invitations that they have allowed themselves to be blinded to the dance. They have devoted far more attention to creating a diverse class of students and minimizing the tensions that inevitably emerge (sometimes at the risk of infantilizing students who are in fact young adults) than promoting substantive exchanges across that diversity once they arrive on campus or modeling how to engage perspectives or statements that are unfamiliar or uncomfortable. As campuses become more diverse and new voices accumulate, this deficit will be all the more glaring. I want to propose that what we have seen play out on campuses in the past several years is not yet a crisis but rather a steady, unremitting beat of frustration at the state of speech whose remedy will require more than a referee.

What our universities need is a more encompassing, affirmative conception of the university's responsibilities toward pluralism that is built for this moment, one that dares to reach beyond admissions (on the one hand) and academic freedom (on the other) to embrace our capacities as educators and community builders. At a point when so many in our society feel more distant from each other than ever, we should be deliberately designing campuses with an eye to engagement and dialogue. We should be working toward a more purposeful pluralism.

What might this look like in practice? It should start with the space of the campus itself. Denison University has already begun reimagining its own campus along pluralistic lines. Declaring that "college campuses should be design studios where students learn to hear different views," Denison President Adam Weinberg launched an initiative to assess every aspect of the physical space, from residential facilities to social life to walkways, for its capacity to connect students across difference.[131] Elon University, likewise, several years ago launched a $100 million restructuring of its residential community after concerns were raised that expensive living quarters were driving some of its students away from campus. Its new residences are centered on "global neighborhoods" in which students are connected across different residence halls through shared facilities and common academic and social programming.[132]

Other schools have revived the practice of roommate assignments. Three years ago, Duke University announced that they would be treating the exposure of students on campus to people of new cultures and interests as an essential part of the educational experience: with few exceptions, incoming first-year students would no longer be allowed to select their roommates. Although the announcement ran into sharp resistance from some students, Duke approached the change with care and rigor, saying they would be sensitive to requests for room changes for reasons of incompatibility, and faculty in the psychology department have participated in an ongoing review of the new policy as it played out.[133] The change appears to have been a success; Duke reports that there was no increase in the number of students requesting room transfers. One Muslim first-year student told *Inside Higher Ed* that she was worried about being paired with a nonreligious roommate, as she prays several times a day. Eventually, however, she came to see the policy as a "blessing" because it led her to engage someone she otherwise might not have about challenging or sensitive topics, like "money, privilege, politics, and race."[134]

Then there is instruction. We now know that universities actually can teach the capacity for pluralist exchange. Studies show that courses that create opportunities for dialogue across difference and encourage the sharing of experiences can produce real gains in students' openness to other people and ideas, which they carry with them long after they graduate.[135] Recently, faculty across the country have been experimenting with new ways to prompt students toward interaction across difference in the classroom. In 2018, two professors in Claremont, California (one a conservative teaching at Claremont McKenna College and another a liberal teaching at Pitzer College) co-taught "The University Blacklist," a course in which students read and discussed the most provocative and controversial—and frequently reviled—books of the past several years.[136] Perhaps more interesting than the content of the course, however, is its structure, which puts debate across difference at its center. The professors began the semester by sparring with each other, and one of the requirements to pass was attendance at several group dinners designed to be extensions of the formal discussions in class.[137] *The Chronicle of Higher Education* reported that hearing their professors debate led students to realize, "We don't have different values . . . We just have different ways of looking at the issues and different ways to solve problems."[138]

Are there ways in which universities can weave the norms of encounter and interaction more vibrantly into campus life beyond the classroom walls, as well? In 2017, George La Noue, a political science professor at the University of Maryland, Baltimore County, published a study showing that most universities rarely sponsor debates or forums about public policy issues that incorporate different perspectives.[139] In fact, when one excludes the most elite research universities that house think tanks and policy institutes, it almost never happens: La Noue calculated that there is only about one such debate annually per campus. When La Noue was first reporting these results, he polled attendees at academic conferences about debates at their own institutions: "I asked audiences whether any faculty group or administrative office was responsible to see that there were open campus discussions of a variety of public policies from diverse viewpoints. No hands went up. Next, I asked how faculty or outside stakeholders would go about trying to discover whether such debates or forums had taken place on their campus in recent years. Again there was silence."[140]

La Noue's research speaks to a reality about the nature of idea transmission and discourse on campus. To a striking degree, our campuses have come to be constructed around the isolated speaker rather than debate or exchange. Classes are predominantly taught by a single teacher or lecturer. Outside speakers brought to campus are usually just that: speakers. Our most storied and celebrated ceremonies, such as commencement, are memorialized with individual speakers who hold forth before a captive audience. And although debate societies still exist, they are no longer the center of academic life in the way vibrant college literary societies were in the nineteenth century. This is significant, I think, because it suggests to our students that the highest ideal of a thinker is proclamation, and that ideas are meant to be developed hermetically and then broadcast to the world rather than cultivated in an ongoing dialogue with others who might disagree or refine them. There are exceptions, of course, including conversations in classrooms and panel discussions on academic papers, but especially on the most complex and divisive issues on campus, our universities too often model speaking *to* someone, rather than *with* someone, as the Platonic ideal of discourse. How can university leaders and faculty complain that our students don't know how to debate or disagree effectively when we don't even try to reveal to them what it looks like?

Universities can change this situation. There are ways to do this programmatically. Universities could, for instance, begin reshaping the college lecture circuit economy to require that individual speakers show up with someone who disagrees with them, or create new incentives for students planning to extend an invitation to a single speaker on critical social and policy issues if they also invite one or more others with competing viewpoints.

The bottom line is that university leaders and faculty need to be more creative in seeking opportunities to model for our students productive interactions across difference. Sometimes these can be forecast and planned; at other times, they might be spontaneous. In 2019, Middlebury College professor Matthew J.

Dickinson saw an opportunity when Ryszard Legutko, a far-right Polish politician who had incited controversy with his comments about LGBTQ rights, had an invitation to speak at the college rescinded at the last minute after the size of anticipated protests to the event swelled. When Dickinson learned that Legutko was staying in a nearby hotel, he asked his political science seminar students if they would be willing to invite the politician to class to critique his arguments in person. The students unanimously agreed. Dickinson had his students spend the first hour of class researching Legutko's views and formulating questions. When Legutko arrived, a respectful but probing dialogue ensued; as word spread around campus, scores of other students joined the seminar. Dickinson described the event to a reporter as "one of the best teaching experiences I've had." A student in the class said that after the conversation, "I feel more confident in my ability to defend my views."[141]

I began this chapter with a story from the Johns Hopkins campus that also, in its own way, contains the promise of a purposeful pluralism. Feeling that they weren't being heard or treated fairly, Johns Hopkins students organized in 2015 for greater equity for their peers, their professors, and our staff. They held our feet to the fire with reason and facts, and they organized a forum where they ensured views were openly exchanged. The result was a radically transparent university-wide road map for greater diversity and inclusion, which recently celebrated its fifth anniversary and is the foundation upon which we're building a new iteration to guide the next five years.

Still, it remains a sobering truth that such experiences are all too fleeting and, it seems, increasingly so. The pluralist endeavor is deeply challenging, and not every attempt to engage in dialogue and debate in the collective effort to arrive at mutual understanding and—where appropriate—compromise will be successful, either on our campuses or off. This is especially true at a moment in our national history when vital calls for racial justice are more ardent and urgent than at any time in decades, even as invidious bigotry and racial resentment fester in—and are even fueled by—what passes for national discourse.

Our universities should be at the forefront of modeling a healthy, multiethnic democracy. They are communities that draw together students from far-reaching locales and diverse backgrounds. They are driven by a deep and abiding fidelity to the notion that learning occurs through dialogue, debate, and reasonable disagreement. And they are home to cutting-edge researchers who can lean into the pluralist ideal, extraordinary instructors who can model that ideal for students, and passionate student affairs professionals who know how best to work alongside students to nurture their development into future democratic citizens. They owe to the democratic experiment an unequivocal commitment both to fulfilling the highest ideals of democratic discourse and to folding all our students into the always unfinished and ever-expanding conversation of democratic life.

>>>><<<<

Conclusion

THE IDEAS FOR THIS BOOK were seeded in 2017, a time when so many of us were becoming increasingly concerned about the various threats posed to liberal democracy in America and beyond. Antidemocratic populists across the globe were ascending to power in once secure democratic nations, and attacks on global alliances made it seem as if the liberal international order was splintering. With the election of Donald Trump to the US presidency, I—along with so many others—watched with consternation and concern as to how (or even, more distressingly, if) the core institutions of democracy would accommodate a person whose rise had been predicated upon violating norms.

I am writing this conclusion in 2021, mere weeks after the violent attack on the US Capitol by a riotous mob of insurgents who vandalized and ransacked the building, attacked and injured police officers, called for Vice President Mike Pence (who was in the Capitol building at the time) to be hanged for his role in officiating over the Senate's expected approval of the Electoral College vote, and seem to have been prepared to kidnap legislators in the interests of halting the peaceful transfer of power from one elected administration to the next. The insurrection was more than an unhinged protest against a fair and free election; it was a blow aimed at the very institutions of constitutional democracy. In storming the Capitol building, the rioters sought both to desecrate the physical emblem of democratic process and majority rule, and disrupt a constitutional mechanism designed to ensure the orderly transfer of power. One could hardly have imagined a more fitting and tragic conclusion to a presidency defined by eroding norms and anti-institutional fervor.

Because of the social distancing strictures imposed by the COVID-19 pandemic, no one could have reasonably expected that the 2021 presidential inauguration several weeks later would be "normal." There was little doubt that the time-honored pageantry of elegant balls, boisterous parades, and well-attended speeches would bend to public health imperatives, and force a scaled down celebration. But as much as we understood and expected a more muted set of festivities, we were ill-prepared for the specter of our nation's capital being sealed off from its citizens by twenty-five thousand national guardsmen assigned to protect the city from further acts of violence. Seeing the city surrounded by concrete blockades, seven-foot-high fencing topped with razor wire, and guardsmen moving in formation was haunting and somber, more akin to how political power is asserted or seized in countries with weak or nonexistent democratic traditions. It is an unfamiliar sight for how power is meant to be transferred in the world's oldest functioning democracy.

The concerns that motivated this book seem more salient than ever: liberal democracy and its institutions remain more fragile than many of us imagined, and we cannot for a moment take their survival and flourishing for granted. It is thus incumbent upon the institutions that are implicated in the liberal democratic experiment to work more intentionally, tirelessly, and energetically toward the realization of its promise. And if, as I have argued throughout these pages, the university stands among these bulwark institutions that are indispensable to liberal democracy, then it is crucial that our universities act in a manner that is commensurate with this role and correlative obligation.

Throughout this book, I have sought to develop a holistic mapping of the role that the university plays in liberal democracy by focusing on four key functions: promoting social mobility, educating for citizenship, checking power with facts and knowledge, and modeling and promoting pluralism. In each of these functional areas, I showed how universities in the United States evolved to take on these responsibilities and how well (or not well) they were requiting them today. Then I suggested avenues for reform.

Here is what I have proposed:

1. *End legacy admissions and restore federal financial aid.* To promote social mobility, selective colleges and universities must redouble efforts to make their institutions accessible and affordable to all talented students. This will not be solved by zero-tuition mandates—which run the risk of depriving public universities of cash and displacing some financial burden on poor families in order to supplement the tuition of affluent families—or by eliminating standardized testing. What we need instead is a massive recommitment of the federal government to the historic government-university compact through programs like Pell Grants and assistance to public universities at the state

level. But there is also a move that colleges and universities can enact immediately to mitigate the imbalanced transfer of advantage from parents to children in a way at odds with the democratic promise of mobility: ending legacy admissions. As I argued in chapter 1, in a highly competitive admissions process, every student admitted to a school deprives another student of a seat. Legacy students tend to be wealthier and whiter, and to have college-educated parents, which means that there are fewer seats for low-income, underrepresented minority, and first-generation applicants. Eliminating legacy admissions is an essential step for creating opportunity and burnishing the promise of higher education as a place for all meritorious students.

2. *Institute a democracy requirement for graduation.* To better educate citizens, colleges and universities need to infuse their campuses and curricula with opportunities to engage and learn about democracy. For too many decades, American higher education has been content to let K–12 education carry the burden of an education in democracy. Recent civics research tells us that good citizenship consists of a multifaceted set of competencies: a knowledge of democratic history, theory, and practice; skills of reasoning, persuasion, and interaction with political institutions and community organizations; an embrace of core democratic values like tolerance and the dignity of all people; and aspirations toward cooperation and collective action. Instilling these competencies is something well within the capacity of universities, which receive students precisely as they are on the cusp of assuming the responsibilities of citizenship. But universities—which have mostly been content with volun-

teer service opportunities to stand in for a robust democratic education—must go much further than they have in recent decades. To begin, colleges and universities that acknowledge their role in citizenship education should ensure that every student they teach is required to engage in some training in democratic citizenship.

3. *Embrace open science with guardrails.* For universities to fulfill their role as stewards of expertise in an era where the very nature of fact in our public debates seems to be eroding, we need first to address one of the deepest problems facing the scientific research enterprise: the reproducibility crisis. If important scientific claims cannot be replicated, then how can the public and policy makers believe what we publish? The COVID-19 pandemic shined a light on the extraordinary promise of technology as a source for democratizing knowledge, for weeding out spurious science, and for burnishing the trust of the public in expertise. The scientific community has proven how swiftly research, data, and insights can be shared, and the results they have achieved both for science and for democracy have been extraordinary. But we have also seen that such unfettered openness comes with its own set of risks: the absence of some of the traditional gatekeepers of scientific publication creates the potential for false claims bearing the imprimatur of a trustworthy researcher or institution to spread through social media. The answer to this dilemma is for our research universities to embrace open science with guardrails, moving toward greater speed and transparency in research while simultaneously building new mechanisms for preserving the review and integrity of research in an ever more open world.

4. *Reimagine student encounters on campus and infuse debate into campus programming.* Finally, to foster pluralism on their campuses, colleges and universities will need to undertake a reassessment of what opportunities students from different backgrounds have to encounter one another and whether they're being taught to speak across their differences effectively. American higher education has, on the whole, done an admirable job of diversifying student bodies, but it has often neglected to consider how students engage with one another after they arrive. Addressing this will require a more purposeful approach to pluralism. Universities should structure their campuses to ensure that students receive opportunities to interact with one other across different backgrounds and perspectives. One key reform is to institute—or, as the case may be, reinstitute—random first-year roommate assignments in residence halls. Beyond that, universities should take more proactive steps to promote thoughtful and healthy engagement when students interact—not by policing student behavior after the fact, but by modeling what healthy debate looks like as part of the educational function. One concrete action here would be to revert the trend on campus of prioritizing lone speakers, and instead construct debates around policy or social issues as a campus ideal.

These reforms are possibilities rather than prescriptions. The four areas of need I describe in this book are urgent, but the answers for each might well be different on different campuses. As I have insisted throughout this book, part of the rich bounty of the diversity of colleges and universities across the United States is that it offers boundless scope for experimentation and innovation. Although I have drawn some of these reforms from my own experience at the University of Toronto, the University of Pennsylvania, and Johns Hopkins University, others are derived from peer institutions that have successfully developed innovations worthy of replication. The many examples I have shared underscore the degree to which there is, across the vast landscape of the United States, considerable experience to draw upon if we, the community of American universities, decide that the time is nigh for us to more sedulously prosecute an agenda that is tethered unabashedly to liberal democracy's revival.

But demonstrating that there are several examples where institutions have decided to "lean into" the task of promoting liberal democracy does not necessarily mean that our campuses will rally to the call for a more purposeful and holistic realization of this role. The task of galvanizing our institutions for this role will invite opposition and critique, and there will be no shortage of reservations expressed.

Some will doubt the capacity of universities to have any meaningful impact on the state of American democracy. They will claim that the university is simply too remote, its role too inconsequential to respond to the challenges currently besetting American democracy. They will argue that rather than focusing on internal reform, the institution should direct its gaze outward, lending its intellectual energies to the task of reforming other institutions of democracy. The country is in urgent need of racial justice, voting rights reform, or curbs on redistricting, among other things, and the university is an important source of ideas on how to achieve these ends. The fear might be that attention to the agenda I have suggested for the university will divert scarce intellectual energy and effort from the pressing problems of the world around us toward a "small bore" set of reforms that only affect members of our arguably cloistered campuses.

Of course, there is no reason that the university cannot simultaneously pursue both inward and outward looking reforms. To borrow a phrase made famous by President Lyndon Johnson, our universities can walk and chew gum at the same time. The agenda I've articulated here is not so overwhelming that it risks exhausting the university's time-honored role in fueling public debate over institutional and policy reform through our research and educational activities. For me, one of the exciting aspects of the reforms I have detailed is how they enlist individuals in virtually every facet of the university, including many who are not traditionally implicated in the discussions surrounding the university's role in liberal democracy, which have tended to focus on the role for, and content of, a liberal arts education. This debate is typically rooted in the faculty of arts and sciences schools, but the program I propose here engages colleagues in those divisions while also touching stakeholders in areas as diverse as admissions, student life, and housing. This means that more of the university's community of staff, students, and researchers can see themselves and their actions as being directly linked to the university's guardianship responsibilities for liberal democracy.

More than that, I believe that there are vast benefits to be realized from working to strengthen our own institutions' standing in democracy. For one, the reforms I have outlined in areas such as education and research are intended to strengthen our capacity and reach to inform public debate on matters of democracy in direct and immediate ways. Beyond that, in light of the deep hostility to the university harbored by contemporary populists—for the way we are seen to have perpetuated intergenerational advantages in our admissions, conferred degree credentials that widen economic inequality, or acted in a manner that is regarded as condescending or contemptuous of the less educated—one can expect that reforms intended to strengthen the university's accessibility, or that take more seriously the responsibilities of inculcating ideals of citizenship in our students, or provide greater assurance of our capacity for the accuracy of our claims, would have important symbolic value in tempering corrosive populist cynicism. After all, the populist narrative that is hostile to elite institutions and meritocratic values does not see the university as peripheral to its cynicism and distrust, but as a central enabler of it. And if we have demonstrated resolve and courage in adopting reforms that are difficult, and that trench on vested interests and well-established patterns of behavior in our own institutions, then our credibility in advocating reforms that are equally difficult to devise and implement by others will be enhanced.

I am not so naive to believe that the faithful adoption of the program I have detailed will be the silver bullet that heals American democracy. Yet the implementation of concrete reforms along these lines has the potential to draw poison from the wounds that are festering in so many parts of our country. It would matter if America's most elite universities publicly and irrevocably repudiated their time-honored use of legacy admissions—a practice, as I argued earlier, that manifests a stark and indefensible assault on bedrock notions of equal opportunity. It would matter if our universities and colleges were to summon the resolve to unabashedly embrace the challenge of ensuring that every graduating student understood the democratic ideals at the heart of our republic, their connection to the ideas and influences of the enlightenment, the laws and institutions that our founders conceived to give flight to them, the many ways we have fallen short, and the possibilities for remediation. It would matter if our universities embraced the ambitious ideals of a science that is more transparent and open. And it would matter if our universities could demonstrate in clear and unequivocal terms the bounty of pluralism that comes from living, studying, and arguing cheek by jowl with people who bear little resemblance—culturally, politically, racially, or religiously—to the clusters of sameness that surround most American families.

I can well imagine that even if the salutary prospects of this agenda are conceded, many will doubt universities' will, or even capacity, for reform. Here the claim might be that universities are by design far too fragmented, far too heterogeneous to be able to muster the intensity of commitment needed to prosecute this agenda. In this vein, Clark Kerr, the celebrated and visionary chancellor of the University of California system, once memorably described the modern American university as "a series of individual faculty entrepreneurs held together by a common grievance over parking."[1] In this frame, it may well be the case that a well-intentioned university president or board of trustees may want to seize the mantle of this agenda, but they are no match for the university's true denizens—the deans, the chairs, and the faculty—who will have little truck for a project that offers only distant and uncertain future rewards but entails real costs today: painstaking and protracted debates over curricular reform and the essence of American citizenship, changes to admissions policies that risk alienating alumni or donors, or disruptions of familiar patterns of faculty research production or dissemination.

From the time that I took on my first academic leadership position a quarter century ago, I have had to contend with this relatively bleak narrative about the prospects for change in the academy. It is hard to deny that the norms and structures of the university don't lend themselves to rapid and dramatic decision-making. The leader advocating change must surmount many hurdles: the innate skepticism of the faculty, the multiple fora in which stakeholders must be consulted and input sought, the need to articulate detailed arguments that are based on clearly defined principles and concrete fact, and, of course, the endless, endless consultation.

These "up-front" costs don't mean that change can't happen, only that it proceeds at a different pace than what one finds in other organizations. It requires infinite patience on the part of its advocates. The clear articulation of principles and goals. The careful assembly and dissemination of relevant facts and data. And deference to the role and prerogatives of a multiplicity of different stakeholders, each of whom holds an expectation of having a voice in the proposed course of action. But at the end of these seemingly interminable deliberative processes, there is the prospect of not only nontrivial change, but also durability.[2]

In building the case for engaging, in a holistic and systematic manner, the university's role in liberal democracy, and in considering the ways in which this role can be augmented and made more relevant to our moment, leadership will need to convince the university's many stakeholders that liberal democracy is worth the fight. But in so doing, it is important to be clear as to what is in play. I am not suggesting that in declaring our support for liberal democracy that we are championing any particular form of liberal democracy. Decisions regarding how communitarian a democracy should be, how goods are to be allocated, or how historical wrongs are to be remedied all fall squarely within the remit of legitimate debate over how liberal democracy's promise is best realized. The claim I make here is more foundational: the university cannot, as an institution, be agnostic about, or indifferent to, its opposition to authoritarianism, its support for human dignity and freedom, its commitment to a tolerant multiracial society, or its insistence on truth and fact as the foundation for collective decision-making.

Would such an explicit commitment to liberal democracy by the university in the various domains I have discussed risk subverting our commitment to academic freedom? For instance, is there a chance that a faculty member or student who were to argue in a research or a classroom setting for the superiority of authoritarian political arrangements over liberal democracy be subject to discipline? Here, I think that one can safely cabin off these activities from the university's more global commitment to the imperatives of liberal democracy in the spheres I have discussed. Faculty and students should be free to analyze and argue for different political institutions and ideologies in their academic pursuits, and their right to do so should be vigorously protected. Indeed, in protecting this right of dissent in our scholarship and teaching, we demonstrate our fidelity to one of liberal democracy's core commitments—the freedom of thought and expression. The animating genius of liberal democracy—and one of the reasons it demands protection—is that it permits, and even encourages, criticism of liberal democracy itself.

*   *   *

The insurrection at the Capitol building may have failed, but the forces that fueled it have not left us. We cannot be blithe about democracy's prospects. It is incumbent upon our fellow citizens and our bulwark institutions to look unflinchingly and intensely at how we came to this place where our democracy feels as if it is coming undone. There is no better place to start this conversation, this self-reflection, than the university. Not only must this indispensable institution seize this opportunity to understand what ails our liberal democracy, but it must also go further in discerning its own role in fostering liberal democracy, its contributions and its failures, and then must act with fierce and unstinting resolve in remedying the places where it has stumbled. It is hardly hyperbole to say that nothing less than the protection of our basic liberties is at stake.

ACKNOWLEDGMENTS

LIBERAL DEMOCRACIES AND UNIVERSITIES are both collective enterprises whose existence depends on the vigorous contestation of ideas. The same could be said of this book, which throughout its development has benefited immeasurably from the support of scores of friends, colleagues, and family members.

First, I wish to thank my extraordinary coauthors Grant Shreve and Phillip Spector for their invaluable contributions at every step of this project and to every page of the book. This book is framed by my more than three decades as a university professor, provost, and president, but the arguments I develop in it, and the research I was able to invoke in support of them, owe much to my coauthors' unflagging efforts and insight. I am grateful also to Hannah Stommel, a researcher in my office from 2017 to 2020, who not only gathered and synthesized the research for this book but also was instrumental in helping to refine its core ideas.

This book benefited from the keen perspectives of many readers. I am thankful for the deep reservoirs of expertise brought to the chapters by several Hopkins colleagues: Kerry Ates, Kelly Barry, Ashley Berner, Cybele Bjorklund, Gundula Bosch, Katrina Caldwell, Arturo Casadevall, G. Sayeed Choudhury, Rachel Dawson, Lauren

Gardner, Hahrie Han, Sunil Kumar, Yascha Mounk, David Phillips, Lainie Rutkow, Smita Ruzicka, Fritz Schroeder, Alanna Shanahan, and Marianne von Nordeck. I also count myself fortunate to have so many friends and peers beyond Baltimore who supported the book throughout its development. Vicki Jackson gave me the opportunity to present the core thesis at the annual meeting of the Association of American Law Schools in 2020. Many others generously agreed to read the manuscript and to provide sage comments that vastly strengthened it. To Bob Birgeneau, Jonathan Cole, Joel Klein, Judith Resnik, Janice Stein, Shirley Tilghman, Michael Trebilcock, and George Triantis, thank you.

I would be remiss if I did not acknowledge the Johns Hopkins undergrads who took one of the two seminars I offered on universities and democracy, the first in January 2020 and the second over Zoom in Spring 2021. These students were a pleasure to teach, and their candor and intellectual acuity sharpened the ideas in this book.

Of course, the most exacting readers in my life have always been those closest to me—my family. I cannot thank my wife, Joanne, and my children, Ryan, Drew, and Ally, enough for graciously allowing me to foist this manuscript upon them and for offering their astute—and unvarnished—feedback, as well as for being part of, and supporting, the wonderful adventure that we have charted together.

Finally, special thanks go to Greg Britton, Kathryn Marguy, Ashleigh McKown, Juliana McCarthy, Adriahna Conway, and the entire team at Johns Hopkins University Press (which, as the oldest university press in continual operation in the United States, also features in chapter 3) for shepherding this book through the publication process.

NOTES

Introduction

1. See Griff Witte, "Amid Illiberal Revolution in Hungary, a University with U.S. Roots Fights to Stay," *Washington Post*, September 3, 2018. See also Act XXV of 2017 on the amendment of Act CCIV of 2011 on National Tertiary Education, *Magyar Közlöny* 53 (April 10, 2017): 4327–4328.

2. Palko Karasz, "Hungary's Parliament Passes Law Targeting George Soros's University," *New York Times*, April 4, 2017, https://nyti.ms/2oygdRi.

3. "CEU Signs MOU with Bard College, Retains Aim to Stay in Budapest," *Central European University*, October 3, 2017, https://www.ceu.edu/article/2017-10-03/ceu -signs-mou-bard-college-retains-aim-stay-budapest; "The Central European University Is Moving to Vienna," *Economist*, December 5, 2018, https://www.economist.com /europe/2018/12/05/the-central-european-university-is-moving-to-vienna.

4. Quoted in Ronald J. Daniels, "Central European University Is a Remarkable School. It Should Stay in Hungary," *Washington Post*, January 22, 2019, https:// www.washingtonpost.com/opinions/central-european-university-is-a-remarkable -school-it-should-stay-in-hungary/2019/01/22/518a2fc6-1e61-11e9-9145-3f740 70bbdb9_story.html.

5. See George Soros, "Central European University: A Statement of Intent," *CEU Gazette* 1, no. 1 (April 1991); Alfred Stepan, "The Early Years of Central European University as a Network: A Memoir," *Social Research* 76, no. 2 (2009): 687–710; and *George Soros and the Founding of Central European University* (Durham, NC: Sanford School of Public Policy, Duke University, 2007), https:// cspcs.sanford.duke.edu/sites/default/files/SorosCEUOriginsfinal.pdf.

6. See "Alumni," Central European University website, accessed March 16, 2021, https://www.ceu.edu/about/facts-figures/alumni; Central European University, *Admissions Bulletin 2007–2008*, http://web.ceu.hu/downloads /admissions_bulletin_2007_2008.pdf, p. 11.

7. "CEU Vienna: Official Inauguration Marks a 'Momentous Day' for the University," Central European University website, November 17, 2019, https://www.ceu.edu/article/2019-11-17/ceu-vienna-official-inauguration-marks-momentous-day-university.

8. "Meet the President and Rector: Message from Michael Ignatieff," Central European University, accessed April 2, 2021, https://www.ceu.edu/about/rector.

9. "Italian Universities under Fascism," in *Universities under Dictatorship*, ed. John Connelly and Michael Grüttner (Philadelphia: Pennsylvania State Press, 2005); Petr Svobodny, "Universities in Central Europe: Changing Perspectives in the Troubled Twentieth Century," in *Sciences in the Universities of Europe, Nineteenth and Twentieth Centuries*, ed. Ana Simões, Maria Paula Diogo, and Kostas Gavroglu (Dordrecht: Springer Netherlands, 2015), 116; Hal Piper, "Polish Intellectuals Show Increasing Unrest," *Baltimore Sun*, March 31, 1978, 2. See Jan Józef Lipski, *K.O.R.: A History of the Worker's Defense Committee in Poland, 1976–1981*, trans. Olga Amsterdamska and Gene M. Moore (Berkeley: University of California Press, 1985), 210–211; see also Michael Getler, "History Is Uncensored in Poland's 'Flying Universities,'" *Washington Post*, July 5, 1978, https://www.washingtonpost.com/archive/politics/1978/07/05/history-is-uncensored-in-polands-flying-universities/cfc9c67d-2801-475f-b1f0-5bd88540198b/?utm_term=.97b5e2bdbd36; Hannah Buczynska-Garewicz, "The Flying University in Poland, 1978–1980," *Harvard Educational Review* 55, no. 2 (1985): 22.

10. See Zoltán Lakner, "Links in the Chain: Patron-Client Relations in the Mafia State," in *Twenty-Five Sides of a Post-Communist Mafia State*, ed. Bálint Magyar and Júlia Vásárhelyi (Budapest: Central European University Press, 2017), 163. See also Alison Abbott, "Hungarian Government Takes Control of Research Institutes Despite Outcry," *Nature*, July 8, 2019, https://www.nature.com/articles/d41586-019-02107-4; Kovács Zoltán, "Hungarian Academy of Sciences Stripped of Its Research Network," *Index*, July 2, 2019, https://index.hu/english/2019/07/02/hungarian_academy_of_sciences_research_network_taken_away_academic_freedom_ministry_of_innovation_and_technology/; and "MTA Submitted Suggestions for Draft Law Amendment," *Hungarian Academy of Sciences*, June 4, 2019, https://mta.hu/english/mta-submitted-suggestions-for-draft-law-amendment-109786. In 2013, Article X(3) of the Fundamental Law, which maintained the autonomy of institutions of higher education in selecting teaching and research content, was altered to give the government far greater authority over the management of universities' finances. See "Hungary," European University Association, accessed March 16, 2021, https://www.university-autonomy.eu/countries/hungary/; Zselyke Csaky, "The End of Viktor Orbán's Peacock Dance," *Foreign Policy*, September 14, 2018, https://foreignpolicy.com/2018/09/14/the-end-of-viktor-orbans-peacock-dance-hungary-eu-article-7-epp-european-parliament/; Kata Karáth, "Hungarian Scientists Are on Edge as Country Is Poised to Force Out Top University," *Science*, May 10, 2018, https://www.sciencemag.org/news/2018/05/hungarian-scientists-are-edge-country-poised-force-out-top

-university; and "'Lectori Salutem,'" VERITAS Research Institute and Archives, accessed April 18, 2021, https://www.veritasintezet.hu/en/.

11. See "Turkey: Government Targeting Academics," *Human Rights Watch*, May 14, 2018, https://www.hrw.org/news/2018/05/14/turkey-government -targeting-academics; and Carlotta Gall, "Erdogan, Flush with Victory, Seizes New Powers in Turkey," *New York Times*, July 19, 2018, https://nyti.ms/2LvNqFk.

12. See Grigory Yudin, "Overzealous Regulators Are Closing In on Russian Universities," *Moscow Times*, July 10, 2018, https://www.themoscowtimes.com /2018/07/10/overzealous-regulators-are-closing-in-on-russian-universities-a62187; and Ararat Osipian, "Can Autocracies Cope with International Universities?," *University World News*, April 7, 2017, https://www.universityworldnews.com/post .php?story=20170403180053696.

13. See Elizabeth Redden, "In Brazil, a Hostility to Academe," *Inside Higher Ed*, May 6, 2019, https://www.insidehighered.com/news/2019/05/06/far-right -government-brazil-slashes-university-funding-threatens-cuts-philosophy-and.

14. Jeff Kaplan, "Donald Trump Jr.'s UNT Speech Raised Record Money, but before His Record Expenses," *Fort Worth Star-Telegram*, December 12, 2017, https://www.star-telegram.com/news/local/fort-worth/article189324009.html.

15. President's Advisory 1776 Commission, *The 1776 Report* (Washington, DC: January 2021).

16. See Elizabeth Redden, "Major Changes to Student Visa Rules Proposed," *Inside Higher Ed*, September 25, 2020. The decision to initiate a civil rights investigation into a September 2020 letter (in the wake of the George Floyd unrest) written by Princeton President Christopher L. Eisgruber in which he acknowledged that the persistence of racism in the university and in society "sometimes by conscious intention but more often through unexamined assumptions and stereotypes, ignorance or insensitivity, the systemic legacy of past decisions and policies" is an example of a targeted institutional attack. See Anemona Hartocollis, "Princeton Admitted Past Racism. Now It Is under Investigation," *New York Times,* September 17, 2020, https://www.nytimes.com/2020/09/17/us/princeton-racism-federal -investigation.html. So, too, are the public shaming efforts that President Trump and senior members of his administration made to limit, without lawful authority, the right of several leading universities to avail themselves of Coronavirus Aid, Relief, and Economic Security (CARES) Act funding designed to assist low-income students in managing through the COVID-19 pandemic. See Doug Lederman, "Trump Administration Takes Aim at Wealthy Universities," *Insider Higher Ed*, April 23, 2020, https://www.insidehighered.com/news/2020/04/23/under-pressure -trump-administration-wealthy-colleges-forgo-stimulus-funds.

17. "Academic Research and Development," in *Science and Engineering Indicators* (Alexandria, VA: National Science Board, 2020); Bill McCarthy, "Trump's Exaggerated Claim That He 'Saved' HBCUs with 2019 Funding Bill," *PolitiFact*, October 27, 2020.

18. Kim Parker, "The Growing Partisan Divide in Views of Higher Education," Pew Research Center, January 30, 2019, https://www.pewresearch.org/social-trends /2019/08/19/the-growing-partisan-divide-in-views-of-higher-education-2/.

19. See Daniel Markovits, *The Meritocracy Trap* (New York: Penguin, 2019) and Michael Sandel, *The Tyranny of Merit* (New York: Farrar, Straus and Giroux, 2020).

20. William Rainey Harper, "The University and Democracy," in *The Trend in Higher Education* (Chicago: University of Chicago Press, 1905), 4.

21. Andreas Schleicher, "China Opens a New University Every Week," *BBC*, March 16, 2016, https://www.bbc.com/news/business-35776555.

22. See *Obstacles to Excellence: Academic Freedom and China's Quest for World-Class Universities* (New York: Scholars at Risk Academic Freedom Monitoring Project, 2019).

23. "China's Xi Calls for Universities' Allegiance to the Communist Party," *Reuters,* December 9, 2016, https://www.reuters.com/article/us-china-education /chinas-xi-calls-for-universities-allegiance-to-the-communist-party -idUSKBN13Y0B5.

24. Dennis Normile, "Science Suffers as China's Internet Censors Plug Holes in Great Firewall," *Science*, August 30, 2017, https://www.sciencemag.org/news/2017 /08/science-suffers-china-s-internet-censors-plug-holes-great-firewall; Javier C. Hernandez, "Study Finds Chinese Students Excel in Critical Thinking. Until College," *New York Times*, July 30, 2016, https://www.nytimes.com/2016/07/31 /world/asia/china-college-education-quality.html.

25. *Obstacles to Excellence*, 6.

26. Count de Montalembert, "The Victory of the North in the United States," *Littell's Living Age* (1867). For the suggestion that Montalembert coined "liberal democracy" as we currently understand it, see Helena Rosenblatt, *The Lost History of Liberalism* (Princeton, NJ: Princeton University Press, 2018), 3.

27. Montalembert, "Victory of the North," 343.

28. Montalembert, "Victory of the North," 343.

29. See Rosenblatt, *Lost History of Liberalism*, 164.

30. Abraham Lincoln, "Address at Gettysburg Pennsylvania, November 19, 1863," in *Lincoln: Speeches and Writings, 1859–1865* (New York: Literary Classics of the United States, 1989), 536.

31. Gordon Graham, "Liberalism and Democracy," *Journal of Applied Philosophy* 9, no. 2 (1992): 149.

32. Larry Diamond, *The Spirit of Democracy: The Challenge of Building Free Societies throughout the World* (New York: Henry Holt, 2008), 21.

33. See Arlene W. Saxonhouse, "Athenian Democracy: Modern Mythmakers and Ancient Theorists," *PS: Political Science and Politics* 26, no. 3 (1993): 486–490.

34. L. T. Hobhouse, "Liberalism," in *Liberalism and Other Writings*, ed. James Meadowcroft (Cambridge: Cambridge University Press, 1994).

35. Rosalie Silberman Abella and Matthew Diller, "A Conversation with the Honorable Rosalie Silberman Abella and Dean Matthew Diller," *Fordham Law*

Review 87, no. 3 (2018): 848. See also Daniel Bell, *Reordering the World: Essays on Liberalism and Empire* (Princeton, NJ: Princeton University Press, 2016), 62–90; Rosenblatt, *Lost History of Liberalism*, 265–277.

36. See Kelly M. McMann, Brigitte Seim, Jan Teorell, and Staffan Lindberg, "Why Low Levels of Democracy Promote Corruption and High Levels Diminish It," *Political Research Quarterly* 73, no. 4 (2019): 1–15; James W. McGuire, "Political Regime and Social Performance," *Comparative Politics* 19, no. 1 (2013): 55–75; and Daron Acemoglu, Suresh Naidu, Pascual Restrepo, and James A. Robinson, "Democracy Does Cause Growth," *Journal of Political Economy* 127, no. 1 (2019): 47–100.

37. Jack S. Levy, "Domestic Politics and War," in *The Origin and Prevention of Major Wars*, ed. Robert I. Rotberg and Theodore K. Rabb (Cambridge: Cambridge University Press, 1989), 88.

38. See Simon Wigley and Arzu Akkoyunlu-Wigley, "The Impact of Regime Type on Health: Does Redistribution Explain Everything?," *World Politics* 63, no. 4 (2011): 647–677.

39. Amartya Sen, *Development as Freedom* (New York: Random House, 1999), 51.

40. See "Racial and Ethnic Disparities Continue in Pregnancy-Related Deaths," Centers for Disease Control and Prevention, September 5, 2019, https://www.cdc.gov/media/releases/2019/p0905-racial-ethnic-disparities-pregnancy-deaths.html; "Disparities," Indian Health Service, October 2019, https://www.ihs.gov/newsroom/factsheets/disparities/.

41. Fareed Zakaria, "The Rise of Illiberal Democracy," *Foreign Affairs*, November 1, 1997, https://www.foreignaffairs.com/articles/1997-11-01/rise-illiberal-democracy.

42. Yascha Mounk, *The People vs. Democracy: Why Our Freedom Is in Danger and How to Save It* (Cambridge, MA: Harvard University Press, 2018), 48; Alexis de Tocqueville, *Democracy in America*, 2 vols., trans. Henry Reeve (London: Longman, Green, Longman, and Roberts, 1862), 2:381.

43. Anna Lührmann and Staffan I. Lindberg, eds., *Democracy Facing Global Challenges: V-Dem Annual Democracy Report 2019* (Gothenburg: Varieties of Democracy Institute, 2019).

44. Anna Lührmann and Staffan I. Lindberg, eds., *Autocratization Surges—Resistance Grows: Democracy Report 2020* (Gothenburg: Varieties of Democracy Institute, 2020).

45. Anna Lührmann and Staffan I. Lindberg, eds., *Democracy for All? V-Dem Annual Democracy Report 2018* (Gothenburg: Varieties of Democracy Institute, 2018), 18.

46. Larry Diamond, "Facing Up to the Democratic Recession," *Journal of Democracy* 26, no. 1 (2015): 141.

47. "Public Trust in Government: 1958–2019," Pew Research Center, April 11, 2019, https://www.people-press.org/2019/04/11/public-trust-in-government-1958

-2019/; "Confidence in Institutions," Gallup, accessed April 18, 2021, https://news
.gallup.com/poll/1597/confidence-institutions.aspx.

48. Yascha Mounk, "Democracy in Poland Is in Mortal Danger," *The Atlantic*,
October 9, 2019, https://www.theatlantic.com/ideas/archive/2019/10/poland
-could-lose-its-democracy/599590/.

49. Regine Cabato, "'Ready the Places Where You'll Be Buried': Philippine
Priests Say They Are under Threat," *Washington Post*, March 12, 2019, https://www
.washingtonpost.com/world/asia_pacific/ready-the-places-where-youll-be-buried
-philippine-priests-say-they-are-under-threat/2019/03/12/ae9239f4-44a2-11e9
-9726-50f151ab44b9_story.html?utm_term=.eaf0003bf20f.

50. Colby Itkowitz, "Trump Threatens Reporter with Prison Time during
Interview," *Washington Post*, June 21, 2019, https://www.washingtonpost.com
/politics/trump-threatens-reporter-with-prison-time-during-interview/2019/06/21
/b622b84c-9420-11e9-b58a-a6a9afaa0e3e_story.html?utm_term=.7db1f4cd3696;
Ruth Marcus, "Trump's Attacks on the Judiciary Are Dangerous. Good for This
Judge for Speaking Up," *Washington Post*, November 8, 2019, https://www
.washingtonpost.com/opinions/trumps-attacks-on-the-judiciary-are-dangerous
-good-for-this-judge-for-speaking-up/2019/11/08/f5bd51a8-0255-11ea-9518
-1e76abc088b6_story.html.

51. Margaret Harris and Carol Milofsky, "Mediating Structures: Their
Organization in Civil Society," *Nonprofit Policy Forum* 10, no. 2 (2019): 1–11.

52. *Crisis in Democracy: Renewing Trust in America—The Report of the Knight
Commission on Trust, Media and Democracy* (Washington, DC: Aspen Institute, 2019).

53. Arthur M. Cohen and Carrie B. Kisker, *Shaping of American Higher
Education: Emergence and Growth of the Contemporary System* (San Francisco:
Jossey-Bass, 2010), 63; Colin B. Burke, *American Collegiate Populations: A Test of
the Traditional View* (New York: New York University Press, 1982), 14.

54. Absalom Peters, *A Discourse Delivered in the Park Presbyterian Church before
the Society for the Promotion of Collegiate and Theological Education at the West* (New
York: John F. Trow, 1851).

55. "Characteristics of Degree-Granting Postsecondary Institutions," National
Center for Education Statistics, last modified May 2020, https://nces.ed.gov
/programs/coe/indicator_csa.asp; "Characteristics of Postsecondary Students,"
National Center for Education Statistics, last modified April 2020, https://nces.ed
.gov/programs/coe/indicator_csb.asp; "Characteristics of Postsecondary Faculty,"
National Center for Education Statistics, last modified May 2020, https://nces.ed
.gov/programs/coe/indicator_csc.asp; Jeffrey Mervis, "As Pandemic Pounds U.S.
Universities, Federal Support Helps Their Labs Stay Afloat," *Science*, June 5, 2020,
https://www.sciencemag.org/news/2020/06/pandemic-pounds-us-universities
-federal-support-helps-their-labs-afloat.

56. One study of dozens of democracies from 1960 to 2000 found that a
1 percent increase in a nation's university enrollment is associated with nearly a full

point increase in a twenty-one-point democracy index. See Edward L. Glaeser, Giacomo A. M. Ponzetto, and Andrei Shleifer, "Why Does Democracy Need Education?," Working Paper 12128 (Cambridge, MA: National Bureau of Economic Research, 2006).

57. "Report of the Board of Commissioners for the University of Virginia to the Virginia General Assembly, [4 August] 1818," National Archives, accessed April 18, 2021, https://founders.archives.gov/documents/Madison/04-01-02-0289.

58. President's Commission on Higher Education, *Higher Education for American Democracy*, 6 vol. (Washington, DC: US Government Printing Office, 1947), 1:102.

59. Nicholas Apergis, "Education and Democracy: New Evidence from 161 Countries," *Economic Modelling* 71 (2018): 59–67; Nicholas Apergis and James Payne, "From Education to Democracy: Evidence from Long-Run Time-Varying Estimates," *International Review of Economics* 64, no. 4 (2017): 313–325; Piergiuseppe Fortunato and Ugo Panizza, "Democracy, Education and the Quality of Government," *Journal of Economic Growth* 20, no. 4 (2015): 333–363; Eduardo Alemán and Yeaji Kim, "The Democratizing Effect of Education," *Research and Politics* 2, no. 4 (2015): 1–7; Howard Sanborn and Clayton L. Thyne, "Learning Democracy: Education and the Fall of Authoritarian Regimes," *British Journal of Political Science* 44, no. 4 (2014): 773–797; Amparo Castelló-Climent, "On the Distribution of Education and Democracy," *Journal of Development Economics* 87, no. 2 (2008): 179–190; Elias Papaioannou and Gregorios Siourounis, "Economic and Social Factors Driving the Third Wave of Democratization," *Journal of Comparative Economics* 36 (2008): 365–387; Matteo Bobba and Decio Coviello, "Weak Instruments and Weak Identification, in Estimating the Effects of Education, on Democracy," *Economics Letters* 96, no. 3 (2007): 301–306; Glaeser et al., "Why Does Democracy Need Education?"; Edward L. Glaeser, Rafael La Porta, Florenico Lopez-De-Silanes, and Andrei Shleifer, "Do Institutions Cause Growth?," *Journal of Economic Growth* 9 (2004): 271–303; see also Gang Wang, Liyun Wu, and Rongbin Han, "College Education and Attitudes toward Democracy in China: An Empirical Study," *Asia Pacific Education Review* 16, no. 3 (2015): 399–412. One study by Daron Acemoglu and colleagues was unable to validate this claim, but a number of authors have since challenged that paper on methodological grounds; see Daron Acemoglu, Simon Johnson, James A. Robinson, and Pierre Yared, "From Education to Democracy?," *American Economic Review* 95, no. 2 (2005): 44–49.

60. Allan Bloom, *The Closing of the American Mind* (New York: Simon & Schuster, 1987).

61. Anthony Kronman, *The Assault on American Excellence* (New York: Free Press, 2019); Greg Lukianoff and Jonathan Haidt, *The Coddling of the American Mind: How Good Intentions and Bad Ideas Are Setting Up a Generation for Failure* (New York: Penguin Press, 2018).

62. Michael J. Trebilcock, *Dealing with Losers: The Political Economy of Policy Transitions* (Oxford: Oxford University Press, 2014), 140.

ONE: American Dreams

1. See Ronald J. Daniels, "Why We Ended Legacy Admissions at Johns Hopkins," *The Atlantic*, January 18, 2020.

2. James Truslow Adams, *The Epic of America* (Boston: Little, Brown, 1931).

3. Adams quoted in Lawrence R. Samuel, *The American Dream: A Cultural History* (Syracuse, NY: Syracuse University Press, 2012).

4. Adams had even hoped to title his book *The American Dream* but was told by his publisher that "no red-blooded American would pay $3.50 for a dream." See Allan Nevins, ed., *James Truslow Adams: Select Correspondence* (London: Routledge, 2017), 296.

5. Alexis de Tocqueville, *Democracy in America*, ed. Harvey C. Mansfield and Delba Winthrop (Chicago: University of Chicago Press, 2000), 432.

6. See Peter M. Blau and Otis Dudley Duncan, *The American Occupational Structure* (New York: Free Press, 1978), 439.

7. Robert D. Putnam, *Our Kids: The American Dream in Crisis* (New York: Simon & Schuster, 2015); White House Office of the Press Secretary, "Remarks by the President on Economic Mobility," press release, December 4, 2013, https:// obamawhitehouse.archives.gov/the-press-office/2013/12/04/remarks-president -economic-mobility; Raj Chetty, Nathaniel Hendren, Patrick Kline, and Emmanuel Saez, "Where Is the Land of Opportunity? The Geography of Intergenerational Mobility in the United States," *Quarterly Journal of Economics* 129, no. 4 (2014): 1553–1623; Christian Houle, "Social Mobility and Political Instability," *Journal of Conflict Resolution* 63, no. 1 (2019): 85–111; Tak Wing Chan, "Social Mobility and the Well-Being of Individuals," *British Journal of Sociology* 69, no. 1 (2018): 183–206; Frank Bruni, "America the Shrunken," *New York Times*, May 3, 2014, https://www.nytimes.com/2014/05/04/opinion/sunday/bruni-america-the-shrunken .html; Knight Commission on Trust, Media and Democracy, *Crisis in Democracy: Renewing Trust in America* (Washington, DC: Aspen Institute, February 2019).

8. Christian Houle and Michael K. Miller, "Social Mobility and Democratic Attitudes: Evidence from Latin America and Sub-Saharan Africa," *Comparative Political Studies* 52, no. 11 (2019): 1610–1647.

9. Houle and Miller, "Social Mobility and Democratic Attitudes," 1636.

10. Tocqueville, *Democracy in America*, 50.

11. Joseph P. Ferrie, "The End of American Exceptionalism? Mobility in the United States Since 1850," *Journal of Economic Perspectives* 19, no. 3 (Summer 2005): 199–215; Jason Long and Joseph Ferrie, "Intergenerational Occupational Mobility in Great Britain and the United States since 1850," *American Economic Review*, 103, no. 4 (2013): 1109–1137; Jérôme Bourdieu, Joseph Ferrie, and Lionel Kesztenbaum, "Vive la différence? Intergenerational Mobility in France and the United States during the Nineteenth and Twentieth Centuries," *Journal of Interdisciplinary History* 39, no. 4 (Spring 2009): 523–557.

12. Claudia Olivetti and M. Daniele Paserman, "In the Name of the Son (and the Daughter): Intergenerational Mobility in the United States, 1850–1940," *American Economic Review* 105, no. 8 (August 2015): 2695–2724; Avery M. Guest, Nancy Susan Landale, and James C. McCann, "Intergenerational Occupational Mobility in the Late 19th Century United States," *Social Forces* 68, no. 2 (1989): 351–378.

13. Wojciech Kopczuk, Emmanuel Saez, and Jae Song, "Earnings Inequality and Mobility in the United States: Evidence from Social Security Data Since 1937," *Quarterly Journal of Economics* 125, no. 1 (February 2010): 91–128.

14. Richard V. Reeves and Eleanor Krause, "Raj Chetty in 14 Charts: Big Findings on Opportunity and Mobility We Should All Know," Brookings Institution, January 11, 2018, https://www.brookings.edu/blog/social-mobility-memos /2018/01/11/raj-chetty-in-14-charts-big-findings-on-opportunity-and-mobility-we -should-know/. See also Markus Jäntti et al., *American Exceptionalism in a New Light: A Comparison of Intergenerational Earnings Mobility in the Nordic Countries, the United Kingdom, and the United States* (Bonn: Institute for the Study of Labor, 2006); Marie Connolly, Miles Corak, and Catherine Haeck, *Intergenerational Mobility between and within Canada and the United States*, Working Paper 25735 (Cambridge, MA: National Bureau of Economic Research, April 2019).

15. Nazifa Alizada et al., *Autocratization Turns Viral: Democracy Report 2021* (Gothenburg: V-Dem Institute, 2021).

16. Julia B. Isaacs, Isabel V. Sawhill, and Ron Haskins, *Getting Ahead or Losing Ground: Economic Mobility in America* (Washington, DC: Brookings Institution, 2016).

17. Raj Chetty et al., *Is the United States Still a Land of Opportunity? Recent Trends in Intergenerational Mobility*, Working Paper 19844 (Cambridge, MA: National Bureau of Economic Research, 2014).

18. Richard V. Reeves and Kimberly Howard, *The Glass Floor: Education, Downward Mobility, and Opportunity Hoarding* (Washington, DC: Brookings Institution, 2013).

19. Isabel Sawhill, "Inequality and Social Mobility: Be Afraid," Brookings Institution, May 27, 2015, https://www.brookings.edu/blog/social-mobility-memos /2015/05/27/inequality-and-social-mobility-be-afraid/.

20. Gabriel Zuckman, *Global Wealth Inequality*, Working Paper 25462 (Cambridge, MA: National Bureau of Economic Research, January 2019); Peter H. Lindert and Jeffrey G. Williamson, *Unequal Gains: American Growth and Inequality since 1700* (Princeton, NJ: Princeton University Press, 2016). See, e.g., Christian Houle, "Inequality and Democracy: Why Inequality Harms Consolidation but Does Not Affect Democratization," *World Politics* 61, no. 4. (Oct. 2009): 589–622.

21. See Seymour Martin Lipset and Reinhard Bendix, *Social Mobility in Industrial Society* (Berkeley: University of California Press, 1959), 76–113; Seymour Martin Lipset, "The Political Consequences of Social Mobility," in *Social Mobility and Political Attitudes: Comparative Perspectives*, ed. Frederick C. Turner (New

Brunswick, NJ: Transaction, 1992), xv–xxiii; James Fallows, *More Like Us: Making America Great Again* (Boston: Houghton Mifflin Harcourt, 1989); Julia B. Isaacs, "International Comparisons of Economic Mobility," in *Getting Ahead or Losing Ground: Economic Mobility in America* (Washington, DC: Brookings Institution, 2016), 37–44.

22. See Lipset and Bendix, *Social Mobility in Industrial Society*; Lipset, "Political Consequences of Social Mobility"; Martin V. Day and Susan T. Fiske, "Movin' on Up? How Perceptions of Social Mobility Affect Our Willingness to Defend the System," *Social Psychological and Personality Science* 8, no. 3 (2017): 267–274; Ambar Narayan et al., "Fair Progress? Economic Mobility across Generations around the World," World Bank, May 2018, https://www.worldbank.org/en/topic/poverty/publication/fair-progress-economic-mobility-across-generations-around-the-world.

23. See Dana Milbank, "Americans' Optimism Is Dying," *Washington Post*, August 12, 2014, https://www.washingtonpost.com/opinions/dana-milbank-americans-optimism-is-dying/2014/08/12/f81808d8-224c-11e4-8593-da634b334390_story.html; Chris Cillizza, "The Single Most Depressing Number in the New NBC-Wall Street Journal Poll," *Washington Post*, August 6, 2014, https://www.washingtonpost.com/news/the-fix/wp/2014/08/06/the-single-most-depressing-number-in-the-new-nbc-wall-street-journal-poll/; "NBC News/Wall Street Journal Poll," PollingReport.com, August 10–14, 2019, https://www.pollingreport.com/life.htm.

24. Five percent of adult children without a college degree from the bottom quartile of parental income reach the top income quintile. Nineteen percent of children with a college degree from the bottom quintile reach the top. That's a fourteen-point difference, or a 280 percent increase. Put differently, people who earn college degrees from the lowest quintile are 3.8 times more likely to reach the highest income quintile than those without college degrees. Ron Haskins, "Education and Economic Mobility," in *Getting Ahead or Losing Ground: Economic Mobility in America* (Washington, DC: Brookings Institution, 2008), 95.

25. Philip Trostel, *It's Not Just the Money: The Benefits of College Education to Individuals and to Society* (Indianapolis: Lumina Foundation, 2015), 10, 14.

26. Jaison R. Abel and Richard Deitz, "Despite Rising Costs, College Is Still a Good Investment," *Liberty Street Economics*, June 5, 2019.

27. Raj Chetty et al., *Mobility Report Cards: The Role of Colleges in Intergenerational Mobility*, Working Paper 23618 (Cambridge, MA: National Bureau of Economic Research, July 2017).

28. Chetty et al., *Mobility Report Cards*, 41.

29. Chetty et al., *Mobility Report Cards*, 26.

30. Michael J. Sandel, *The Tyranny of Merit: What's Become of the Common Good* (New York: Farrar, Straus and Giroux, 2020), 169.

31. "Some Colleges Have More Students from the Top 1 Percent Than the Bottom 60. Find Yours," *New York Times*, January 18, 2017, https://www.nytimes

.com/interactive/2017/01/18/upshot/some-colleges-have-more-students-from-the-top-1-percent-than-the-bottom-60.html.

32. *Postsecondary Attainment: Differences by Socioeconomic Status* (National Center for Education Statistics, May 2015), https://nces.ed.gov/programs/coe/indicator_tva.asp.

33. See Richard Reeves, *Dream Hoarders: How the American Middle Class Is Leaving Everyone Else in the Dust, Why That Is a Problem, and What to Do about It* (Washington, DC: Brookings Institution, 2017), 81. See also *Education Longitudinal Study of 2002 (ELS:2002): A First Look at 2002 High School Sophomores 10 Years Later* (National Center for Education Statistics, 2014), https://nces.ed.gov/pubs2014/2014363.pdf, p. 8. To put a finer point on this claim, 59 percent of children whose parents have postgraduate degrees graduate from a four-year college, as do 45 percent of children born to parents who possess only a bachelor's degree. Only 40 percent of children born to parents in the highest quintile income bracket go on to stay in that bracket.

34. "An Hereditary Meritocracy," *The Economist*, January 22, 2015, https://www.economist.com/briefing/2015/01/22/an-hereditary-meritocracy.

35. "Highest Educational Levels Reached by Adults in U.S. Since 1940," US Census Bureau, March 30, 2017, https://www.census.gov/newsroom/press-releases/2017/cb17-51.html; "U.S. Census Bureau Releases New Educational Attainment Data," US Census Bureau, March 30, 2020, https://www.census.gov/newsroom/press-releases/2020/educational-attainment.html.

36. "Immediate College Enrollment Rate," National Center for Education Statistics, last updated April 2020, https://nces.ed.gov/programs/coe/indicator_cpa.asp.

37. See Samuel Eliot Morison, *The Founding of Harvard College* (Cambridge, MA: Harvard University Press, 1963), 303–310.

38. See Rupert Wilkinson, *Aiding Students, Buying Students: Financial Aid in America* (Nashville, TN: Vanderbilt University Press, 2005), 2–3.

39. See Arthur M. Cohen and Carrie B. Kisker, *Shaping of American Higher Education*, 2nd ed. (San Francisco: Jossey-Bass, 2009), 63–65.

40. See Cohen and Kisker, *Shaping of American Higher Education*, 63; Colin B. Burke, *American Collegiate Populations: A Test of the Traditional View* (New York: New York University Press, 1982), 14; see David B. Potts, "'College Enthusiasm!' As Public Response, 1800–1860," *Harvard Educational Review* 47, no. 1 (February 1977).

41. Thomas Snyder, *120 Years of American Education: A Statistical Portrait* (Washington, DC: National Center for Education Statistics, 1993), 75.

42. Absalom Peters, *A Discourse Delivered in the Park Presbyterian Church* (New York: John F. Trow, 1851).

43. See Potts, "'College Enthusiasm!'"

44. Burke, *American Collegiate Populations*, 138.

45. See Matthew B. Fuller, "A History of Financial Aid to Students," *Journal of Student Financial Aid* 44, no. 1 (2014): 46.

46. David F. Allmendinger Jr., *Paupers and Scholars: The Transformation of Student Life in Nineteenth-Century New England* (New York: St. Martin's Press, 1975), 11.

47. See George Gary Bush, *History of Higher Education in Massachusetts* (Washington, DC: US Government Printing Office, 1891), 95.

48. Allmendinger, *Paupers and Scholars*, 11; Stanley A. Guralnik, *Science and the Ante-bellum College* (Philadelphia: American Philosophical Society, 1975).

49. Lyman Beecher, *An Address Delivered at the Tenth Anniversary Celebration of the Union Literary Society of Miami University, September 29, 1835* (Cincinnati: Cincinnati Journal Office, 1835), 5.

50. Edward A. Goedeken, "From Model Farm to a College with Students: Benjamin Gue, Peter Melendy, Adonijah Welch, and the Iowa Agricultural College and Model Farm, 1867–1869," *Annals of Iowa* 76, no. 2 (2017): 205.

51. *Addresses Delivered at the Opening of the Iowa State Agricultural College, March 17, 1869* (Davenport, IA: Gazette, 1869), 11.

52. Justin Smith Morrill, "Agricultural Colleges," Cong. Globe, 37th Cong., 2nd sess. 256 (June 6, 1862).

53. Earle D. Ross, *Democracy's College: The Land-Grant Movement in the Formative Stage* (Ames: Iowa State College Press, 1942).

54. An Act Donating Public Lands to the Several States and Territories Which May Provide Colleges for the Benefit of Agriculture and the Mechanic Arts, 7 U.S.C. § 301 (1862).

55. Nathan M. Sorber and Roger L. Geiger, "The Welding of Opposite Views: Land-Grant Historiography at 150 Years," in *Higher Education: Handbook of Theory and Research*, ed. Michael B. Paulsen (New York: Springer, 2014), 29:386.

56. See Nathan M. Sorber, *Land-Grant Colleges and Popular Revolt: The Origins of the Morrill Act and the Reform of Higher Education* (Ithaca, NY: Cornell University Press, 2018), 67–74.

57. Nathan M. Sorber, "Early Land-Grant Colleges and Students in the Northeastern United States: A History of Regional Access and Mobility Patterns in Maine, Massachusetts, and New York, 1862–1878," *Agricultural History* 92, no. 1 (Winter 2018): 102.

58. J. Gregory Behle, "Educating the Toiling Peoples," in *The Land-Grant Colleges and the Reshaping of American Higher Education*, ed. Roger L. Geiger and Nathan M. Sorber (New Brunswick, NJ: Transaction, 2013), 79.

59. See Sorber, "Early Land-Grant Colleges," 108–112. According to Sorber, the "median wealth of the graduating classes ($2,350)" at Maine State College was nearly double the average for the state as a whole (107).

60. Julian B. Roebuck and Komanduri S. Murty, *Historically Black Colleges and Universities: Their Place in American Higher Education* (Westport, CT: Praeger, 1993), 27–28; Earnest N. Bracey, "The Significance of Historically Black Colleges and Universities (HBCUs) in the 21st Century: Will Such Institutions of Higher

Learning Survive?," *American Journal of Economics and Sociology* 76, no. 3 (May 2017): 673.

61. Racial Discrimination by Colleges Restricted, 7 U.S.C. §323 (1890).

62. For more on these schools as "separate but equal," see M. Christopher Brown II and James Earl Davis, "The Historically Black College as Social Contract, Social Capital, and Social Equalizer," *Peabody Journal of Education* 76, no. 1 (2001): 31–49.

63. Several Black colleges did receive 1862 funds, though not until after 1890: Alcorn State University was established with the 1862 Morrill Act but was designated land-grant status under the Morrill Act of 1890. See "Council of 1890s Institutions," Association of Public and Land-Grant Universities, accessed April 18, 2021, https://www.aplu.org/members/councils/1890-universities/council-of-1890s -institutions.html; National Research Council, *Colleges of Agriculture at the Land Grant Universities: A Profile* (Washington, DC: National Academies Press, 1995), 3.

64. Robert L. Jenkins, "The Black Land-Grant Colleges in Their Formative Years, 1890—1920," *Agricultural History* 65, no. 2 (1991): 65.

65. See W. E. B. Du Bois, "The Talented Tenth," in *The Negro Problem: A Series of Articles by Representative American Negroes of Today* (New York: James Pott, 1903), 50.

66. See William J. Collins and Robert A. Margo, "Historical Perspectives on Racial Differences in Schooling in the United States," in *Handbook of the Economics of Education*, vol. 1, ed. Eric A. Hanushek and Finis Welch (Amsterdam: Elsevier, 2006), 111–122.

67. "Letter from W. E. B. Du Bois to Samuel May, Jr." December 24, 1907, http://credo.library.umass.edu/view/pageturn/mums312-b003-i325/#page/1/mode /1up.

68. Snyder, *120 Years of American Education*, 76.

69. See John R. Thelin, *A History of American Higher Education* (Baltimore: Johns Hopkins University Press, 2004), 155–157. Claudia Goldin and Lawrence F. Katz, "The Shaping of Higher Education: The Formative Years in the United States, 1890 to 1940," *Journal of Economic Perspectives* 13, no. 1 (Winter 1999): 41, 44, found that in the early twentieth century, "the estimated return to a year of college from a standard log earnings regression was over 12 percent a year for young workers."

70. "The Colleges Turn Out Their 1937 Models: American Boy and Girl," *Life Magazine*, June 7, 1937, 23.

71. Goldin and Katz, "Shaping of Higher Education."

72. *Historical Statistics of the United States, Colonial Times to 1970*, part 2 (Washington, DC: US Bureau of the Census, 1975), https://www2.census.gov /library/publications/1975/compendia/hist_stats_colonial-1970/hist_stats_colonial -1970p1-chH.pdf?#, p. 1128.

73. Goldin and Katz, "Shaping of Higher Education," 51.

74. Goldin and Katz, "Shaping of Higher Education," 50.

75. Cited in Laurence R. Veysey, *The Emergence of the American University* (Chicago: University of Chicago Press, 1970), 107. See Joe Corry and James Gooch, "The Wisconsin Idea: Extending the Boundaries of a University," *Higher Education Quarterly* 46, no. 4 (1992): 305–320.

76. See *Historical Statistics of the United States, Colonial Times to 1970*, 382; John H. Frye, "The Rhetoric of Professional Educators and the Definition of Public Junior Colleges from 1900 to 1940," *Community College Review* 20, no. 4 (1993): 13.

77. Debra D. Bragg, "Community College Access, Mission, and Outcomes: Considering Intriguing Intersections and Challenges," *Peabody Journal of Education* 76, no. 1 (2001): 97–98.

78. Ernest Martin Hopkins, "An Aristocracy of Brains," *Dartmouth Alumni Magazine* 15, no. 1 (November 1922): 8.

79. Hopkins, "Aristocracy of Brains," 9.

80. "Classified Ad 6—Harvard University," *New York Times*, September 20, 1870, 6.

81. See Jerome Karabel, *The Chosen: The Hidden History of Admission and Exclusion at Harvard, Yale, and Princeton* (New York: Houghton Mifflin, 2005), 129.

82. Robert A. McCaughey, *Stand, Columbia: A History of Columbia University in the City of New York, 1754–2004* (New York: Columbia University Press, 2003), 257.

83. McCaughey, *Stand, Columbia*, 257; Karabel, *The Chosen*, 119.

84. Karabel, *The Chosen*, 44.

85. Karabel, *The Chosen*, 23, 88.

86. See Jason Kalman, "Dark Places around the University: The Johns Hopkins University Admissions Quota and the Jewish Community, 1945–1951," *Hebrew Union College Annual* 81 (2010): 233–279.

87. See Roger L. Geiger, *To Advance Knowledge* (New York: Routledge, 2017), 136. See also idem, *The History of American Higher Education: Learning and Culture from the Founding to World War II* (Princeton, NJ: Princeton University Press, 2016), 453.

88. Franklin D. Roosevelt, "Fireside Chat on Progress of War and Plans for Peace, July 28, 1943," in *The Public Papers and Addresses of Franklin D. Roosevelt*, ed. Samuel Irving Rosenman (New York: Harper & Brothers, 1950), 327–328; Thelin, *History of American Higher Education*, 262.

89. Servicemen's Readjustment Act of 1944, S. 1767 (1944), secs. 700, 500, 400.

90. Stanley Frank, "The G.I.'s Reject Education," *Saturday Evening Post*, August 18, 1945, 102.

91. Robert Maynard Hutchins, "The Threat to American Education," *Collier's*, December 30, 1944, 21.

92. Keith W. Olson, "The G.I. Bill and Higher Education: Success and Surprise," *American Quarterly* 25, no. 5 (December 1973): 596.

93. See Suzanne Mettler, *Soldiers to Citizens: The G.I. Bill and the Making of the Greatest Generation* (New York: Oxford University Press, 2005), 95–97.

94. Robert J. Sampson and John H. Laub, "Socioeconomic Achievement in the Life Course of Disadvantaged Men: Military Service as a Turning Point, Circa 1940–1965," *American Sociological Review* 61, no. 3 (June 1996): 347–367.

95. See Wilkinson, *Aiding Students, Buying Students*, 115. The G.I. Bill was renewed and reimagined after nearly every subsequent American conflict and has continued to be a vital source of opportunity for veterans.

96. Lyndon B. Johnson, "Remarks at Southwest Texas State College upon Signing the Higher Education Act of 1965," American Presidency Project, November 8, 1965, https://www.presidency.ucsb.edu/node/241092.

97. "Higher Education Act of 1965," P.L. 89-329 (1965), sec. 402.

98. See "Average Undergraduate Tuition and Fees and Room and Board Rates Charged for Full-Time Students in Degree-Granting Institutions, by Type and Control of Institution: 1964–65 through 2006–07," National Center for Education Statistics, accessed April 18, 2021, https://nces.ed.gov/programs/digest/d07/tables /dt07_320.asp. See also Suzanne Mettler, *Degrees of Inequality: How the Politics of Higher Education Sabotaged the American Dream* (New York: Basic Books, 2014), 59.

99. Christopher M. Mullin, "Past, Present, and Possibilities for the Future of the Pell Grant Program," *Journal of Education Finance* 39, no. 1 (2013): 4.

100. Clark Kerr, *The Gold and the Blue: A Personal Memoir of the University of California, 1949–1967* (Berkeley: University of California Press, 2001), 183.

101. Kerr, *The Gold and the Blue*, 186.

102. Kerr, *The Gold and the Blue*, 187–188.

103. *Reviews of National Policies for Education: Higher Education in California* (Paris: Organisation for Economic Co-operation and Development, 1990), 32.

104. Geoffrey Kabaservice, *The Guardians: Kingman Brewster, His Circle, and the Rise of the Liberal Establishment at Yale* (New York: Henry Holt, 2004), 269.

105. Nicholas Lemann, *The Big Test: The Secret History of the American Meritocracy* (New York: Farrar, Straus and Giroux, 2000), 149.

106. Buckley quoted in Kabaservice, *The Guardians*, 269.

107. Wilkinson, *Aiding Students, Buying Students*, 133.

108. Quoted in Kabaservice, *The Guardians*, 264.

109. Wilkinson, *Aiding Students, Buying Students*, 133.

110. Bowen, *Ever the Teacher*, 466; Wilkinson, *Aiding Students, Buying Students*, 134–135.

111. Bowen, *Ever the Teacher*, 508.

112. The cuts, which went into effect on October 1, 1981, curtailed Pell Grants, eliminated all support for students whose families qualified for Social Security, and set new restrictions on guaranteed student loans. See Edward B. Fiske, "After the Federal Cutbacks, a New Era in Paying for College," *New York Times*, November 15, 1981, https://www.nytimes.com/1981/11/15/education/after-the-federal -cutbacks-a-new-era-in-paying-for-college.html.

113. Edward B. Fiske, "Strain on Student Aid," *New York Times*, October 27, 1982, B1, https://www.nytimes.com/1982/10/27/nyregion/strain-on-student-aid-news-analysis.html; Fred M. Hechinger, "Federal Aid Policy and U.S. Colleges," *New York Times*, February 19, 1985, C15, https://www.nytimes.com/1985/02/19/science/about-education-federal-aid-policy-and-us-colleges.html.

114. Edward B. Fiske, "Colleges Struggle to Cope with U.S. Aid Cuts," *New York Times*, February 16, 1982, 1, https://www.nytimes.com/1982/02/16/us/colleges-struggle-to-cope-with-us-aid-cuts.html.

115. Leon Botstein, "Colleges Offer More Bad News for the Poor," *New York Times*, April 25, 1982, 65, https://www.nytimes.com/1982/04/25/education/colleges-offer-more-bad-news-for-the-poor.html.

116. Botstein, "Colleges Offer More Bad News."

117. *Indicators of Higher Education Equity in the United States: 2020 Historical Trend Report* (Washington, DC: Pell Institute for the Study of Opportunity in Higher Education, 2020), 108.

118. In 2018, 64 percent of students enrolled at for-profit colleges were federal grant recipients, compared to 36 percent of the student body at public four-year institutions. *Indicators*, 84.

119. *Diminishing Funding and Rising Expectations: Trends and Challenges for Public Research Universities* (Washington, DC: National Science Foundation, 2012), https://www.nsf.gov/nsb/publications/2012/nsb1245.pdf.

120. James Fallows, "The Early-Decision Racket," *The Atlantic* (September 2001): https://www.theatlantic.com/magazine/archive/2001/09/the-early-decision-racket/302280/.

121. Christopher Avery, Andrew Fairbanks, and Richard Zeckhauser, *The Early Admissions Game* (Cambridge, MA: Harvard University Press, 2004), 32.

122. Wendy Nelson Espeland and Michael Sauder, *Engines of Anxiety: Academic Rankings, Reputation, and Accountability* (New York: Russell Sage Foundation, 2016), 10.

123. See Michael N. Bastedo and Nicholas A. Bowman, "U.S. News & World Report College Rankings: Modeling Institutional Effects on Organizational Reputation," *American Journal of Education* 116, no. 2 (2010): 163.

124. Colleges usually will release students from early decision if they receive a financial aid offer that does not make it economically feasible to attend. Still, the director of admissions at Carnegie Mellon put it bluntly in 2000: "If financial aid is important to you, it is best to apply for regular admissions." Edward B. Fiske, "Financial Aid Free-For-All As Students and Colleges Seek Deals," *New York Times*, November 12, 2000, https://www.nytimes.com/2000/11/12/education/admissions-financial-aid-free-for-all-as-students-and-colleges-seek-deals.html.

125. Leonard Buder, "Colleges Pick Freshmen; Method Is Vexing to Both," *New York Times*, May 18, 1958, 1, 80; Marcia Winn, "Colleges Face a Big Application

Muddle," *Chicago Daily Tribune*, May 17, 1959, 1; Jay Mathews, "Early Admission Later Cost?," *Washington Post*, Feb. 23, 2000, A1.

126. James A. Dearden et al., "Demonstrated Interest: Signaling Behavior in College Admissions," *Contemporary Economic Policy* 35, no. 4 (October 2017): 630–657.

127. Melissa E. Clinedinst, *2019 State of College Admission* (Alexandria, VA: National Association for College Admission Counseling, 2019), https://www .nacacnet.org/globalassets/documents/publications/research/2018_soca/soca2019 _all.pdf, p. 15.

128. In 1993, 46 percent of colleges reported assigning "considerable importance" to test scores. That share climbed to 58 percent by 2000 and 60 percent by 2004. It has since fallen back below 50 percent, but remains among the most important admissions factors. Clinedinst, *2019 State of College Admission*, 15; David A. Hawkins and Jessica Lautz, *State of College Admission* (Alexandria, VA: National Association for College Admission Counseling, 2005), https://files.eric.ed .gov/fulltext/ED489862.pdf; Marc Meredith, "Why Do Universities Compete in the Ratings Game? An Empirical Analysis of the Effects of the U.S. News and World Report College Rankings," *Research in Higher Education* 45, no. 5 (August 2004): 443–461; Briana Boyington, "Infographic: 30 Editions of the U.S. News Best Colleges Rankings," *U.S. News & World Report*, September 9, 2014, https://www.usnews.com/education/best-colleges/articles/2014/09/09/infographic -30-editions-of-the-us-news-best-colleges-rankings.

129. Andrew M. Perry, "Students Need More Than an SAT Adversity Score, They Need a Boost in Wealth," Brookings Institution, May 17, 2019, https://www .brookings.edu/blog/the-avenue/2019/05/17/students-need-more-than-an-sat -adversity-score-they-need-a-boost-in-wealth/.

130. Perry, "Students Need More"; Joshua Goodman, Oded Gurantz, and Jonathan Smith, "Take Two! SAT Retaking and College Enrollment Gaps," *American Economic Journal* (forthcoming).

131. Douglas Belkin, Jennifer Levitz, and Melissa Korn, "Many More Students, Especially Affluent, Get Extra Time to Take the SAT," *Wall Street Journal*, May 21, 2019, https://www.wsj.com/articles/many-more-students-especially-the-affluent-get -extra-time-to-take-the-sat-11558450347?mod=hp_lead_pos5.

132. Andrew S. Belasco, Kelly O. Rosinger, and James C. Hearn, "The Test-Optional Movement at Liberal Arts Colleges," in *Measuring Success: Testing, Grades, and the Future of College Admissions*, ed. Jack Buckley, Lynn Letukas, and Ben Wildavsky (Baltimore: Johns Hopkins University Press, 2018), 280.

133. Jennifer Giancola and Richard D. Kahlenberg, *True Merit: Ensuring Our Brightest Students Have Access to Our Best Colleges and Universities* (Leesburg, VA: Jack Kent Cooke Foundation, January 2016), https://www.jkcf.org/research/true -merit-ensuring-our-brightest-students-have-access-to-our-best-colleges-and -universities/; Scott Jaschik, "High School Grades: Higher and Higher," *Inside*

Higher Ed, July 17, 2017, https://www.insidehighered.com/admissions/article/2017 /07/17/study-finds-notable-increase-grades-high-schools-nationally.

134. Robert Cribb, "Star Investigation: Cash for Marks Gets Kids into University," *Toronto Star*, September 16, 2011; "'It Was a Joke': Students Describe Lax Standards, Easy High Marks at Private Schools Known as 'Credit Mills,'" CBC Radio, January 28, 2020.

135. Joshua Hyman, "ACT for All: The Effect of Mandatory College Entrance Exams on Postsecondary Attainment and Choice," *Education Finance and Policy* 12, no. 3 (2017): 281–312; Susan M. Dynarski, "ACT/SAT for All: A Cheap, Effective Way to Narrow Income Gaps in College," Brookings Institution, February 8, 2018, https://www.brookings.edu/research/act-sat-for-all-a-cheap-effective-way-to-narrow -income-gaps-in-college/.

136. Mikhail Zinshteyn, "Will the New SAT Better Serve Poor Students," *The Atlantic*, March 5, 2016, https://www.theatlantic.com/education/archive/2016/03/will -the-new-sat-better-serve-poor-students/472311/; "Landscape Comprehensive Data and Methodology Overview," College Board, accessed April 18, 2021, https://secure -media.collegeboard.org/landscape/comprehensive-data-methodology-overview.pdf. Famously, the dashboard came under fire (from the political Left as well as the political Right) for its "adversity score," which consolidated this information into a single score for every student that would sit alongside the SAT score. The College Board eventually abandoned the adversity score, but it is still making the specific information in the dashboard available. Anemona Hartocollis, "SAT 'Adversity Score' Is Abandoned in Wake of Criticism," *New York Times*, August 27, 2019, https://www.nytimes.com /2019/08/27/us/sat-adversity-score-college-board.html.

137. Douglas Belkin, "SAT to Give Students 'Adversity Score' to Capture Social and Economic Background," *Wall Street Journal*, May 16, 2019, https://www.wsj .com/articles/sat-to-give-students-adversity-score-to-capture-social-and-economic -background-11557999000; "Incoming Class of 2022 Sets Record for Socio-Economic Diversity and Yield," *YaleNews*, August 23, 2018, https://news.yale.edu /2018/08/23/incoming-class-2022-sets-record-socio-economic-diversity-and-yield.

138. Robert Morse and Eric Brooks, "What's New in the 2019 U.S. News Best Colleges Rankings," *U.S. News & World Report*, September 10, 2018, https://www .usnews.com/education/blogs/college-rankings-blog/articles/2018-09-10/whats-new -in-the-2019-us-news-best-colleges-rankings; Robert Morse, Eric Brooks, and Matt Mason, "How U.S. News Calculated the 2020 Best Colleges Rankings," *U.S. News & World Report*, September 8, 2019, https://www.usnews.com/education/best -colleges/articles/how-us-news-calculated-the-rankings.

139. "Elimination of Student Loans Opens Doors of Opportunity for Hopkins Undergraduates," *The Hub*, November 26, 2018, https://hub.jhu.edu/2018/11/26 /bloomberg-gift-hopkins-student-impact/.

140. Nick Anderson, "Princeton and Williams Still Top U.S. News College Rankings—But New Formula Scrambles the Annual Lists," *Washington Post*,

September 10, 2018, https://www.washingtonpost.com/local/education/princeton
-and-williams-still-top-us-news-college-rankings--but-new-formula-scrambles-the
-annual-lists/2018/09/08/a7f798b0-b2b1-11e8-a20b-5f4f84429666_story.html;
Deepti Sailappan, "UChicago's U.S. News Ranking Slips to No. 6, after Three Years
at No. 3," *Chicago Maroon*, September 9, 2019, https://www.chicagomaroon.com
/article/2019/9/9/uchicago-u-news-ranking-slips-6-three-years-3/; Sarah Lindenfeld
Hall, "UVA Takes a Tumble in U.S. News' 2020 Rankings," *Virginia Magazine*
(Winter 2019): https://uvamagazine.org/articles/uva_takes_a_tumble_in_u.s_news
_2020_rankings.

141. Alan Finder, "Yale Set to Increase Spending from Its Endowment by
40 Percent," *New York Times*, January 8, 2008, https://www.nytimes.com/2008/01
/08/world/americas/08iht-yale.1.9074997.html.

142. Scott Jaschik, "New Tactic in Aid Arms Race," *Inside Higher Ed*, August 30, 2010, https://www.insidehighered.com/news/2010/08/30/new-tactic-aid
-arms-race; "Tuition: The Price-Break Problem," *Newsweek*, March 3, 2008,
https://www.newsweek.com/tuition-price-break-problem-83779.

143. This calculation relies on College Board figures for the 2007–2008 and
2009–2010 school years in constant 2020 dollars. *Trends in College Pricing and
Student Aid 2020* (New York: College Board, 2020), 19. Some point to a number
of US Department of Justice investigations in the late 1980s that ended a practice
of many universities of discussing financial aid packages with one another as also
playing a role in the unleashing of competition in financial aid packages in the 2000s.
Jaschik, "New Tactic in Aid Arms Race."

144. Nicholas Hillman, *Economic Diversity among Selective Colleges: Measuring
the Enrollment Impact of "No-Loan" Programs* (Washington, DC: Institute for
Higher Education Policy, 2012), 2; Anthony Abraham Jack, *The Privileged Poor:
How Elite Colleges Are Failing Disadvantaged Students* (Cambridge, MA: Harvard
University Press, 2019), 6.

145. *Trends in College Pricing 2020,* 19.

146. "In Year Punctured by Pandemic, Higher Education Endowments Provide
More Than $23 Billion to Support Students, Mission," National Association of
College and University Business Officers, February 19, 2021, https://www.nacubo
.org/Press-Releases/2021/Higher%20Education%20Endowments%20Provide%20
More%20Than%2023%20Billion%20to%20Support%20Students%20Mission.

147. Doug Lederman, "Underrepresented Students, Unintended Consequences," *Inside Higher Ed*, January 28, 2019, https://www.insidehighered.com
/admissions/article/2019/01/28/study-pressure-enroll-more-pell-eligible-students
-has-skewed-colleges.

148. Jon Marcus, "In an Era of Inequity, More and More College Financial Aid
Is Going to the Rich," *Hechinger Report*, December 7, 2017, https://hechingerreport
.org/era-inequity-college-financial-aid-going-rich/.

149. *Indicators of Higher Education Equity in the United States*, 145.

150. Karin Fischer, "Engine of Inequality," *Chronicle of Higher Education*, January 17, 2016, https://www.chronicle.com/article/Engine-of-Inequality/234952.

151. *Two Decades of Change in Federal and State Higher Education Funding* (New York: Pew Charitable Trusts, 2019), 5; *Public Research Universities: Why They Matter* (Cambridge, MA: American Academy of Arts and Sciences, 2015), https://www.amacad.org/multimedia/pdfs/publications/researchpapersmonographs /PublicResearchUniv_WhyTheyMatter.pdf.

152. *Trends in College Pricing 2020*, 18 (in 2020 dollars).

153. Michael Mitchell, Michael Leachman, and Kathleen Masterson, "A Lost Decade in Higher Education Funding," Center on Budget and Policy Priorities, August 23, 2017, https://www.cbpp.org/research/state-budget-and-tax/a-lost -decade-in-higher-education-funding.

154. Kery Murakami, "Colleges: Financial Toll of Coronavirus Worse Than Anticipated," *Inside Higher Ed*, September 29, 2020, https://www.insidehighered .com/quicktakes/2020/09/29/colleges-financial-toll-coronavirus-worse-anticipated.

155. Victoria Yuen, "Mounting Peril for Public Higher Education During the Coronavirus Pandemic," Center for American Progress, June 11, 2020, https://www .americanprogress.org/issues/education-postsecondary/reports/2020/06/11/485963 /mounting-peril-public-higher-education-coronavirus-pandemic.

156. *Fall 2020 Current Term Enrollment Estimates* (Herndon, VA: National Student Clearinghouse Research Center, December 17, 2020), https:// nscresearchcenter.org/current-term-enrollment-estimates/; Madeleine St. Amour, "Enrollment Still Down," *Inside Higher Ed*, November 12, 2020, https://www .insidehighered.com/news/2020/11/12/enrollment-declines-continue-national -student-clearinghouse-finds.

157. Esteban M. Aucejo, Jacob French, Maria Paola Ugalde Araya, and Basit Zafar, "The Impact of COVID-19 on Student Experiences and Expectations: Evidence from a Survey," *Journal of Public Economics* 191 (2020).

158. "How Has the Pandemic Affected Your Ability to Afford School?," *OneClass* [blog], June 1, 2020, https://oneclass.com/blog/featured/179420-how-has -the-pandemic-affected-your-ability-to-afford-school3F.en.html.

159. Ronald Daniels and Michael J. Trebilcock, "Towards a New Compact for University Education in Ontario," in *Taking Public Universities Seriously*, ed. Frank Iacobucci and Carolyn Tuohy (Toronto: University of Toronto Press, 2005).

160. Paul Tough, "Who Gets to Graduate?," *New York Times Magazine*, May 15, 2014, https://www.nytimes.com/2014/05/18/magazine/who-gets-to -graduate.html.

161. *The Pell Partnership: Ensuring a Shared Responsibility for Low-Income Student Success* (Washington, DC: Education Trust, 2015), 1, 3.

162. David J. Deming, *Increasing College Completion with a Federal Higher Education Matching Grant*, Policy Proposal 2017-03 (Washington, DC: Hamilton Project, April 2017).

163. *Where Financial Aid Began: Partnering with Campuses and States* (Washington, DC: Institute for Higher Education Policy, 2015), 9.

164. *Fiscal Year 2011 Budget: Summary and Background Information* (Washington, DC, US Department of Education, 2011), https://www2.ed.gov/about/overview/budget/budget11/summary/11summary.pdf, p. 75.

165. For a forceful call for such a matching program on behalf of the American Association of State Colleges and Universities, and the need for greater co-investment and maintenance of effort requirements in federal grants, see Daniel J. Hurley, Thomas L. Harnisch, and Barmak Nassirian, *A Proposed Federal Matching Program to Stop the Privatization of Public Higher Education* (Washington, DC: American Association of State Colleges and Universities, January 2014).

166. See Sandy Baum and Sarah Turner, "Pricing 'Free College,'" *Urban Wire: Education and Training* [blog], May 3, 2019, https://www.urban.org/urban-wire/pricing-free-college. This is also why I favor income-contingent loans over a universal loan forgiveness program. The Becker Friedman Institute found that full loan forgiveness in the United States would give $192.5 billion to those in the top 20 percent of earners, but only $29.5 billion to the bottom 20 percent. See Sylvain Catherine and Constantine Yannelis, *The Distributional Effects of Student Loan Forgiveness*, Working Paper 2020-169 (Cambridge, MA: National Bureau of Economic Research, December 2020).

167. *Expanding Opportunity for Lower-Income Students: Three Years of the American Talent Initiative* (American Talent Initiative, 2020), 30.

168. "Big Philanthropic Investments a Bright Spot for HBCUs amid Financial Uncertainty Worsened by Pandemic," Georgetown University, July 30, 2020, https://feed.georgetown.edu/access-affordability/big-philanthropic-investments-a-bright-spot-for-hbcus-amid-financial-uncertainty-worsened-by-pandemic/.

169. See Valerie Strauss, "Bloomberg Promises to End Legacy Preferences in College Admissions—And Threatens to Limit Federal Funds to Schools That Refuse," *Washington Post*, February 19, 2020, https://www.washingtonpost.com/education/2020/02/19/bloomberg-promises-end-legacy-preferences-college-admissions-threatens-limit-federal-funds-schools-that-refuse/.

170. See Sandel, *Tyranny of Merit*; Daniel Markovits, *The Meritocracy Trap: How America's Foundational Myth Feeds Inequality, Dismantles the Middle Class, and Devours the Elite* (New York: Penguin, 2019).

171. Daniel Golden, "An Analytic Survey of Legacy Preferences," in *Affirmative Action for the Rich: Legacy Preferences in College Admissions*, ed. Richard D. Kahlenberg (New York: Century Foundation, 2010), 71.

172. See Steve D. Shadowen, "Personal Dignity, Equal Opportunity, and the Elimination of Legacy Preferences," *Civil Rights Law Journal* 21, no. 1 (2010): 31. A 2018 survey by *Inside Higher Ed* of nearly five hundred of the senior-most admissions and enrollment officers at US colleges and universities found that 42 percent of private institutions (although only 6 percent of public ones) consider

legacy status in their admissions process. Scott Jaschik and Doug Lederman, *2018 Survey of College and University Admissions Directors: A Study by Inside Higher Ed and Gallup* (Washington, DC: Inside Higher Ed, 2018).

173. Thomas J. Espenshade, Chang Y. Chung, and Joan L. Walling, "Admission Preferences for Minority Students, Athletes, and Legacies at Elite Universities," *Social Science Quarterly* 85, no. 5 (December 2004): 1431.

174. Michael Hurwitz, "The Impact of Legacy Status on Undergraduate Admissions at Elite Colleges and Universities," *Economics of Education Review* 30, no. 3 (June 2011): 486.

175. Peter Arcidiacono, Josh Kinsler, and Tyler Ransom, *Divergent: The Time Path of Legacy and Athlete Admissions at Harvard*, Working Paper 26315 (Cambridge, MA: National Bureau of Economic Research, 2019), 2.

176. *Parenting in America: Outlook, Worries, Aspirations Are Strongly Linked to Financial Situation* (Washington, DC: Pew Research Center, 2015), 65–72.

177. A helpful comparative chart of legacy numbers was published in Zoe Light, "Vanderbilt Brings Back Legacy Admissions as Factor in Admissions," *Vanderbilt Hustler*, January 12, 2020, https://vanderbilthustler.com/29597/featured/vanderbilt -brings-back-legacy-admissions-preference/. See also Brandon Kochkodin, "Notre Dame and Baylor Admit More Legacies Than Harvard and Yale," *Bloomberg*, March 21, 2019, https://www.bloomberg.com/news/articles/2019-03-21/notre -dame-baylor-top-harvard-yale-for-most-legacies-admitted.

178. See Peter Arcidiacono, Josh Kinsler, and Tyler Ransom, *Legacy and Athlete Preferences at Harvard*, Working Paper 26316 (Cambridge, MA: National Bureau of Economic Research, 2019), 2.

179. Arcidiacono et al., *Legacy and Athlete Preferences*, 17.

180. Jerome Karabel, "The Legacy of Legacies," *New York Times*, September 13, 2004, https://www.nytimes.com/2004/09/13/opinion/the-legacy-of-legacies.html.

181. "Admissions 'Caste System' Attacked," *Philadelphia Daily News*, December 20, 1990, 14.

182. William Douglas, "End Preference for Alumni Kids, Be Diverse, Bush Says," *Detroit Free Press*, August 7, 2004, 9A.

183. Chris Peterson, "Just to Be Clear: We Don't Do Legacy," *MIT Admissions* [blog], June 25, 2012, https://mitadmissions.org/blogs/entry/just-to-be-clear-we -dont-do-legacy/.

TWO: Free Minds

1. This education was limited to male citizens, which speaks to Athens's constrained vision of citizenship. See Derek Heater, *A History of Education for Citizenship* (New York: Routledge, 2004), 1–25.

2. Plato, "Laws, Book I," in *The Collected Dialogues of Plato*, ed. Edith Hamilton and Huntington Cairns (Princeton, NJ: Princeton University Press, 1961), 1243.

3. Montesquieu, "Part I, Chapter 5: On Education in Republican Government," in *The Spirit of the Laws*, ed. Anne M. Cohler, Basia C. Miller, and Harold S. Stone (Cambridge: Cambridge University Press, 1989), 35.

4. "From Thomas Jefferson to Littleton W. Tazewell, January 5, 1805," University of Virginia Press, accessed April 18, 2021, https://rotunda.upress.virginia.edu/founders/default.xqy?keys=FOEA-print-04-01-02-0958.

5. John Dewey, "The Need of an Industrial Education in an Industrial Democracy," in *The Middle Works, 1899–1924*, ed. Jo Ann Boydston (Carbondale: Southern Illinois University Press, 1980), 139.

6. "Who We Are," CivXNow, accessed April 18, 2021, https://www.civxnow.org/founder.

7. "Rebuilding Civic Education Key to Keeping Democracy Running, Professor Says," Arizona State University, April 4, 2019, https://asunow.asu.edu/20190404-solutions-danielle-allen-rebuilding-civic-education-asu-scetl.

8. David E. Campbell, "What Social Scientists Have Learned about Civic Education: A Review of the Literature," *Peabody Journal of Education* 94, no. 1 (2019): 32–47.

9. Anja Neundorf, Richard G. Niemi, and Kaat Smets, "The Compensation Effect of Civic Education: How School Education Makes Up for Missing Parental Socialization," *Political Behavior* 38, no. 4 (2016): 921–949.

10. Neundorf et al., "Compensation Effect of Civic Education," 945.

11. Allison M. Martens and Jason Gainous, "Civic Education and Democratic Capacity: How Do Teachers Teach and What Works?," *Social Science Quarterly* 94, no. 4 (2013): 959; David E. Campbell, "Voice in the Classroom: How an Open Classroom Climate Fosters Political Engagement among Adolescents," *Political Behavior* 30, no. 4 (2008): 437–454; D. E. Hess and P. McAvoy, *The Political Classroom: Evidence and Ethics in Democratic Education* (New York: Routledge, 2015); Diana Owen and Suzanne Soule, "Civic Education and the Development of Participatory Norms," American Political Science Association 2010 Annual Meeting Paper, https://ssrn.com/abstract=1644389; Ryan T. Knowles, Judith Torney-Purta, and Carolyn Barber, "Enhancing Citizenship Learning with International Comparative Research: Analyses of IEA Civic Education Datasets," *Citizenship Teaching and Learning* 13, no. 1 (2018).

12. Meghan Condon, "Voice Lessons: Rethinking the Relationship between Education and Political Participation," *Political Behavior* 37 (2015): 819–843.

13. Wolfram Schulz et al., *Becoming Citizens in a Changing World: IEA International Civic and Citizenship Education Study 2016 International Report* (Amsterdam: International Association for the Evaluation of Educational Achievement, 2017), 58; Anna Lührmann et al., *Democracy at Dusk? V-Dem Annual Report 2017* (Gothenburg: V-Dem Institute, June 2017).

14. Anatoli Rapoport, "Patriotic Education in Russia: Stylistic Move or a Sign of Substantive Counter-Reform?," *Educational Forum* 73, no. 2 (2009): 141–152.

15. Christian Fernández and Kristian Kriegbaum Jensen, "The Civic Integrationist Turn in Danish and Swedish School Politics," *Comparative Migration Studies* 5, no. 5 (2017).

16. Schulz et al., *Becoming Citizens*, 126, 114, 128.

17. Judith Shklar, *American Citizenship: The Quest for Inclusion* (Cambridge, MA: Harvard University Press, 1998), 4.

18. See The National Task Force on Civic Learning and Democratic Engagement, *A Crucible Moment: College Learning and Democracy's Future* (Washington, DC: Association of American Colleges and Universities, 2012).

19. Ashley Berner, *Pluralism and American Public Education: No One Way to School* (New York: Palgrave Macmillan, 2016), 86.

20. Yascha Mounk and Roberto Stefan Foa, "This Is How Democracy Dies," *The Atlantic*, January 29, 2020, https://www.theatlantic.com/ideas/archive/2020/01/confidence-democracy-lowest-point-record/605686/; see also Roberto S. Foa et al., *The Global Satisfaction with Democracy Report 2020* (Cambridge: Centre for the Future of Democracy, 2020).

21. Roberto Stefan Foa and Yascha Mounk, "The Democratic Disconnect," *Journal of Democracy* 27, no. 3 (July 2016): 8–9.

22. Lee Rainie, Scott Keeter, and Andrew Perrin, *Trust and Distrust in America* (Washington, DC: Pew Charitable Trust, 2019), 29; "Political Polarization in the American Public: How Increasing Ideological Uniformity and Partisan Antipathy Affect Politics, Compromise and Everyday Life," Pew Research Center, June 12, 2014, https://www.pewresearch.org/wp-content/uploads/sites/4/2014/06/6-12-2014-Political-Polarization-Release.pdf; Uri Friedman, "Trust Is Collapsing in America," *The Atlantic*, January 21, 2018, https://www.theatlantic.com/international/archive/2018/01/trust-trump-america-world/550964/.

23. Connie Cass, "Young Generation No Slouches at Volunteering," Associated Press, December 29, 2014, https://www.apnews.com/f2e5ba5a6c11469d9200f114 7ed69fe2; "The AP-GfK Poll, July 2014," GfK Public Affairs and Corporate Communications, accessed April 10, 2021, http://surveys.associatedpress.com/data/GfK/AP-GfK%20July%202014%20Poll%20Topline%20FINAL_Informed.pdf.

24. "Americans' Civics Knowledge Increases but Still Has a Long Way to Go," Annenberg Public Policy Center of the University of Pennsylvania, September 12, 2019, https://cdn.annenbergpublicpolicycenter.org/wp-content/uploads/2019/09/Annenberg_civics_survey_2019.pdf; Michael X. Delli Carpini and Scott Keeter, *What Americans Know about Politics and Why It Matters* (New Haven, CT: Yale University Press, 1997); Carpini, "In Search of the Informed Citizen: What Americans Know about Politics and Why It Matters," *Communication Review*, October 1, 2000.

25. "Election Week 2020: Young People Increase Turnout, Lead Biden to Victory," Center for Information and Research on Civic Learning and Engagement, November 25, 2020, https://circle.tufts.edu/latest-research/election-week

-2020#youth-voter-turnout-increased-in-2020; Deirdre Fernandes and Laura Krantz, "Young Voters Helped Put Biden in the White House. Now They Want Action," *Boston Globe*, January 21, 2021, https://www.bostonglobe.com/2021/01 /21/metro/young-voters-came-out-large-numbers-this-election-helped-put-biden -white-house-now-they-want-action/.

26. See Richard G. Nieme and Julia Smith, "Enrollments in High School Government Classes: Are We Short-Changing Both Citizenship and Political Science Training?," *Political Science and Politics* 34, no. 2 (2001): 281–287; Peter Levine and Kei Kawashima-Ginsberg, *Civic Education and Deeper Learning*, Students at the Center: Deeper Learning Research Series (Boston, MA: Jobs for the Future, 2015), 5; Martha Minow, *Education and Democracy*, Harvard Public Law Working Paper No. 18-03 (Cambridge, MA: Harvard Law Review, October 2017); Jonathan Gould, ed., *Guardian of Democracy: The Civic Mission of Schools* (New York: Carnegie Corporation, 2011), https://www.carnegie.org/media/filer _public/ab/dd/abdda62e-6e84-47a4-a043-348d2f2085ae/ccny_grantee_2011 _guardian.pdf.

27. Jeffrey Mirel, "The Decline of Civic Education," *Daedalus* 131, no. 3 (Summer 2002): 49–55; Charles N. Quigley, "Civic Education: Recent History, Current Status, and the Future" (presented at the American Bar Association Symposium, Center for Civic Education, Washington, DC, February 25–26, 1999), http://www.civiced.org/papers/papers_quigley99.html; Edward B. Fiske, "With Old Values and New Titles, Civics Courses Make a Comeback," *New York Times*, June 7, 1987, https://www.nytimes.com/1987/06/07/us/with-old-values-and -new-titles-civics-courses-make-a-comeback.html.

28. Kristina Rizga, "Why Teaching Civics in America's Classrooms Must Be a Trump-Era Priority," *Mother Jones* (January/February 2017): https://www .motherjones.com/politics/2017/02/civics-education-trump-bullying/#correction; Martin West, "Testing, Learning, and Teaching: The Effects of Test-Based Accountability on Student Achievement and Instructional Time in Core Academic Subjects," in *Beyond the Basics: Achieving a Liberal Education for All Children*, ed. Chester E. Finn Jr. and Diane Ravitch (Washington, DC: Thomas B. Fordham Institute, 2007), 45–61.

29. Alyson Klein, "Students Get 'Too Little' Civics Teaching, Principals Say," *Education Week*, June 28, 2018, https://www.edweek.org/leadership/students-get -too-little-civics-teaching-principals-say/2018/06.

30. Many organizations are making noble efforts on this front. See "National Endowment for the Humanities and U.S. Department of Education Award $650,000 to iCivics," iCivics, November 5, 2019, https://www.icivics.org/news/news-story /national-endowment-humanities-us-department-education-award-650000-icivics.

31. Meira Levinson and Ellis Reid, "Polarization, Partisanship, and Civic Education," in *Philosophical Perspectives on Moral and Civic Education: Shaping Citizens and Their Schools* (New York: Routledge, 2019), 103.

32. Sarah Shapiro and Catherine Brown, "The State of Civics Education," Center for American Progress, February 21, 2018, https://www.americanprogress.org/issues/education-k-12/reports/2018/02/21/446857/state-civics-education/; Michael Hansen, Elizabeth Levesque, Jon Valant, and Diana Quintero, *The 2018 Brown Center Report on American Education: How Well are American Students Learning?* (Washington, DC: Brookings Institution, June 2018), https://www.brookings.edu/wp-content/uploads/2018/06/2018-Brown-Center-Report-on-American-Education_FINAL1.pdf.

33. See Lawrence C. Stedman, "The NAEP Long-Term Trend Assessment: A Review of Its Transformation, Use, and Findings," *Teaching, Learning and Educational Leadership Faculty Scholarship* 2 (2008): https://orb.binghamton.edu/cgi/viewcontent.cgi?article=1001&context=education_fac, p. 13; "NAEP Report Card: Civics (2018)," National Assessment of Educational Progress, accessed February 28, 2021, https://www.nationsreportcard.gov/civics.

34. "NAEP Report Card: Civics (2018)"; "NAEP Report Card: Civics (2010)," National Assessment of Educational Progress, accessed April 16, 2021, https://nces.ed.gov/nationsreportcard/pdf/main2010/2011466.pdf.

35. Charles N. Quigley, "Civic Education: Recent History, Current Status, and the Future," *Albany Law Review* 62, no. 4 (1999): 1431.

36. "Report of the Board of Commissioners for the University of Virginia to the Virginia General Assembly," Founders Online, August 4, 1818, https://founders.archives.gov/documents/Madison/04-01-02-0289.

37. Derek Bok, "The Crisis of Civic Education," *Chronicle of Higher Education*, October 1, 2017, https://www.chronicle.com/article/the-crisis-of-civic-education/.

38. See "Age Distribution among College Students, Fall 2017," *Almanac of Higher Education 2019* 65, no. 40 (August 2019): https://www.chronicle.com/article/Age-Distribution-Among-College/246866; David O. Sears, "Political Socialization," in *Handbook of Political Science*, vol. 2, ed. F. I. Greenstein and N. W. Polsby (Reading, MA: Addison-Wesley, 1975): 93–153; R. G. Niemi and M. K. Jennings, *Generations and Politics: A Panel Study of Young Adults and Their Parents* (Princeton, NJ: Princeton University Press, 1981); David O. Sears and Sheri Levy, "Childhood and Adult Political Development," in *The Oxford Handbook of Political Psychology*, 2nd ed., ed. Leonie Huddy, David O. Sears, and Jack S. Levy (Oxford: Oxford University Press, 2003), 60–109; Anja Neundorf, Kaat Smets, and Gema M. García-Albacete, "Homemade Citizens: The Development of Political Interest during Adolescence and Young Adulthood," *Acta Politica* 48 (2013): 105; David E. Campbell, *Why We Vote: How Schools and Communities Shape Our Civic Life* (Princeton, NJ: Princeton University Press, 2006).

39. Elizabeth Beaumont, Anne Colby, Thomas Ehrlich, and Judith Torney-Purta, "Promoting Political Competence and Engagement in College Students: An Empirical Study," *Journal of Political Science Education* 2, no. 3 (2006): 249–

270; Alison Rios Millett McCartney, Elizabeth A. Bennion, and Dick Simpson, eds., *Teaching Civic Engagement: From Student to Active Citizen* (Washington, DC: American Political Science Association, 2013); Kim Edward Spiezio, Kerrie Q. Baker, and Kathleen Boland, "General Education and Civic Engagement: An Empirical Analysis of Pedagogical Possibilities," *Journal of General Education* 54, no. 4 (2006): 273–292; Andrew J. Perrin and Alanna Gillis, "How College Makes Citizens: Higher Education Experiences and Political Engagement," *Socius: Sociological Research for a Dynamic World* 5 (2019): 1–16. For influential treatments of the theory underlying an education in citizenship at colleges and universities, see Amy Gutmann, *Democratic Education* (Princeton, NJ: Princeton University Press, 1999), 172–232, and Martha C. Nussbaum, *Cultivating Humanity: A Classical Defense of Reform in Liberal Education* (Cambridge, MA: Harvard University Press, 1997).

40. "Immediate College Enrollment Rate," National Center for Education Statistics, last modified May 2021, https://nces.ed.gov/programs/coe/indicator _cpa.asp.

41. Benjamin Rush to Richard Price, May 25, 1786, quoted in David Madsen, *The National University* (Detroit, MI: Wayne Press, 1966), 16.

42. John R. Vile, *The Constitutional Convention of 1787: A Comprehensive Encyclopedia of America's Founding* (Santa Barbara, CA: ABC-Clio, 2015), 1:516.

43. "From George Washington to the United States Senate and House of Representatives, 8 January 1790," Founders Online, accessed April 18, 2021, https://founders.archives.gov/documents/Washington/05-04-02-0361.

44. "George Washington's Last Will and Testament, July 9, 1799," George Washington's Mount Vernon, accessed April 18, 2021, https://www.mountvernon .org/education/primary-sources-2/article/george-washingtons-last-will-and -testament-july-9-1799/.

45. Frederick Rudolph, *Curriculum: A History of the American Undergraduate Course of Study since 1636* (San Francisco: Jossey-Bass, 1977), 90.

46. *Reports on the Course of Instruction in Yale College; By a Committee of the Corporation, and the Academical Faculty* (New Haven, CT: Hezekiah Howe, 1828), 15, available from http://collegiateway.org/reading/yale-report-1828/.

47. George P. Schmidt, as cited in Frederick Rudolph, *Mark Hopkins and the Log: Williams College, 1836–1872* (New Haven, CT: Yale University Press, 1956), 46.

48. See Rudolph, *Curriculum*, 90.

49. Theodore Dwight Jr., *President Dwight's Decisions of Questions Discussed by the Senior Class in Yale College in 1813 and 1814* (New York: Jonathan Leavitt, 1833), 5–6.

50. Daniel Coit Gilman, "Commemorative Address," *Johns Hopkins University Circular* 21, no. 156 (March 1902): 38. See Julie A. Reuben, *The Making of the Modern University: Intellectual Transformation and the Marginalization of Morality* (Chicago: University of Chicago Press, 1996), 36–60.

51. William James, "The Teaching of Philosophy in Our Colleges," *The Nation*, September 21, 1876, 178.

52. See Dorothy Ross, "Development of the Social Sciences," in *The Organization of Knowledge in Modern America, 1860–1920*, ed. Alexandra Oleson and John Voss (Baltimore: Johns Hopkins University Press, 1979), 113–115.

53. See Jon H. Roberts and James Turner, *The Sacred and the Secular University* (Princeton, NJ: Princeton University Press, 2000), 83–93; John Higham, "Specialization in a Democracy," in *Hanging Together: Unity and Diversity in American Culture*, ed. Carl J. Guarneri (New Haven, CT: Yale University Press, 2001), 78–79.

54. Ellen Condliffe Lagemann and Harry Lewis, eds., "Renewing the Civic Mission of American Higher Education," in *What Is College For? The Public Purpose of Higher Education* (New York: Teachers College Press, 2015). See also Benjamin Barber, "The Apprenticeship of Liberty: Schools for Democracy," School Superintendents Association, accessed April 18, 2021, http://www.aasa.org/SchoolAdministratorArticle.aspx?id=15264.

55. David Snedden, "The Achievements and Shortcomings of the American College," *School Review* 18, no. 6 (June 1910): 387.

56. Charles A. Ellwood, "How Should Sociology Be Taught as a College or University Subject?," *American Journal of Sociology* 12, no. 5 (March 1907): 592.

57. Charles Hart Handschin, "The American College, as It Looks from the Inside," *Popular Science Monthly* 82 (June 1913), 557.

58. Ross, "Development of the Social Sciences," 113.

59. *Annual Report of the American Historical Association for the Year 1898* (Washington, DC: US Government Printing Office, 1899), 439.

60. *Proceedings of the American Political Science Association at Its Tenth Annual Meeting Held at Washington, D.C., December 30, 1913–January 1, 1914* (Baltimore: Waverly Press, 1914), 264. The other two duties were "to prepare for professions, such as law, journalism, teaching and public service" and "to train experts for government positions."

61. Snedden, "Achievements and Shortcomings," 387; *Teaching of Government: Report to the American Political Science Association by the Committee on Instruction* (New York: Macmillan, 1916), 135–224.

62. Abraham Flexner, *The American College: A Criticism* (New York: Century, 1908), 131.

63. See W. A. Schaper, "What Do Students Know about American Government, before Taking College Courses in Political Science? A Report to the Section on Instruction in Political Science," *Proceedings of the American Political Science Association* 2 (1905): 207–228.

64. Schaper, "What Do Students Know," 212.

65. Schaper, "What Do Students Know," 227.

66. See Roger L. Geiger, *The History of American Higher Education: Learning and Culture from the Founding to World War II* (Princeton, NJ: Princeton University

Press, 2014), 423–426; Benjamin F. Shearer, "An Experiment in Military and Civilian Education: The Students' Army Training Corps at the University of Illinois," *Journal of the Illinois State Historical Society* 72, no. 3 (1979): 213.

67. Frank Aydelotte, *Final Report of the War Issues Course of the Students' Army Training Corps* (Washington, DC: US War Department, 1919), 9.

68. Aydelotte, *Final Report*, 18.

69. Aydelotte, *Final Report*, 90.

70. Herbert E. Hawkes quoted in Timothy P. Cross, *An Oasis of Order: The Core Curriculum at Columbia College* (New York: Columbia College, 1995), https://www.college.columbia.edu/core/oasis.

71. Cross, *Oasis of Order*.

72. John W. Boyer, *The University of Chicago: A History* (Chicago: University of Chicago Press, 2015), 231–252; Anne H. Stevens, "The Philosophy of General Education and Its Contradictions: The Influence of Hutchins," *Journal of General Education* 50, no. 3 (2001): 165–191.

73. Alston Chase, "The Rise and Fall of General Education: 1945–1980," *Academic Questions* 6, no. 2 (Spring 1993), 22.

74. Earl James McGrath, "The General Education Movement," *Journal of General Education* 1, no. 1 (October 1946): 3.

75. Committee on the Objectives of a General Education in a Free Society, *General Education in a Free Society* (Cambridge, MA: Harvard University Press, 1945), x.

76. See Chase, "Rise and Fall of General Education," 43; Committee on the Objectives of a General Education in a Free Society, *General Education in a Free Society*, 53.

77. "Letter of Appointment of Commission Members," in *Higher Education for American Democracy: A Report of the President's Commission on Higher Education* (New York: Harper & Brothers, 1947).

78. *Higher Education for American Democracy*, 102.

79. *Higher Education for American Democracy*, 69.

80. *Higher Education for American Democracy*, 49.

81. *Higher Education for American Democracy*, 59.

82. See Roger L. Geiger, *American Higher Education since World War II* (Princeton, NJ: Princeton University Press, 2019), 21.

83. See Molly Worthen, *Apostles of Reason: The Crisis of Authority in American Evangelicalism* (New York: Oxford University Press, 2014); and Robert Glenn Salter, "A 'Christian America' Restored: The Rise of the Evangelical Christian School Movement in America, 1920–1952" (PhD diss., University of Tennessee, 2012), 122–123.

84. Mario Savio, "Put Your Bodies upon the Gears," speech on December 2, 1964, in *Essential Documents in the History of American Higher Education*, ed. John R. Thelin (Baltimore: Johns Hopkins University Press, 2014), 250–252.

85. See Robert Bellah et al., *Habits of the Heart: Individualism and Commitment in American Life* (Berkeley: University of California Press, 1985), viii.

86. John Saltmarsh and Matthew Hartley, "A Brief History of the Civic Engagement Movement in American Higher Education," in *The Cambridge Handbook of Service-Learning and Community Engagement*, ed. Corey Dolgon, Tania D. Mitchell, and Timothy K. Eatman (Cambridge: Cambridge University Press, 2017), 113.

87. See Keith Morton and Marie Troppe, "From the Margin to the Mainstream: Campus Compact's Project on Integrating Service with Academic Study," *Journal of Business Ethics* 15, no. 1 (1996): 21–32.

88. Tony C. Chambers, "The Special Role of Higher Education in Society: As a Public Good for the Public Good," in *Higher Education for the Public Good: Emerging Voices from a National Movement*, ed. Adrianna J. Kezar, Tony C. Chambers, John C. Burkhardt, and Associates (San Francisco: Jossey-Bass, 2005), 3–22.

89. Saltmarsh and Hartley, "Brief History of the Civic Engagement Movement," 115.

90. *Three Decades of Institutionalizing Change: 2014 Annual Member Survey* (Boston: Campus Compact, 2014), 2; "News from Brown," Brown University News Bureau, April 8, 1999, https://www.brown.edu/Administration/News _Bureau/1998-99/98-087.html; "Who We Are," Campus Compact, accessed March 12, 2020, https://compact.org/who-we-are/.

91. See Mary Prentice, Gail Robinson, and Sara McPhee, *Service-Learning in Community Colleges: 2003 National Survey Results* (Washington, DC: American Association of Community Colleges, 2003), https://files.eric.ed.gov/fulltext /ED500798.pdf, p. 1; *Revitalizing Our Democracy: Building on Our Assets: 2016 Annual Member Survey* (Boston: Campus Compact, 2016); National Survey of Student Engagement, *Engagement Insights: Survey Findings on the Quality of Undergraduate Education: Annual Results 2019* (Bloomington: Indiana University Center for Postsecondary Research, 2020), 13.

92. Ellen Porter Honnet and Susan J. Pulsen, *Principles of Good Practice for Combining Service and Learning* (Racine, WI: Johnson Foundation, 1989).

93. Alexander W. Astin, Lori J. Vogelgesang, Elaine K. Ikeda, and Jennifer A. Yee, *How Service-Learning Affects Students* (Los Angeles: Higher Education Research Institute, 2000); Lori Simons and Beverly Cleary, "The Influence of Service-Learning on Students' Personal and Social Development," *College Teaching* 54, no. 4 (2006); Janet Eyler and Dwight E. Giles Jr., *Where's the Learning in Service-Learning?* (San Francisco: Jossey-Bass, 1999).

94. Alexander W. Astin et al., *Understanding the Effects of Service-Learning: A Study of Students and Faculty* (Los Angeles: Higher Education Research Institute, 2006).

95. John Saltmarsh, Matthew Hartley, and Patti Clayton, "Democratic Engagement White Paper," New England Resource Center for Higher Education,

accessed March 21, 2021, https://repository.upenn.edu/cgi/viewcontent.cgi?article
=1252&context=gse_pubs, p. 11.

96. Nathan Dietz and Robert T. Grimm Jr., "Doing Good by the Young and
Old: Forty Years of American Volunteering," *Nonprofit Quarterly* (Fall 2016):
https://nonprofitquarterly.org/good-young-old-forty-years-american-volunteering/;
Cass, "Young Generation No Slouches at Volunteering"; John Gramlich, "Jury
Duty Is Rare, but Most Americans See It as Part of Good Citizenship," Pew
Research, August 24, 2017, https://www.pewresearch.org/fact-tank/2017/08/24
/jury-duty-is-rare-but-most-americans-see-it-as-part-of-good-citizenship/; Katy
Harriger, Jill J. McMillan, Christy M. Buchanan, and Stephanie Gusler, "The
Long-Term Impact of Learning to Deliberate," *Diversity and Democracy* 18, no. 4
(Fall 2015).

97. Cliff Zukin et al., *A New Engagement? Political Participation, Civic Life, and
the Changing American Citizen* (Oxford: Oxford University Press, 2006).

98. Saltmarsh et al., "Democratic Engagement White Paper," 5.

99. Thomas Ehrlich and Elizabeth Hollander, *Presidents' Declaration on the Civic
Responsibility of Higher Education* (Boston: Campus Compact, 1999).

100. National Task Force on Civic Learning and Democratic Engagement, *A
Crucible Moment: College Learning and Democracy's Future* (Washington, DC:
Association of American Colleges and Universities, 2012).

101. George Mehaffy quoted in Keith Melville, John Dedrick, and Elizabeth
Gish, "Preparing Students for Democratic Life: The Rediscovery of Education's
Civic Purpose," *Journal of General Education* 62, no. 4 (2013): 259.

102. Evidence suggests that, unlike in previous generations, military service in
the all-volunteer era has a negative impact on education attainment, meaning that
fewer veterans attend college. See Jay Teachman, "Military Service and Educational
Attainment in the All-Volunteer Era," *Sociology of Education* 80 (2007): 359–374.

103. Chase, "Rise and Fall of General Education," 29.

104. David Randall, *Making Citizens: How American Universities Teach Civics*
(New York: National Association of Scholars, 2017), 9.

105. George Washington, "George Washington's Last Will and Testament, 9
July 1799," Founders Online, https://founders.archives.gov/documents/Washington
/06-04-02-0404-0001.

106. Sandra Feder, "Stanford Pilots a New Citizenship Course for First-Year
Students," *Stanford Today*, March 17, 2021, https://news.stanford.edu/today/2021
/03/17/citizenship-course-piloted/; Kate Chesley, "Faculty Alter New First-Year
Requirement Because of Continuing Pandemic," *Stanford News*, November 3,
2020, https://news.stanford.edu/2020/11/03/faculty-alter-new-first-year
-requirement-continuing-pandemic/.

107. Edgar E. Robinson, "'Problems of Citizenship'—A Course That Every
Stanford Man and Woman Will Hear," *Stanford Illustrated Review* 24, no. 8
(May 1923): 430.

108. Feder, "Stanford Pilots."

109. Feder, "Stanford Pilots."

110. John Carfagno, "Landmark Vote by College Faculty to Approve, Expand New Curriculum," *UVA Today*, October 20, 2019, https://news.virginia.edu /content/landmark-vote-college-faculty-approve-expand-new-curriculum.

111. Rachel Most and Chad Wellmon, "Engaging Students in Advising and General Education Requirements," *Journal of General Education* 64, no. 2 (2015): 109.

112. Trevor Peters, "Daniels Proposes U.S. Facts Exam for Purdue Students to Graduate," WLFI, January 31, 2019, https://www.wlfi.com/content/news /Daniels-proposes-US-facts-exam-for-Purdue-students-to-graduate-505146541 .html.

113. Dave Bangert, "Mitch Daniels' Call for a Civics Exam to Graduate from Purdue Faces Faculty Test," *Journal and Courier*, February 8, 2020, https://www .jconline.com/story/news/2020/02/08/mitch-daniels-call-civics-exam-graduate -purdue-faces-faculty-test/4690314002/.

114. Dave Bangert, "Purdue's Mitch Daniels Bemoans Campus Civics Illiteracy, Calls for Test to Graduate," *Journal and Courier*, January 28, 2019, https://www .jconline.com/story/news/2019/01/28/purdues-mitch-daniels-bemoans-campus -civics-illiteracy-calls-test-graduate/2704554002/.

115. Colleen Flaherty, "And Civics Literacy for All," *Inside Higher Ed*, February 24, 2020, https://www.insidehighered.com/news/2020/02/24/purdue-looks -adopt-civics-knowledge-undergraduate-requirement; "West Lafayette Senate Report, May 2020," May 8, 2020, https://www.pnw.edu/faculty-senate/2020/05 /03/west-lafayette-senate-report-may-2020/.

116. Colleen Flaherty, "Undemocratic Civics at Purdue?," *Inside Higher Ed*, June 11, 2021, https://www.insidehighered.com/news/2021/06/11/some-purdue -professors-say-university-unilaterally-pursuing-civics-requirement.

117. National Task Force on Civic Learning and Democratic Engagement, *Crucible Moment*.

118. Ashley Finley, *A Brief Review of the Evidence on Civic Learning in Higher Education* (Washington, DC: Association of American Colleges and Universities, 2012), https://www.aacu.org/sites/default/files/files/crucible/CivicOutcomesBrief .pdf, p. 3.

119. Dick Simpson, "Teaching Engagement Today," in *Teaching Civic Engagement across the Disciplines*, ed. Elizabeth C. Matto, Alison Rios Millett McCartney, Elizabeth A. Bennion, and Dick Simpson (Washington, DC: American Political Science Association, 2017), 403.

120. See Elizabeth L. Hollander, "Civic Education in Research Universities: Leaders or Followers?," *Education and Training* 53, nos. 2–3 (2011): 166–176.

121. *Our Common Purpose: Reinventing American Democracy for the 21st Century* (Cambridge, MA: American Academy of Arts and Sciences, 2021), 55–56;

Educating for American Democracy: Excellence in History and Civics for All Learners (Cambridge, MA: iCivics, 2021), 10.

122. Maria Henson, "The Making of Future Citizens," *Wake Forest Magazine* (Fall 2016): https://magazine.wfu.edu/2016/09/30/the-making-of-future-citizens/.

123. Harriger et al., "Long-Term Impact of Learning to Deliberate."

124. Henson, "The Making of Future Citizens."

125. Duke University learned this lesson the hard way in 2017 when a five-year effort to streamline major requirements and enhance student decision-making suddenly collapsed. See Colleen Flaherty, "Years of Work, Tabled," *Inside Higher Ed*, April 26, 2017, https://www.insidehighered.com/news/2017/04/26/duke -undergraduate-curricular-reform-vote-tabled-indefinitely-after-years-work.

THREE: Hard Truths

1. "Georgetown Emerging Technology Experts Help Create Online Coronavirus Repository," Georgetown University News, March 16, 2020, https://www .georgetown.edu/news/georgetown-emerging-technology-experts-help-create-online -coronavirus-repository/.

2. "Machine Learning Can Identify Areas Most at Risk from Pandemic," Stony Brook University News, July 8, 2020, https://news.stonybrook.edu/homespotlight /machine-learning-can-identify-areas-most-at-risk-from-pandemic/.

3. "Engineers Developing No-Touch, Mail-In, Fast-Scan Test for COVID-19, Other Outbreaks," *Iowa State University News Service*, July 31, 2020, https://www .news.iastate.edu/news/2020/07/31/nocontacttesting.

4. Tonia Thomas and Rachel Colin-Jones, "Oxford Scientists: How We Developed Our COVID-19 Vaccine in Record Time," *The Conversation*, January 13, 2021, https://theconversation.com/oxford-scientists-how-we-developed-our -covid-19-vaccine-in-record-time-153135.

5. "Johns Hopkins Releases Report on Digital Contact Tracing to Aid COVID-19 Response," *The Hub*, May 26, 2020, https://hub.jhu.edu/2020/05/26/digital -contact-tracing-technologies-report/; "Johns Hopkins Experts Will Aid Baltimore Mayoral Transition Team," December 3, 2020, https://hub.jhu.edu/2020/12/03 /experts-aid-baltimore-mayoral-transition/; Charles Davis, "How Convalescent Plasma Could Be Used to Treat New Variants of the Coronavirus—Especially Where Vaccines Are Scarce," *Business Insider*, March 15, 2021, https://www .businessinsider.com/convalescent-plasma-could-help-against-coroanvirus-variants -2021-3.

6. See Kristen Rogers, "Johns Hopkins' Dashboard: The People behind the Pandemic's Most Visited Site," CNN, July 11, 2020, https://www.cnn.com/2020 /07/11/health/johns-hopkins-covid-19-map-team-wellness-trnd/index.html; Kyle Swenson, "Millions Track the Pandemic on Johns Hopkins's Dashboard. Those Who Built It Say Some Miss the Real Story," *Washington Post*, June 29, 2020,

https://www.washingtonpost.com/local/johns-hopkins-tracker/2020/06/29 /daea7eea-a03f-11ea-9590-1858a893bd59_story.html.

7. Jill Rosen, "Johns Hopkins Coronavirus Resource Center Passes 1 Billion Views," *The Hub*, January 6, 2021, https://hub.jhu.edu/2021/01/06/coronavirus -resource-center-billion-page-views/.

8. Association of American Universities (AAU) survey conducted in April 2020 on file with AAU.

9. See Noah Weiland, Sheryl Gay Stolberg, and Abby Goodnough, "Political Appointees Meddled in C.D.C.'s 'Holiest of the Holy' Health Reports," *New York Times*, September 12, 2020, https://www.nytimes.com/2020/09/12/us/politics /trump-coronavirus-politics-cdc.html; Weiland, "'Like a Hand Grasping': Trump Appointees Describe the Crushing of the C.D.C.," *New York Times*, December 16, 2020, https://www.nytimes.com/2020/12/16/us/politics/cdc-trump.html.

10. John Rawls, "The Idea of Public Reason Revisited," *University of Chicago Law Review* 64, no. 3 (Summer 1997): 765–766.

11. William A. Galston, "Truth and Democracy: Theme and Variations," in *Truth and Democracy*, ed. Jeremy Elkins and Andrew Norris (Philadelphia: University of Pennsylvania Press, 2012), 130.

12. See Iuliia Mendel, "85 Years Later, Ukraine Marks Famine That Killed Millions," *New York Times*, November 24, 2018, https://www.nytimes.com/2018 /11/24/world/europe/ukraine-holodomor-famine-memorial.html; Anne Apple- baum, "How Stalin Hid Ukraine's Famine from the World," *The Atlantic*, Octo- ber 13, 2017, https://www.theatlantic.com/international/archive/2017/10/red -famine-anne-applebaum-ukraine-soviet-union/542610/.

13. See George S. Vascik and Mark R. Sadler, eds., *The Stab-in-the-Back Myth and the Fall of the Weimar Republic: A History in Documents and Visual Sources* (New York: Bloomsbury, 2016), 1–3.

14. Jim Rutenberg, Nick Corasaniti, and Alan Feuer, "Trump's Fraud Claims Died in Court, but the Myth of Stolen Elections Lives On," *New York Times*, December 26, 2020, https://www.nytimes.com/2020/12/26/us/politics/republicans -voter-fraud.html.

15. Czeslaw Milosz, *The Captive Mind*, trans. Jane Zielonko (New York: Vintage Books, 1981), 48.

16. Barbara J. Shapiro, *A Culture of Fact: England, 1550–1720* (Ithaca, NY: Cornell University Press, 2003), 6, 9–12; Mary Poovey, *A History of the Modern Fact: Problems of Knowledge in the Sciences of Wealth and Society* (Chicago: Univer- sity of Chicago Press, 1998), 29.

17. Rudyard Kipling, *From Sea to Sea* (New York: Doubleday, Page, 1913), 180.

18. Sophia Rosenfeld, *Democracy and Truth: A Short History* (Philadelphia: University of Pennsylvania Press, 2019), 19.

19. Sergei Guriev and Daniel Treisma, "Informational Autocrats," *Journal of Economic Perspectives* 33, no. 4 (2019): 100–127.

20. Jonathan Cole, *The Great American University* (New York: PublicAffairs, 2010), 4.

21. See, e.g., Tim Wu, *The Attention Merchants: The Epic Scramble to Get inside Our Heads* (New York: Alfred A. Knopf, 2016). Studies have shown that fake news travels across social media at six times the speed of real news and that the most popular false news stories normally find their way to anywhere between 1,000 and 100,000 people online, while real news almost always fails to reach more than 1,000 recipients. Soroush Vosoughi, Deb Roy, and Sinan Aral, "The Spread of True and False News Online," *Science* 359, no. 6380 (March 2018): 1146–1151.

22. Seth Flaxman, Sharad Goel, and Justin M. Rao, "Filter Bubbles, Echo Chambers, and Online News Consumption," *Public Opinion Quarterly* 80, no. S1 (2016): 298–320; Kartik Hosanagar, "Blame the Echo Chamber on Facebook. But Blame Yourself, Too," *Wired*, November 25, 2016, https://www.wired.com/2016/11/facebook-echo-chamber/.

23. "Confidence in Institutions," Gallup, accessed April 13, 2021, https://news.gallup.com/poll/1597/confidence-institutions.aspx; Cary Funk, Meg Hefferon, Brian Kennedy, and Courtney Johnson, "Trust and Mistrust in Americans' Views of Scientific Experts," Pew Research Center, August 2, 2019, https://www.pewresearch.org/science/2019/08/02/trust-and-mistrust-in-americans-views-of-scientific-experts/; Jasmine Aguilera, "'An Epidemic of Misinformation.' New Report Finds Trust in Social Institutions Diminished Further in 2020," *Time*, January 13, 2021, https://time.com/5929252/edelman-trust-barometer-2021/.

24. Jennifer Kavanagh and Michael D. Rich, *Truth Decay: An Initial Exploration of the Diminishing Role of Facts and Analysis in American Public Life* (Santa Monica, CA: RAND Corporation, 2018).

25. Quoted in Heather Ewing, *The Lost World of James Smithson: Science, Revolution, and the Birth of the Smithsonian* (New York: Bloomsbury, 2007), 331.

26. See Edward Shils, "The Order of Learning in the United States from 1865 to 1920: The Ascendancy of the Universities," *Minerva* 16, no. 2 (Summer 1978): 159–195.

27. Roger L. Geiger, "The Rise and Fall of Useful Knowledge," in *The American College in the Nineteenth Century* (Nashville, TN: Vanderbilt University Press, 2000), 157–160; Frederick Rudolph, *The American College and University* (Athens: University of Georgia Press, 1990), 113–116.

28. "Science in America," *New York Quarterly* (October 1853): 448.

29. See Roger L. Geiger, *The History of American Higher Education: Learning and Culture from the Founding to World War II* (Princeton, NJ: Princeton University Press, 2014), 267.

30. Lori Thurgood, Mary J. Golladay, and Susan T. Hill, *U.S. Doctorates in the 20th Century* (Washington, DC: National Science Foundation, 2006), 3.

31. Robert V. Bruce, *The Launching of Modern American Science, 1846–1876* (Ithaca, NY: Cornell University Press, 1987), 335.

32. Daniel Coit Gilman, "Inaugural Address at Johns Hopkins University," Johns Hopkins University, February 22, 1876, https://www.jhu.edu/about/history/gilman-address/.

33. Laurence R. Vesey, *The Emergence of the American University* (Chicago: University of Chicago Press, 1965), 160–161.

34. Jonathan Cole, *The Great American University* (New York: PublicAffairs, 2013), 20.

35. Rudolph, *The American College and University*, 270–273.

36. See also Claudia Goldin and Lawrence Katz, "The Shaping of American Higher Education: The Formative Years in the United States, 1890 to 1940," *Journal of Economic Perspectives* 13, no. 1 (Winter 1999): 46.

37. Colin Burke, *American Collegiate Populations* (New York: New York University Press, 1982), 21; Daniel Coit Gilman, "Plan for JHU," 1.59–24, D. C. Gilman Papers, Special Collections, Johns Hopkins University.

38. Gilman, "Plan for JHU."

39. Gilman, "Inaugural Address at Johns Hopkins University."

40. Ira Remsen, "Development of Chemical Research in America," *Journal of the American Chemical Society* 37, no. 1 (1915): 5.

41. Abraham Flexner, *Universities: American, English, German* (New Brunswick, NJ: Transaction, 1994), 288.

42. See Deborah Kent, "*The Mathematical Miscellany* and *The Cambridge Miscellany of Mathematics*: Closely Connected Attempts to Introduce Research-Level Mathematics in America, 1836–1843," *Historia Mathematica* 35 (2008): 102–122.

43. Lindsey R. Harmon and Herbert Soldz, *Doctorate Production in United States Universities, 1920–1962* (Washington, DC: National Academy of Sciences, 1963), 11; Thurgood et al., *U.S. Doctorates in the 20th Century*, 7.

44. J. David Hoevler, *John Bascom and the Origins of the Wisconsin Idea* (Madison: University of Wisconsin Press, 2016), 4.

45. Michael J. Keane, *The Wisconsin Legislative Reference Bureau: A Century of Service* (Madison: Wisconsin Legislative Reference Bureau, 2002), 2.

46. LaVern J. Rippley, "Charles McCarthy and Frederic C. Howe: Their Imperial German Sources for the Wisconsin Idea in Progressive Politics," *Monatshefte* 80, no. 1 (1988): 69–70; Charles McCarthy, *The Wisconsin Idea* (New York: MacMillan, 1912), 214.

47. Marion Casey, "Charles McCarthy's 'Idea': A Library to Change Government," *Library Quarterly* 44, no. 1 (1974): 36; Jack Stark, "The Wisconsin Idea: The University's Service to the State," in *1995–1996 Wisconsin Blue Book* (Madison: Wisconsin Legislative Reference Bureau), 10–11, 17–18; McCarthy, *Wisconsin Idea*, 313–317.

48. Casey, "Charles McCarthy's 'Idea,'" 38–40; George B. Galloway, "The Legislative Reference Service of Congress," *Parliamentary Affairs* 8, no. 2 (1954): 261–265.

49. See Sebastian Edwards, "Gold, the Brains Trust, and Roosevelt," *History of Political Economy* 49, no. 1 (2017): 1–30.

50. "How Roosevelt Aides Became 'Brain Trust,'" *New York Times*, June 29, 1933.

51. Russell Owen, "The 'Brain Trust' Mirrors Many Minds," *New York Times*, June 11, 1933.

52. Richard S. Kirkendall, "Roosevelt and the Service Intellectual," *Mississippi Valley Historical Review* 49, no. 3 (December 1962): 458.

53. Kirkendall, "Roosevelt and the Service Intellectual," 468; Warren Moscow, "Taft, Robey Named Advisors," *New York Times*, June 20, 1936.

54. Harold M. Groves, "Richard T. Ely: An Appreciation," *Land Economics* 45, no. 1 (1969): 1.

55. Gerald F. Vaughn, "Richard T. Ely: Economic Reformer and Champion of Academic Freedom," *Choices* (1994): 28.

56. Oliver Wells, "The College Anarchist," *The Nation* 59, July 12, 1894, 27.

57. Quoted in Theodore Herfurth, *Sifting and Winnowing: A Chapter in the History of Academic Freedom at the University of Wisconsin* (Madison: University of Wisconsin, 1949), 11.

58. See Ellen Schrecker, "Subversives, Squeaky Wheels, and 'Special Obligations': Threats to Academic Freedom, 1890–1960," *Social Research* 76, no. 2 (2009): 523.

59. Schrecker, "Subversives," 524.

60. "Declaration of Principles on Academic Freedom and Academic Tenure," American Association of University Professors, accessed March 22, 2021, http://www.aaup-ui.org/Documents/Principles/Gen_Dec_Princ.pdf.

61. Ralph S. Brown and Jordan E. Kurland, "Academic Tenure and Academic Freedom," *Law and Contemporary Problems* 53, no. 3 (1990), 330.

62. See Roger L. Geiger, *To Advance Knowledge* (New York: Routledge, 2017), 256.

63. According to Ashish Arora and colleagues, the number of citations per article coming out of industrial laboratories surpassed those coming out of universities for the first time in 1940. See "The Changing Structure of American Innovation: Some Cautionary Remarks for Economic Growth," *Innovation Policy and the Economy* 20 (2020): 49.

64. See G. Pascal Zachary, *Endless Frontier: Vannevar Bush, Engineer of the American Century* (New York: Free Press, 2018), 113–115; Jerome B. Wiesner, *Vannevar Bush: 1890–1974* (Washington, DC: National Academy of Sciences, 1979), 95.

65. Roger L. Geiger, *Research and Relevant Knowledge: American Research Universities since World War II* (Oxford: Oxford University Press, 1993), 6.

66. "Science Mobilizes a Test-Tube Army," *New York Times*, January 3, 1943, A32.

67. Vannevar Bush, *Science—The Endless Frontier: A Report to the President* (Washington, DC: US Government Printing Office, 1945), vii.

68. Bush, *Science*, 73.

69. Bush, *Science*, 2.

70. "The National Science Foundation: A Brief History," National Science Foundation, July 15, 1994, https://www.nsf.gov/about/history/nsf50/nsf8816.jsp.

71. National Science Foundation Act of 1950, 42 U.S.C. § 1861-75, available at https://www.nsf.gov/about/history/legislation.pdf.

72. See George T. Mazuzan, "'Good Science Gets Funded . . .': The Historical Evolution of Grant Making at the National Science Foundation," *Science Communication* 14, no. 1 (1992); Melinda Baldwin, "Scientific Autonomy, Public Accountability, and the Rise of 'Peer Review' in the Cold War United States," *Isis* 109, no. 3 (2018): 544–547.

73. "Budget," National Institutes of Health, accessed April 14, 2021, https://www.nih.gov/about-nih/what-we-do/budget.

74. For a list of NSF-funded achievements, see "Nifty 50," National Science Foundation, accessed March 22, 2021, https://www.nsf.gov/about/history/nifty50/index.jsp.

75. Bush, *Science*, 13–14.

76. See Roger Pielke Jr., "'Basic Research' as a Political Symbol," *Minerva* 50 (2012): 344.

77. Damian Garde and Jonathan Saltzman, "The Story of mRNA: How a Once-Dismissed Idea Became a Leading Technology in the Covid Vaccine Race," *STAT*, November 10, 2020, https://www.statnews.com/2020/11/10/the-story-of-mrna-how-a-once-dismissed-idea-became-a-leading-technology-in-the-covid-vaccine-race/.

78. See Ellen Schrecker, "Subversives, Squeaky Wheels, and 'Special Obligations': Threats to Academic Freedom, 1890–1960," *Social Research* 76, no. 2 (2009): 513–540.

79. See Stephen H. Aby, "Discretion over Valor: The AAUP during the McCarthy Years," *American Educational History Journal* 36, no. 1 (2009): 126; and John R. Thelin, *A History of American Higher Education* (Baltimore: Johns Hopkins University Press, 2004), 275.

80. Joanne Cavanaugh Simpson, "Seeing Red," *Johns Hopkins Magazine* (September 2000): https://pages.jh.edu/jhumag/0900web/red.html; Lionel S. Lewis, *The Cold War and Academic Governance: The Lattimore Case at Johns Hopkins* (New York: State University of New York Press, 1993).

81. See Aby, "Discretion over Valor," 122; Schrecker, "Subversives, Squeaky Wheels, and 'Special Obligations,'" 516.

82. Michael Hiltzik, *Big Science: Ernest Lawrence and the Invention That Launched the Military-Industrial Complex* (New York: Simon & Schuster, 2016), 333.

83. See John McCumber, "Time in the Ditch: American Philosophy and the McCarthy Era," *Diacritics* 26, no. 1 (1996): 33–49.

84. *A History in Highlights, 1950–2000* (Alexandria, VA: National Science Board, 2000), https://www.nsf.gov/nsb/documents/2000/nsb00215/nsb00215.pdf, p. 11; *The First Annual Report of the National Science Foundation, 1950–51* (Washington, DC: US Government Printing Office, 1951), 26.

85. Joy Rohde, *Armed with Expertise: The Militarization of American Social Research* (Ithaca, NY: Cornell University Press, 2013).

86. Rohde, *Armed with Expertise*, 24.

87. Dwight D. Eisenhower, *Public Papers of the Presidents of the United States, 1953* (Washington, DC: US Government Printing Office, 1960), 293.

88. Office of Technology Assessment, *History of the Department of Defense Federally Funded Research and Development Centers* (Washington, DC: US Government Printing Office, 1995), 17

89. See Ron Robin, *The Making of the Cold War Enemy: Culture and Politics in the Military-Intellectual Complex* (Princeton, NJ: Princeton University Press, 2003), 5; Rohde, *Armed with Expertise,* 48–53.

90. American Academy of Arts and Sciences, "Bachelor's Degrees in the Humanities," Humanities Indicators, accessed March 22, 2021, https://www .amacad.org/humanities-indicators/higher-education/bachelors-degrees-humanities. For the purposes of counting, the "humanities" in this case include English language and literature, history, philosophy, classics, linguistics, and languages and literatures other than English.

91. *Report of the Commission on the Humanities* (New York: American Council of Learned Societies, 1964), 6.

92. "National Endowment for the Humanities (NEH) Funding Levels," Humanities Indicators, https://www.humanitiesindicators.org/content /indicatorDoc.aspx?i=75. Dollar amounts are adjusted for inflation.

93. Richard Macksey and Eugenio Donato, eds., *The Structuralist Controversy: The Languages of Criticism and the Sciences of Man*, 40th anniversary ed. (Baltimore: Johns Hopkins University Press, 2007), xxi–xxv.

94. Bret McCabe, "Structuralism's Samson," *Johns Hopkins Magazine* (Fall 2012): https://hub.jhu.edu/magazine/2012/fall/structuralisms-samson/.

95. Cynthia L. Haven, *Evolution of Desire: A Life of René Girard* (East Lansing: Michigan State University Press, 2018), 121–123.

96. See Thomas Kuhn, *The Structure of Scientific Revolutions* (Chicago: University of Chicago Press, 1962).

97. See Ullica Segerstråle, ed., *Beyond the Science Wars: The Missing Discourse about Science and Society* (New York: State University of New York Press, 2000), 1–40.

98. Robert C. Cowen, "Senator William Proxmire and the Golden Fleece," *Christian Science Monitor*, April 30, 1980, https://www.csmonitor.com/1980/0430 /043035.html.

99. Norman Levitt and Paul Gross, *Higher Superstition: The Academic Left and Its Quarrels* (Baltimore: Johns Hopkins University Press, 1994), 3.

100. See Segerstråle, *Beyond the Science Wars*, 23–24.

101. Jennifer Ruark, "Bait and Switch: How the Physicist Alan Sokal Hoodwinked a Group of Humanists and Why, 20 Years Later, It Still Matters," *Chronicle of Higher Education*, January 1, 2017; Richard Rorty, "Phony Science Wars," *The*

Atlantic (November 1999): https://www.theatlantic.com/magazine/archive/1999/11/phony-science-wars/377882/.

102. Bruno Latour, "Why Has Critique Run Out of Steam? From Matters of Fact to Matters of Concern," *Critical Inquiry* 30, no. 2 (2004): 225, 228.

103. See Derek Bok, *Universities in the Marketplace: The Commercialization of Higher Education* (Princeton, NJ: Princeton University Press, 2003), 57–78; Jonathan R. Cole, *The Great American University* (New York: PublicAffairs, 2009), 163–170; Bronwyn H. Hall, *University-Industry Research Partnerships in the United States*, Working Paper ECO No. 2004/14 (Fiesole, Italy: European University Institute, February 2004), http://cadmus.eui.eu/bitstream/id/1735/EC/.

104. "Innovation's Golden Goose," *The Economist*, December 14, 2002, https://www.economist.com/technology-quarterly/2002/12/14/innovations-golden-goose.

105. "Higher Education R&D Expenditures, by Source of Funds: FYs 1953–2018," National Science Foundation, accessed March 22, 2021, https://ncsesdata.nsf.gov/herd/2018/html/herd18-dt-tab001.html. As a percentage of all university research funding, support from businesses shot up from 2.8 percent in 1972 to 7 percent in 2000. Paul Basken, "How to Protect Your College's Research from Undue Corporate Influence," *Chronicle of Higher Education*, February 25, 2018, https://www.chronicle.com/article/How-to-Protect-Your/242616.

106. David Blumenthal, "Academic-Industrial Relationships in the Life Sciences," *New England Journal of Medicine* 349, no. 25 (2003): 2452–2459. David B. Resnik, "Conflicts of Interest in Scientific Research Related to Regulation or Litigation," *Journal of Philosophy, Science, and Law* 7, no. 1 (April 2007); Ronald Bailey, *Scrutinizing Industry-Funded Science: The Crusade against Conflicts of Interest* (New York: American Council on Science and Health, March 2008); Justin E. Bekelman, "Scope and Impact of Financial Conflicts of Interest in Biomedical Research," *JAMA* 289, no. 4 (January 22/29 2003): 454–465.

107. Bok, *Universities in the Marketplace*, 2.

108. David Blumenthal, Michael Gluck, Karen S. Louis, Michael A. Stoto, and David Wise, "University-Industry Research Relationships in Biotechnology: Implications for the University," *Science* 232, no. 4756 (June 13, 1986): 1361–1366; David Blumenthal, Eric G. Campbell, Nancyanne Causino, and Karen Seashore Louis, "Participation of Life-Science Faculty in Research Relationships with Industry," *New England Journal of Medicine* 335 (December 5, 1996): 1734–1739; and Bekelman, "Scope and Impact of Financial Conflicts."

109. Rick Weiss and Deborah Nelson, "Penn Settles Gene Therapy Suit," *Washington Post*, November 4, 2000; Robin Fretwell Wilson, "The Death of Jesse Gelsinger: New Evidence of the Influence of Money and Prestige in Human Research," *American Journal of Law and Medicine* 36 (2010): 295–325.

110. Weiss and Nelson, "Penn Settles Gene Therapy Suit."

111. Headlines like "Flawed Study Helps Doctors Profit on Drug" and "How a Drug Firm Paid for a University Study—Then Undermined It" became increasingly common during this period.

112. Wilson, "Death of Jesse Gelsinger."

113. Sheldon Krimsky, "Combatting the Funding Effect in Science: What's Beyond Transparency?," *Stanford Law and Policy Review* 21 (2010): 87.

114. M. K. R. Shohara, A. Schissel, and D. Rennie, "Policies on Faculty Conflicts of Interest at US Universities," *Journal of the American Medical Association* 284, no. 17 (2000): 2203–2208; National Academies of Sciences, Engineering, and Medicine, *Fostering Integrity in Research* (Washington, DC: National Academies Press, 2017), table 4-1; National Academies of Sciences, Engineering, and Medicine, *Optimizing the Nation's Investment in Academic Research: A New Regulatory Framework for the 21st Century* (Washington, DC: National Academies Press, 2016), 85–89.

115. "Policy of the American Society of Gene Therapy: Financial Conflict of Interest in Clinical Research," American Society of Gene Therapy, adopted April 5, 2000, https://ccnmtl.columbia.edu/projects/rcr/rcr_conflicts/misc/Ref/AGST_CoI .pdf; "American Society of Clinical Oncology: Revised Conflict of Interest Policy," *Journal of Clinical Oncology* 21, no. 12 (2003): 2394–2396.

116. National Academies, *Fostering Integrity in Research*, table 4-1; Richard S. Saver, "Financial Conflicts in the New Era of Sunshine: What We Know and Still Need to Know," *Indiana Health Law Review* 15 (2018): 67–71.

117. David Randall and Christopher Welser, *The Irreproducibility Crisis of Modern Science* (New York: National Association of Scholars, 2018), 11.

118. Michael Schulson, "Science's 'Reproducibility Crisis' Is Being Used as Political Ammunition," *Wired*, April, 20, 2018, https://www.wired.com/story /sciences-reproducibility-crisis-is-being-used-as-political-ammunition/.

119. Robinson Meyer, "Congress and Trump Won't 'Terminate the EPA,'" *The Atlantic*, February 16, 2017, https://www.theatlantic.com/science/archive/2017/02 /congress-wont-terminate-the-epa/516918/.

120. *Making the EPA Great Again, Hearing before the Comm. on Science, Space, and Technology*, 115th Cong. (2017), https://www.govinfo.gov/content/pkg/CHRG -115hhrg24628/html/CHRG-115hhrg24628.htm.

121. Heidi Vogt, "EPA Wants New Rules to Rely Solely on Public Data," *Wall Street Journal*, April 24, 2018, https://www.wsj.com/articles/epa-wants-new-rules-to -rely-solely-on-public-data-1524599432.

122. Naomi Oreskes, "Beware: Transparency Rule Is a Trojan Horse," *Nature*, May 22, 2018.

123. Rachel Frazin, "Court Tosses Trump EPA's 'Secret Science' Rule," *The Hill*, February 1, 2021.

124. Quoted in Friedrich Steinle, "Stability and Replication of Experimental Results: A Historical Perspective," in *Reproducibility: Principles, Problems, Practices,*

and Prospects, ed. Harald Atmanspacher and Sabine Maasen (New York: Wiley, 2016), 43.

125. Robert Boyle, "The Second Essay, of Un-Succeeding Experiments," Early English Books Online, accessed March 22, 2021, https://quod.lib.umich.edu/e /eebo/A28944.0001.001/1:9?rgn=div1;view=fulltext.

126. See John P. A. Ioannidis, "Why Most Published Research Findings Are False," *PLoS Medicine* 2, no. 8 (2005): e124.

127. Colin F. Camerer et al., "Evaluating the Replicability of Social Science Experiments in Nature and Science between 2010 and 2015," *Nature Human Behavior* 2 (2018): 637–644.

128. Ed Yong, "How Reliable Are Psychology Studies?," *The Atlantic*, August 27, 2015, https://www.theatlantic.com/science/archive/2015/08/psychology -studies-reliability-reproducability-nosek/402466/.

129. See Andrew C. Chang and Phillip Li, *Is Economics Research Replicable? Sixty Published Papers from Thirteen Journals Say "Usually Not,"* Finance and Economics Discussion Series 2015-083 (Washington, DC: Board of Governors of the Federal Reserve System, 2015), http://dx.doi.org/10.17016/FEDS.2015.083.

130. C. Glenn Begley and Lee M. Ellis, "Raise Standards for Preclinical Cancer Research," *Nature* 483 (2012): 532.

131. Lee Kennedy-Schaffer, "Before $p < 0.05$ to beyond $p < 0.05$: Using History to Contextualize p-Values and Significance Testing," *American Statistician* 73, suppl. 1 (2019): 82–90; Tukur Dahiru, "*P*-Value, a True Test of Statistical Significance? A Cautionary Note," *Annals of Ibadan Postgraduate Medicine* 6, no. 1 (June 2008): 21–26.

132. Lee Kennedy-Schaffer, "Before $p < 0.05$ to Beyond $p < 0.05$: Using History to Contextualize p-Values and Significance Testing," *American Statistician* 73, no. 1 (2019): 84.

133. Donald Mainland, "Statistical Ritual in Clinical Journals: Is There a Cure?—I," *BMJ* 288 (March 17, 1984): 842.

134. E. J. Masicampo and Daniel R. Lalande, "A Peculiar Prevalence of p Values Just below .05," *Quarterly Journal of Experimental Psychology* 65, no. 11 (2012): 2271–2279; J. Ridley, N. Kolm, R. P. Freckelton, and M. J. G. Gage, "An Unexpected Influence of Widely Used Significance Thresholds on the Distribution of Reported *P*-Values," *Journal of Evolutionary Biology* 20, no. 3 (2007): 1082–1089; Megan L. Head, Luke Holman, Rob Lanfear, Andrew T. Kahn, and Michael D. Jennions, "The Extent and Consequences of p-Hacking in Science," *PLoS Biology* 13, no. 3 (2015): e1002106.

135. Quoted in Ed Yong, "The Inevitable Evolution of Bad Science," *The Atlantic,* September 21, 2016, https://www.theatlantic.com/science/archive/2016 /09/the-inevitable-evolution-of-bad-science/500609/.

136. Monya Baker, "1,500 Scientists Lift the Lid on Reproducibility," *Nature*, May 25, 2016, https://www.nature.com/news/1-500-scientists-lift-the-lid-on -reproducibility-1.19970.

137. See Daniel Engber, "Is Science Broken?," *Slate*, August 21, 2017; "Scientists Who Cheat," *New York Times*, June 1, 2015; "How Science Goes Wrong," *The Economist*, October 21, 2013.

138. See Friederike Hendriks, Dorothe Kienhuesand, and Rainer Bromme, "Replication Crisis = Trust Crisis? The Effect of Successful vs Failed Replications on Laypeople's Trust in Researchers and Research," *Public Understanding of Science* 29, no. 3 (2020): 270–288; Niels G. Mede, Mike S. Schäfer, Ricarda Ziegler, and Markus Weißkopf, "The 'Replication Crisis' in the Public Eye: Germans' Awareness and Perceptions of the (Ir)reproducibility of Scientific Research," *Public Understanding of Science* 30, no. 1 (2021): 91–102.

139. Kai Kupferschmidt, "More and More Scientists Are Preregistering Their Studies. Should You?," *Science*, September 21, 2018, https://www.sciencemag.org /news/2018/09/more-and-more-scientists-are-preregistering-their-studies-should -you; Brian A. Nosek and D. Stephen Lindsay, "Preregistration Becoming the Norm in Psychological Science," Association for Psychological Science, February 28, 2018, https://www.psychologicalscience.org/observer/preregistration -becoming-the-norm-in-psychological-science.

140. Lucy Goodchild van Hilten, "Why It's Time to Publish Research 'Failures,'" *Elsevier Connect*, May 5, 2015, https://www.elsevier.com/connect/scientists -we-want-your-negative-results-too.

141. "Negative Results: A Crucial Piece of the Scientific Puzzle," *PLOS One*, October 26, 2017, https://everyone.plos.org/2017/10/26/negative-results-a-crucial -piece-of-the-scientific-puzzle/.

142. Ed Yong, "In Science, There Should Be a Prize for Second Place," *The Atlantic*, February 1, 2018.

143. Allan Drazen, Anna Dreber, Erkut Y. Ozbay, and Erik Snowberg, *A Journal-Based Replication of "Being Chosen to Lead,"* Working Paper 20-064 (Cambridge, MA: Harvard Business School, 2019).

144. Arturo Casadevall and Ferric C. Fang, "Is Science in Crisis?," *Baltimore Sun*, July 25, 2015; Arturo Casadevall and Ferric C. Fang, "Reproducible Science," *Infection and Immunity* 77, no. 6 (2009): 2367–2375.

145. Gundula Bosch, "Train PhD Students to Be Thinkers Not Just Specialists," *Nature*, February 4, 2018, https://www.nature.com/articles/d41586-018-01853-1. For an account of the origins and aims of the R3 curriculum, see David Epstein, *Range: Why Generalists Triumph in a Specialized World* (New York: Riverhead Books, 2019), 275–279.

146. Sally Rockey, "What Are the Chances of Getting Funded?," *Extramural Nexus*, June 29, 2015, https://nexus.od.nih.gov/all/2015/06/29/what-are-the -chances-of-getting-funded/.

147. National Academies of Sciences, Engineering, and Medicine, *The Next Generation of Biomedical and Behavioral Sciences Researchers: Breaking Through* (Washington, DC: National Academies Press, 2018), 2.

148. Bruce Alberts, Marc W. Kirschner, Shirley Tilghman, and Harold Varmus, "Rescuing US Biomedical Research from Its Systemic Flaws," *Proceedings of the National Academy of Sciences* 111, no. 16 (2014): 5773, 5774.

149. See *Diminishing Funding and Rising Expectations: Trends and Challenges for Public Research Universities* (Washington, DC: National Science Foundation, 2012), https://www.nsf.gov/nsb/sei/companion2/files/nsb1245.pdf; John Bound, Breno Braga, Gaurav Khanna, and Sarah Turner, *Public Universities: The Supply Side of Building a Skilled Workforce*, Working Paper 25945 (Cambridge, MA: National Bureau of Economic Research, June 2019).

150. See James Manyika, William H. McRaven, and Adam Segal, *Innovation and National Security: Keeping Our Edge* (New York: Council on Foreign Relations, 2019); Caleb Foote and Robert D. Atkinson, "Federal Support for R&D Continues Its Ignominious Slide," Information Technology and Innovation Foundation, August 12, 2019, https://itif.org/publications/2019/08/12/federal-support-rd -continues-its-ignominious-slide; James Pethokoukis, "US Federal Research Spending Is at a 60-Year Low. Should We Be Concerned?," American Enterprise Institute, May 11, 2020, https://www.aei.org/economics/us-federal-research -spending-is-at-a-60-year-low-should-we-be-concerned/.

151. Thomas Lin, "Cracking Open the Scientific Process," *New York Times*, January 16, 2012.

152. *Science as an Open Enterprise* (London: Royal Society Science Center, 2012), 7.

153. Lindsay McKenzie, "Sci-Hub's Cache of Pirated Papers Is So Big, Subscription Journals Are Doomed, Data Analyst Suggests," *Science*, July 27, 2017, https://www.sciencemag.org/news/2017/07/sci-hub-s-cache-pirated-papers-so-big -subscription-journals-are-doomed-data-analyst.

154. "UC Secures Landmark Open Access Deal with World's Largest Scientific Publisher," UC Office of the President, March 16, 2021, https://www .universityofcalifornia.edu/press-room/uc-news-uc-secures-landmark-open-access -deal-world-s-largest-scientific-publisher.

155. Adam Seigel, "Prediction Markets Give Hope to Reproducibility Crisis in Scientific Experiments," Cultivate Labs, accessed April 14, 2021, https://www .cultivatelabs.com/posts/prediction-markets-give-hope-to-reproducibility-crisis-in -scientific-experiments.

156. Kelsey Piper, "Science Has Been in a 'Replication Crisis' for a Decade. Have We Learned Anything?," *Vox*, October 14, 2020, https://www.vox.com/future -perfect/21504366/science-replication-crisis-peer-review-statistics.

157. Anna Dreber, Thomas Pfeiffer, Johan Almenberg, Siri Isaksson, Brad Wilson, Yiling Chen, Brian A. Nosek, and Magnus Johannesson, "Using Prediction Markets to Estimate the Reproducibility of Scientific Research," *PNAS* 112, no. 50 (2015), e15344.

158. Colin F. Camerer et al., "Evaluating the Replicability of Social Science Experiments in *Nature* and *Science* between 2010 and 2015," *Nature Human Behaviour* 72, no. 12 (September 2018): 637–644.

159. Dreber et al., "Using Prediction Markets."

160. "Crisis in Democracy: Renewing Trust in America," Knight Commission on Trust, Media and Democracy, February 4, 2019, https://knightfoundation.org/reports/crisis-in-democracy-renewing-trust-in-america/.

161. "Show Your Work: The New Terms for Trust in Journalism," *PressThink*, December 31, 2017.

162. "America's Great Divide," PBS.org, accessed January 26, 2021, https://www.pbs.org/wgbh/frontline/interview-collection/americas-great-divide/about-this-project/.

163. "The Washington Post Launches 'How to Be a Journalist' Video Series," *Washington Post*, December 8, 2017, https://www.washingtonpost.com/pr/wp/2017/12/08/the-washington-post-launches-how-to-be-a-journalist-video-series/.

164. See Kai Kupferschmidt, "'A Completely New Culture of Doing Research.' Coronavirus Outbreak Changes How Scientists Communicate," *Science*, February 26, 2020, https://www.sciencemag.org/news/2020/02/completely-new-culture-doing-research-coronavirus-outbreak-changes-how-scientists.

165. "Preprints and Rapid Communication of COVID-19 research," ASAPBio, accessed March 22, 2021, https://asapbio.org/preprints-and-covid-19; Diana Kwon, "How Swamped Preprint Servers Are Blocking Bad Coronavirus Research," *Nature*, May 7, 2020, https://www.nature.com/articles/d41586-020-01394-6.

166. Amalie Trewartha and John Dagdelen, "We Built an AI-powered Search Tool for 60,000 COVID-19 Research Papers," Fast Company, May 14, 2020, https://www.fastcompany.com/90504265/we-built-an-ai-powered-search-tool-for-60000-covid-19-research-papers.

167. Holly Else, "How a Torrent of COVID Science Changed Research Publishing—In Seven Charts," *Nature*, December 16, 2020, https://www.nature.com/articles/d41586-020-03564-y.

168. Kupferschmidt, "'Completely New Culture of Doing Research.'"

169. Kwon, "How Swamped Preprint Servers Are Blocking Bad Coronavirus Research"; Ivan Oransky and Adam Marcus, "Quick Retraction of a Faulty Coronavirus Paper Was a Good Moment for Science," *STAT*, February 3, 2020, https://www.statnews.com/2020/02/03/retraction-faulty-coronavirus-paper-good-moment-for-science/; Holly Else, "How to Bring Preprints to the Charged Field of Medicine," *Nature*, June 6, 2019, https://www.nature.com/articles/d41586-019-01806-2.

170. Jason Beaubien, "WHO Halts Hydroxychloroquine Trial over Safety Concerns," National Public Radio, May 25, 2020, https://www.npr.org/sections/coronavirus-live-updates/2020/05/25/861913688/who-halts-hydroxychloroquine-trial-over-safety-concerns.

171. Catherine Offord, "The Surgisphere Scandal: What Went Wrong?," *The Scientist*, October 1, 2020, https://www.the-scientist.com/features/the-surgisphere-scandal-what-went-wrong--67955.

172. See Andrew Joseph, "Lancet, New England Journal Retract COVID-19 Studies, Including One That Raised Safety Concerns about Malaria Drugs," *STATNews*, June 4, 2020; Sarah Bosley and Melissa Davey, "COVID-19: Lancet Retracts Paper That Halted Hydroxychloroquine Trials," *The Guardian*, June 4, 2020, https://www.theguardian.com/world/2020/jun/04/covid-19-lancet-retracts-paper-that-halted-hydroxychloroquine-trials.

173. Allysia Finley, "The Lancet's Politicized Science on Antimalarial Drugs," *Wall Street Journal*, June 1, 2020.

174. The effect of open peer review on disadvantaged groups is still unclear, with studies showing contrasting results. Charles W. Fox and C. E. Timothy Paine, "Gender Differences in Peer Review Outcomes and Manuscript Impact at Six Journals of Ecology and Evolution," *Ecology and Evolution* 9, no. 6 (2019): 3599–3619, showed that "papers with female first authors obtained, on average, slightly worse peer review scores and were more likely to be rejected after peer review" than those with male first authors. Amelia R. Cox and Robert Montgomerie, "The Case for and against Double-Blind Reviews," *PeerJ* 7 (2019): e6702, found no gender bias in peer review of ornithology journals, but discussed papers showing double-blind reviewing may reduce institutional and geographic biases as well as the incidence of nepotism.

FOUR: Purposeful Pluralism

1. John Stuart Mill, *The Principles of Political Economy: With Some of Their Applications to Social Philosophy*, book v, chap. xvii, sec. 3 (1848), 594.

2. Jurgen Habermas, *The Structural Transformation of the Public Sphere: An Inquiry into a Category of Bourgeois Society*, trans. Thomas Burger (Cambridge: Massachusetts Institute of Technology Press, 1992), 36.

3. Cass Sunstein, "Is the Internet Really a Blessing for Democracy?," *Boston Review* (Summer 2001): https://bostonreview.net/archives/BR26.3/sunstein.html.

4. See Bill Bishop, *The Big Sort: Why the Clustering of Like-Minded America Is Tearing Us Apart* (Boston, MA: Houghton Mifflin, 2008); James A. Thomson and Jesse Sussell, *Are Changing Constituencies Driving Rising Polarization in the U.S. House of Representatives?* (Santa Monica, CA: RAND Corporation, 2015); Andrew Garner and Harvey Palmer, "Polarization and Issue Consistency over Time," *Political Behavior* 33 (2011): 225–246; James G. Gimpel and Iris Hui, "Inadvertent and Intentional Partisan Residential Sorting," *Annals of Regional Science* 58, no. 3 (May 2017); Matt Motyl, "Liberals and Conservatives Are (Geographically) Dividing," in *Bridging Ideological Divides: The Claremont Symposium for Applied Social Psychology*, ed. P. Valdesolo and J. Graham (Newbury Park, CA: Sage, 2016).

5. See Ross Butters and Christopher Hare, "Polarized Networks? New Evidence on American Voters' Political Discussion Networks," *Political Behavior* (2020).

6. See Diana Mutz, *Hearing the Other Side: Deliberative versus Participatory Democracy* (New York: Cambridge University Press, 2006).

7. See Jean M. Twenge, W. Keith Campbell, and Nathan T. Carter, "Declines in Trust in Others and Confidence in Institutions among American Adults and Late Adolescents, 1972–2012," *Psychological Science* 25, no. 10 (2014): 1914–1923; Kevin Vallier, "Why Are Americans So Distrustful of Each Other?," *Wall Street Journal*, December 17, 2020, https://www.wsj.com/articles/why-are-americans-so-distrustful -of-each-other-11608217988.

8. "Partisanship and Political Animosity in 2016," Pew Research Center, June 22, 2016, https://www.pewresearch.org/politics/2016/06/22/partisanship-and -political-animosity-in-2016/.

9. Shanto Iyengar, Gaurav Sood, and Yphtach Lelkes, "Affect, Not Ideology: A Social Identity Perspective on Polarization," *Public Opinion Quarterly* 76, no. 3 (2012): 419.

10. Iyengar et al., "Affect, Not Ideology," 417. See also *Political Polarization in the American Public* (Washington, DC: Pew Research Center, 2014), 48.

11. Iyengar et al., "Affect, Not Ideology."

12. James Gimpel and Iris Hui, "Seeking Politically Compatible Neighbors? The Role of Neighborhood Partisan Composition in Residential Sorting," *Political Geography* 48 (February 2015).

13. M. J. Crockett, "Moral Outrage in the Digital Age," *Nature Human Behavior* (2017): 771.

14. See William J. Bowen and Derek Bok, *The Shape of the River: Long-Term Consequences of Considering Race in College and University Admissions* (Princeton, NJ: Princeton University Press, 1998), 231; and Thomas J. Espenshade and Alexandria Walton Radford, *No Longer Separate, Not Yet Equal: Race and Class in Elite College Admission and Campus Life* (Princeton, NJ: Princeton University Press, 2009), 183.

15. Patricia Gurin, "Expert Report of Patricia Gurin," *Michigan Journal of Race and Law* 5 (1999): 387. Studies in this area present challenges, and some of Gurin's findings drew criticism in the months and years after her report. Broadly speaking, however, subsequent analyses have borne out her conclusions, with studies continuing to show that interactional diversity in college is connected to a wide range of educational and civic outcomes. James H. Kuklinski, "The Scientific Study of Campus Diversity and Students' Educational Outcomes," *Public Opinion Quarterly* 70, no. 1 (Spring 2016): 99–120; Nicholas A. Bowman, "Promoting Participation in a Diverse Democracy: A Meta-Analysis of College Diversity Experiences and Civic Engagement," *Review of Educational Research* 81, no. 1 (March 2010); Nicholas A. Bowman, "College Diversity Experiences and Cognitive Development; A Meta-Analysis," *Review of Educational Research* 81, no. 1 (March 2010); Gary Pike and George Kuh, "Relationships among Structural

Diversity, Informal Peer Interactions and Perceptions of the Campus Environment," *Review of Higher Education* 29, no. 4 (2006): 425–450.

16. See Beverly Tatum, *Why Are the Black Kids Sitting Together in the Cafeteria?* (New York: Basic Books, 1997).

17. Carla Yanni, *Living on Campus: An Architectural History of the American Dormitory* (Minneapolis: University of Minnesota Press, 2019), 8–9.

18. "Magistrates and Ministers of the Massachusetts, August 21, 1671," in *The Correspondence of John Owen (1616–1683): With an Account of His Life and Work*, ed. Peter Toon (Eugene, OR: Wipf and Stock, 2018), 150.

19. "From George Washington to Robert Brooke, 16 March 1795," Founders Online, accessed March 24, 2021, https://founders.archives.gov/documents /Washington/05-17-02-0443, emphasis added.

20. Colin Burke, *American Collegiate Populations: A Test of the Traditional View* (New York: New York University Press, 1982), 109.

21. See Gordon S. Wood, *Empire of Liberty: A History of the Early Republic, 1789–1815* (New York: Oxford University Press, 2009), 343–344; and Alan Taylor, *Thomas Jefferson's Education* (New York: W. W. Norton, 2019), 268.

22. George Ticknor, *The Life of William Prescott* (Philadelphia: J. B. Lippincott, 1863). See also Richard Stott, *Jolly Fellows: Male Milieus in Nineteenth-Century America* (Baltimore: Johns Hopkins University Press, 2009).

23. Samuel Taylor Coleridge, *Annotated Copy of Shakespeare* (London: 1807), https://www.bl.uk/collection-items/coleridges-annotated-copy-of-shakespeare; see Stott, *Jolly Fellows*, 26–30.

24. See Helen Lefkowitz Horowitz, *Campus Life: Undergraduate Cultures from the End of the Eighteenth Century to the Present* (New York: Alfred A. Knopf, 1987).

25. Lowell Simpson, "The Little Republics: Undergraduate Literary Societies at Columbia, Dartmouth, Princeton, and Yale, 1753–1865" (EdD diss., Columbia University, 1976), 1.

26. Quoted in Simpson, "The Little Republics," 44.

27. See James McLachlan, "The *Choice of Hercules*: American Student Societies in the Early 19th Century," in *The University in Society: Europe, Scotland, and the United States from the 16th to the 20th Century*, vol. 2, ed. Lawrence Stone (Princeton, NJ: Princeton University Press, 1974), 472.

28. Cyrus Hamlin, *My Life and Times* (Boston: Congregational Sunday-School and Publishing Society, 1893), 122.

29. Thomas Spencer Harding, *College Literary Societies: Their Contribution to Higher Education in the United States, 1815–1876* (New York: Pageant, 1971), 45.

30. Harding, *College Literary Societies*, 193–194.

31. Brooks Mather Kelley, *Yale: A History* (New Haven, CT: Yale University Press, 1974), 222.

32. *Yale Literary Magazine* 17, no. 1 (October 1851): 36. The magazine promised a statement explaining the dissolution; it appears to have never been published.

33. See Nicholas L. Syrett, *The Company He Keeps: A History of White College Fraternities* (Chapel Hill: University of North Carolina Press, 2009), 162.

34. Eric Foner, "South Carolina's Forgotten Black Political Revolution," *Slate*, January 31, 2018, https://slate.com/human-interest/2018/01/the-many-black -americans-who-held-public-office-during-reconstruction-in-southern-states-like -south-carolina.html; Stephen Middleton, *Black Congressmen during Reconstruction: A Documentary Sourcebook* (New York: Praeger, 2002).

35. Shannon H. Wilson, *Berea College: An Illustrated History* (Lexington: University Press of Kentucky, 2006), 2.

36. Wilson, *Berea College*, 23.

37. Quoted in Marion B. Lucas, "Berea College in the 1870s and 1880s," *Register of the Kentucky Historical Society* 98, no. 1 (2000): 9–10.

38. Michael David Cohen, *Reconstructing the Campus: Higher Education and the American Civil War* (Charlottesville: University of Virginia Press, 2012), 119.

39. T. McCants Stewart, "From South Carolina," *New National Era*, July 9, 1874, 1.

40. Charles William Eliot, "Aims of Higher Education," in *Educational Reform: Essays and Addresses* (New York: Century, 1898), 239.

41. Charles William Eliot, "Liberty in Education," in *The Rise of the Research University: A Sourcebook*, ed. Louis Menand, Paul Reitter, and Chad Wellmon (Chicago: University of Chicago Press, 2017), 278.

42. "Secretary's Report of the Class of 1870," Hathi Trust Digital Library, accessed March 24, 2021, https://babel.hathitrust.org/cgi/pt?id=hvd.3204410 7297053&view=1up&seq=11, pp. 5–6.

43. "Secretary's First Report of the Class of 1909," Hathi Trust Digital Library, accessed March 24, 2021, https://babel.hathitrust.org/cgi/pt?id=hvd.3204410 7299174&view=1up&seq=31, pp. 12–13, 15–16.

44. Eliot, "Aims," 239.

45. Charles William Eliot to Bruce L. Keenan, August 9, 1907, quoted in Marcia G. Synnott, "The Admission and Assimilation of Minority Students at Harvard, Yale, and Princeton, 1900–1970," *History of Education Quarterly* 19, no. 3 (Autumn 1979): 293.

46. Charles William Eliot, "The Private Dormitory," *Religious Education* 4, no. 1 (April 1909): 58.

47. A. Lawrence Lowell, "Inaugural Address," *Harvard Graduates' Magazine* 18, no. 70 (December 1909): 220.

48. See John J. Farrell, "The Catholic Chaplain at the Secular University," July 11, 1907, Hathi Trust Digital Library, accessed April 9, 2021, https://babel .hathitrust.org/cgi/pt?id=hvd.32044079786646&view=1up&seq=1, 8; and John Whitney Evans, *The Newman Movement: Roman Catholics in American Higher Education* (Notre Dame, IN: University of Notre Dame Press, 1980), 47.

49. In 1910, W. E. B. Du Bois surveyed 107 colleges (excluding historically Black colleges and universities) to assess how many Black students attended and graduated. He found that from 1880 to 1884, these schools collectively graduated 36 Black

students; from 1905 to 1909, that number had risen to 149. See W. E. B. Du Bois, *The College-Bred Negro American* (Atlanta: Atlanta University Press, 1910).

50. John Whitney Evans, "The Newman Idea in Wisconsin, 1883–1920," *Wisconsin Magazine of History* 54, no. 3 (1971): 205.

51. See Daniel Greene, *The Jewish Origins of Cultural Pluralism: The Menorah Association and American Diversity* (Bloomington: Indiana University Press, 2011), 35, 38.

52. Jenna Weissman Joselit, "Without Ghettoism: A History of the Intercollegiate Menorah Association, 1906–1930," *American Jewish Archives* 30 (1978): 141n20.

53. "Lionel Trilling to Elliot Cohen, December 2, 1929," in *Life in Culture: Selected Letters of Lionel Trilling*, ed. Adam Kirsch (New York: Farrar, Straus and Giroux, 2018), 32.

54. See Deborah E. Whaley, "Links, Legacies, and Letters: A Cultural History of Black Greek-Letter Organizations," in *Brothers and Sisters: Diversity in College Fraternities and Sororities*, ed. Craig L. Torbenson and Gregory S. Parks (Cranbury, NJ: Rosemont, 2009), 58–59.

55. Carol Kammen, *Part and Apart: The Black Experience at Cornell, 1865–1945* (Ithaca, NY: Cornell University Library, 2009), 47.

56. Felix L. Armfield, Stefan M. Bradley, Kenneth I. Clarke Sr., Gregory S. Parks, and Jeremy M. Harp, "Defining the 'Alpha' Identity," in *Alpha Phi Alpha: A Legacy of Greatness, the Demands of Transcendence*, ed. Gregory S. Parks and Stefan M. Bradley (Lexington: University Press of Kentucky, 2012), 40.

57. See Christine G. O'Malley, "'First of All': The Founding of Alpha Phi Alpha and the Search for Fraternal Space at Cornell University, 1905–1920," *Building and Landscapes: Journal of the Vernacular Architecture Forum* 26, no. 1 (2019): 48–72; Andre McKenzie, "In the Beginning: The Early History of the Divine Nine," in *African American Fraternities and Sororities: The Legacy and the Vision*, ed. Tamara L. Brown, Gregory S. Parks, and Clarenda M. Phillips (Lexington: University Press of Kentucky, 2005), 181–210; Whaley, "Links, Legacies, and Letters."

58. See Sarah Turner and John Bound, *Closing the Gap or Widening the Divide: The Effects of the G.I. Bill and World War II on the Educational Outcomes of Black Americans*, Working Paper 9044 (Washington, DC: National Bureau of Economic Research, 2002); Suzanne Mettler, "'The Only Good Thing Was the G.I. Bill': Effects of the Education and Training Provisions on African-American Veterans' Political Participation," *Studies in American Political Development* 19 (2005): 31–52.

59. John R. Thelin, *A History of American Higher Education* (Baltimore: Johns Hopkins University Press, 2011), 305.

60. Calvin H. Plimpton quoted in Anthony S. Chen and Lisa M. Stulberg, "Before *Bakke*: The Hidden History of the Diversity Rationale," University of Chicago Law Review Online, October 30, 2020, https://lawreviewblog.uchicago.edu/2020/10/30/aa-chen-stulberg/.

61. See Gareth Davies, "Richard Nixon and the Desegregation of Southern Schools," *Journal of Policy History* 19, no. 4 (2007): 367–394.

62. See Peter Wallenstein, "Black Southerners and Non-Black Universities: Desegregating Higher Education, 1935–1967," *History of Higher Education Annual* 19 (1999): 121–148.

63. William L. Tetlow Jr., "Preliminary Investigations on the Academic Performance of Minority Group Students at Cornell University" (presented at the 137th Annual Meeting of the American Association for the Advancement of Science, Chicago, IL, December 27, 1970).

64. Tetlow, "Preliminary Investigations," 3; Donald Alexander Downs, *Cornell '69: Liberalism and the Crisis of the American University* (Ithaca, NY: Cornell University Press, 1999), 49.

65. Tetlow, "Preliminary Investigations," 14–15.

66. Downs, *Cornell '69*, 55.

67. See Thomas Jones, *From Willard Straight to Wall Street* (Ithaca, NY: Cornell University Press, 2019).

68. See Wayne Clifford Glasker, "The Paradoxes of Integration: A Case Study of the Black Student Movement at the University of Pennsylvania, 1965–1990" (PhD diss., University of Pennsylvania, 1994), 257.

69. "Mundheim Report," *Daily Pennsylvanian* 84, no. 37 (September 17, 1968): 2.

70. Shelley Cox, "Univ. Council Sets Rules to Discipline Demonstrators," *Daily Pennsylvanian* 84, no. 3 (March 21, 1968): 5.

71. "Guidelines on Open Expression," *Daily Pennsylvanian* 84, no. 105 (February 3, 1969): 3.

72. Judith Ann Fowler, "Six Days in College Hall," *Pennsylvania Gazette* (March 1969): 15.

73. Ted Asregadoo, "A Bulwark against Radicalism: Protest Movements at the University of Pennsylvania and the Struggle for Reform, 1965–1969," *Peace and Change: A Journal of Peace Research* 42, no. 3 (2017): 428.

74. Quoted in Fowler, "Six Days in College Hall."

75. See Ernest Holsendolph, "Black Presence Grows in Higher Education," *New York Times*, November 14, 1976; "Status and Trends in the Education of Racial and Ethnic Minorities: Table 24.1," National Center for Education Statistics, accessed March 24, 2021, https://nces.ed.gov/pubs2010/2010015/tables/table_24_1.asp; Courtney Rozen, "What to Know about Affirmative Action as the Harvard Trial Begins," National Public Radio, October 16, 2018, https://www.npr.org/2018/10/16/657499646/what-to-know-about-affirmative-action-as-the-harvard-trial-begins; Gene I. Maeroff, "Issue and Debate: Court to Rule in College Admissions Case," *New York Times*, December 27, 1976.

76. The US Supreme Court did not issue a decision regarding the constitutionality of race-conscious admissions in *DeFunis v. Odegaard*, 416 U.S. 312 (1974), as it determined that the case was moot.

77. See Regents of Univ. of California v. Bakke, 438 U.S. 265 (1978), 311.

78. *Bakke*, at 312.

79. Peter Schmidt, "'Bakke' Set a New Path to Diversity for Colleges," *Chronicle of Higher Education*, June 20, 2008, https://www.chronicle.com/article/Bakke-Set-a -New-Path-to/13231.

80. Bok and Bowen, *Shape of the River*, 231.

81. Thomas J. Espenshade and Alexandria Walton Radford, *No Longer Separate, Not Yet Equal: Race and Class in Elite College Admission and Campus Life* (Princeton, NJ: Princeton University Press, 2009), 183.

82. Denise K. Magner, "Amid the Diversity, Racial Isolation Remains at Berkeley," *Chronicle of Higher Education*, November 14, 1990.

83. Ellen Uzelac, "Cultures Course Sets Off Explosive Debate at UC Berkeley," *Seattle Times*, November 27, 1988.

84. "For Berkeley, Diversity Means Many Splinters," *New York Times*, October 3, 1990.

85. "Title IX, Education Amendments of 1972," US Department of Labor, accessed April 22, 2021, https://www.dol.gov/agencies/oasam/centers-offices/civil -rights-center/statutes/title-ix.

86. Nancy Weiss Malkiel, *"Keep the Damned Women Out": The Struggle for Coeducation* (Princeton, NJ: Princeton University Press, 2016), 147.

87. Malkiel, *"Keep the Damned Women Out,"* 140, 286.

88. Karen Thorsen, "An Intimate Revolution in Campus Life: Co-Ed Dorms Put Boys and Girl Together," *Life Magazine* 69, no. 21 (November 20, 1970): 36.

89. Between 1950 and 1990, the number of international students at US colleges and universities grew by a factor of nearly fifteen, from 26,000 to more than 380,000. As of 2019, more than one million international students were enrolled in colleges and universities in the United States. See Emma Israel and Jeanne Batalova, "International Students in the United States," Migration Policy Institute, January 14, 2021, https://www.migrationpolicy.org/article/international -students-united-states-2020.

90. Anthony Depalma, "Separate Ethnic Worlds Grow on Campus," *New York Times*, May 18, 1991, 1; Mary Jordan, "College Dorms Reflect Trend of Self-Segregation," *Washington Post*, March 6, 1994, A1.

91. Jon Marcus, "Why Segregation in College Increases after Freshman Year," *The Atlantic*, September 26, 2016, https://www.theatlantic.com/education/archive /2016/09/segregated-by-dormitory/501602/.

92. See Yanni, *Living on Campus*; William Archibald Irwin, "A Study of the Historical Development of On-Campus Housing at the Ohio State University" (PhD diss., Ohio State University, 1977), 40.

93. Yanni, *Living on Campus*, 105–106, 197; Valerie Michelman, Joseph Price, and Seth D. Zimmerman, *Old Boys' Clubs and Upward Mobility among the*

Educational Elite, Working Paper 28583 (Cambridge, MA: National Bureau of Economic Research, 2021); Valerie Michelman and Bruce Sacerdote, "Peer Effects with Random Assignment: Results for Dartmouth Roommates," *Quarterly Journal of Economics*, 116, no. 2 (2001): 681–704; Alice Dembner, "Harvard Puts End to Selective Living," *Boston Globe*, June 6, 1996; Mary Jordan, "Self-Segregated Dorms a Trend and an Uproar: Universities Accede to Students' Demands, Organize Housing by Ethnicity, Race, Sexual Orientation," *Los Angeles Times*, April 3, 1994.

94. Colette Van Laar, Shana Levin, and Jim Sidanius, "Ingroup and Outgroup Contact: A Longitudinal Study of the Effects of Cross-Ethnic Friendships, Dates, Roommate Relationships and Participation in Segregated Organizations," in *Improving Intergroup Relations*, ed. Ulrich Wagner, Linda R. Tropp, Gillian Finchilescu, and Colin Tredoux (New York: Blackwell, 2008), 134; and Sarah E. Gaither and Samuel R. Sommers, "Living with an Other-Race Roommate Shapes Whites' Behavior in Subsequent Diverse Settings," *Journal of Experimental Social Psychology* 49, no. 2 (2013): 272–276.

95. See Logan Strother et al., "College Roommates Have a Modest but Significant Influence on Each Other's Political Ideology," *PNAS* 118, no. 2 (2021): 4; and Casey Klofstad, "Exposure to Political Discussion in College Is Associated with Higher Rates of Political Participation over Time," *Political Communication* 32, no. 2 (2015): 292–309.

96. Johanne Boisjoly, Greg J. Duncan, Michael Kremer, Dan M. Levy, and Jacque Eccles, "Empathy or Antipathy? The Impact of Diversity," *American Economic Review* 96, no. 5 (1890–1905); Dan Levy, Michael Kremer, Johanne Boisjoly, Greg Duncan, and Jacque Eccles, "Peer Effects, Diversity, and College Roommates in the United States," accessed April 22, 2021, https://www.povertyactionlab.org/evaluation/peer-effects-diversity-and-college-roommates-united-states.

97. Elizabeth Chuck, "Match Made on Facebook: More College Freshmen Choose Their Own Roommates," NBC News, June 26, 2015, https://www.nbcnews.com/feature/freshman-year/match-made-facebook-more-college-students-choosing-their-roommates-n381036.

98. Sarah Willets, "Surprise! Duke's Next Incoming Class Won't Get to Choose Roommates," IndyWeek, February 27, 2018, https://indyweek.com/news/archives/surprise-duke-s-next-incoming-class-get-choose-roommates/; Scott Simon, "Why Duke University Won't Honor Freshman Roommate Requests This Fall," National Public Radio, April 21, 2018, https://www.npr.org/2018/04/21/602270265/why-duke-university-wont-honor-freshman-roommate-requests-this-fall; "Why a Random Roommate Policy Builds a More Inclusive University," Duke Today, December 6, 2019, https://today.duke.edu/2019/12/why-random-roommate-policy-builds-more-inclusive-university; Diane Krieger, "USC's First-Year Roommates Use Social Media to Play the Match Game," *USC News*, August 20, 2015, https://news.usc.edu/85297/uscs-first-year-roommates-use-social-media-to-play-the-match-game/.

99. See Elizabeth Garber Paul, "The New Science of Pairing College Room-mates," *Rolling Stone*, August 19, 2014, https://www.rollingstone.com/culture/culture-news/the-new-science-of-pairing-college-roommates-192068/.

100. Nick Anderson, "Should Colleges Let Students Choose Their First Room-mate? Some Say No," *Washington Post*, June 11, 2018, https://www.washingtonpost.com/local/education/should-colleges-let-students-choose-their-first-roommate-some-say-no/2018/06/10/bd2a1d1a-4edf-11e8-af46-b1d6dc0d9bfe_story.html; Sam Zern, "First-Year Housing Selection Transitions to Fully University-Matched System," *Vanderbilt Hustler*, October 11, 2019, https://vanderbilthustler.com/26858/featured/first-year-housing-selection-transitions-to-fully-university-matched-system/.

101. Greta Anderson, "Living Together—Apart," *Inside Higher Education*, April 7, 2021, https://www.insidehighered.com/news/2021/04/07/study-finds-campus-residence-halls-have-racialized-labels; Rebecca Burns, "Luxury Private Student Housing Further Divides Rich and Poor Campuses," *Hechinger Report*, August 27, 2019, https://hechingerreport.org/luxury-private-student-housing-further-divides-rich-and-poor-on-campuses/; Ali Breland, "If the Tuition Doesn't Get You, the Cost of Student Housing Will," *Bloomberg*, August 13, 2019, https://www.bloomberg.com/news/features/2019-08-13/if-the-tuition-doesn-t-get-you-the-cost-of-student-housing-will; Jon Marcus, "Why Segregation in College Increases after Freshman Year," *The Atlantic*, September 26, 2016, https://www.theatlantic.com/education/archive/2016/09/segregated-by-dormitory/501602/.

102. Burns, "Luxury Private Student Housing."

103. Kevin Fosnacht, Robert M. Gonyea, and Polly A. Graham, "The Relation-ship of First-Year Residence Hall Roommate Assignment Policy with Interactional Diversity and Perceptions of the Campus Environment," *Journal of Higher Education* 91, no. 5 (2020): 1.

104. See Robert Putnam, *Bowling Alone: The Collapse and Revival of American Community* (New York: Simon & Schuster, 2001), 22–24.

105. J. W. Powell, "The Tyranny of the College Major," *The Atlantic*, January 24, 2014; Robert Zemsky and Lisa Banning, *Checklist for Change: Making American Higher Education a Sustainable Enterprise* (New Brunswick, NJ: Rutgers University Press, 2013), 81–83; *General Education in the 21st Century: A Report of the University of California Commission on General Education in the 21st Century* (Berkeley, CA: Center for Studies in Higher Education, 2007).

106. "Final Report: Second Commission on Undergraduate Education," Johns Hopkins University website, https://provost.jhu.edu/wp-content/uploads/sites/4/2020/11/CUE2-Final-Report.pdf.

107. "Campus Contest Stirs Controversy," *Washington Post and Times Herald*, March 18, 1956, D15.

108. Frank Newport and Brandon Busteed, "Why Are Republicans Down on Higher Ed?," Gallup, August 16, 2017, https://news.gallup.com/poll/216278/why-republicans-down-higher.aspx.

109. See Paul Lazarsfeld and Wagnar Thielens, *The Academic Mind: Social Scientists in a Time of Crisis* (Glencoe, IL: Free Press, 1958); Everett Carll Ladd Jr. and Seymour Martin Lipset, *The Divided Academy: Professors and Politics* (New York: McGraw-Hill, 1976); Michael A. Faia, "The Myth of the Liberal Professor," *Sociology of Education* 47, no. 2 (Spring 1974): 171–202.

110. See Neil Gross and Ethan Fosse, "Why Are Professors Liberal?," *Theory and Society* 41 (2012): 131.

111. Samuel J. Abrams, "There Are Conservative Professors. Just Not in These States," *New York Times*, July 1, 2016. The data show some divergence across fields, with conservatives comprising more than 20 percent of faculty in disciplines like engineering, business, and health, but less than 10 percent in most social sciences and humanities disciplines. See Abrams, "The Contented Professors: How Conservative Faculty See Themselves within the Academy," draft manuscript, 2016.

112. Mitchell Langbert, Anthony J. Quain, and Daniel B. Klein, "Faculty Voter Registration in Economics, History, Journalism, Law, and Psychology," *Econ Journal Watch* 13, no. 3 (September 2016): 423, 425. A separate report found that nearly 40 percent of the top liberal arts colleges have zero faculty members in any field who are Republican. Michael Langbert, "Homogenous: The Political Affiliations of Elite Liberal Arts College Faculty," *Academic Questions* (Summer 2018).

113. Neil Gross, *Why Are Professors Liberal and Why Do Conservatives Care?* (Cambridge, MA: Harvard University Press, 2013), 4.

114. Jeffrey Adams Sachs, "Do Universities Have a Self-Censorship Problem?," *Washington Post*, April 16, 2020; Markus Kemmelmeir, Cherry Danielson, and Jay Basten, "What's in a Grade? Academic Success and Political Orientation," *Personality and Psychology Bulletin* 31, no. 10 (2005): 1386–1399.

115. Patricia Cohen summarizes the research in "Professors' Liberalism Contagious? Maybe Not," *New York Times*, November 2, 2008, https://www.nytimes.com/2008/11/03/books/03infl.html.

116. Studies show that think tanks in particular have long served as a safe harbor for conservative intellectuals. See, for instance, Thomas Medvetz, "The Merits of Marginality: Think Tanks, Conservative Intellectuals, and the Liberal Academy," in *Professors and Their Politics*, ed. Neil Gross and Solon Simmons (Baltimore: Johns Hopkins University Press, 2014), 291–308.

117. For the close relationship between identity and to whom students gravitate as mentors, see Kevin N. Rask and Elizabeth M. Bailey, "Are Faculty Role Models? Evidence from Major Choice in an Undergraduate Institution," *Journal of Economic Education* 33, no. 2 (2002): 99–124.

118. Abby Jackson, "Liberal Colleges Are Recruiting Conservative Professors to 'Stir Up Some Trouble,'" *Business Insider*, August 10, 2017, https://www.businessinsider.com/affirmative-action-conservative-professors-liberal-colleges-2017-8.

119. Jackson, "Liberal Colleges Are Recruiting."

120. See, for instance, David Brooks, "Understanding Student Mobbists," *New York Times*, March 8, 2018, https://www.nytimes.com/2018/03/08/opinion/student-mobs.html.

121. Jesse Panuccio, "Remarks on Free Speech at the 2019 Harvard Alumni Symposium Hosted by the Harvard Law School Federalist Society Chapter," US Department of Justice, March 30, 2019, https://www.justice.gov/opa/speech/principal-deputy-associate-attorney-general-jesse-panuccio-delivers-remarks-free-speech.

122. See "Disinvitation Database," FIRE, accessed March 24, 2021, https://www.thefire.org/research/disinvitation-database.

123. Knight Foundation, *The First Amendment on Campus 2020 Report: College Students' Views of Free Expression* (Washington, DC: Gallup, 2020), 34.

124. Madeleine Kearns, "Are We Setting a Generation Up for Failure? Part II," *National Review*, September 8, 2018, https://www.nationalreview.com/2018/09/jonathan-haidt-coddling-of-the-american-mind-college-experience/; Jeffrey Adam Sachs, "There Is No Campus Free Speech Crisis: A Close Look at the Evidence," Niskanen Center, April 27, 2018, https://www.niskanencenter.org/there-is-no-campus-free-speech-crisis-a-close-look-at-the-evidence/.

125. Rivky Stern and Aid Elbaz, "The Hate Speech of Tucker Max," *JHU Newsletter*, November 11, 2009, https://www.jhunewsletter.com/article/2009/11/the-hate-speech-of-tucker-max-77663.

126. "Academic Freedom," Johns Hopkins University Office of the Provost, September 11, 2015, https://provost.jhu.edu/about/academicfreedom/.

127. See, for instance, "Joint Statement on Rights and Freedoms of Students," American Association of University Professors, accessed March 24, 2021, https://www.aaup.org/AAUP/pubsres/policydocs/contents/stud-rights.htm#1.

128. Robert Zimmer, "Free Speech Is the Basis of a True Education," *Wall Street Journal*, August 26, 2016, https://www.wsj.com/articles/free-speech-is-the-basis-of-a-true-education-1472164801.

129. *Spotlight on Speech Codes 2021: The State of Free Speech on Our Nation's Campuses* (Philadelphia, PA: Foundation for Individual Rights in Education, 2021), https://www.thefire.org/resources/spotlight/reports/spotlight-on-speech-codes-2021/, p. 2.

130. Verna Myers quoted in Laura Sherbin and Ripa Rashid, "Diversity Doesn't Stick without Inclusion," *Harvard Business Review*, February 1, 2017, https://hbr.org/2017/02/diversity-doesnt-stick-without-inclusion.

131. Adam Weinberg, "Promoting Civic Agency and Free Speech on College Campuses," *Huffington Post*, February 15, 2017, https://www.huffpost.com/entry/civic-agency-and-free-speech-on-college-campuses_b_58a4ad3be4b080bf74f0439e.

132. Eric Townsend, "Fully Completed Global Neighborhood Opens for 2014–15," August 21, 2014, https://www.elon.edu/u/news/2014/08/21/fully-completed-global-neighborhood-opens-for-2014-15/.

133. See Jeremy Bauer-Wolf, "Random Roommates Only," *Inside Higher Ed*, March 2, 2018, https://www.insidehighered.com/news/2018/03/02/duke -university-blocks-students-picking-their-roommates-freshman-year.

134. Jeremy Bauer-Wolf, "Duke's Random Roommates," *Inside Higher Ed*, December 19, 2018, https://www.insidehighered.com/news/2018/12/19/little -drama-dukes-random-roommate-policy. Other universities are doing the same: New York University, for instance, prohibits first-year students from selecting their own roommates and purposefully pairs roommates who are from different zip codes. Anderson, "Should Colleges Let Students Choose Their First Roommate?"

135. See Katy Harriger, Jill J. McMillan, Christy M. Buchanan, and Stephanie Gusler, "The Long-Term Impact of Learning to Deliberate," *Diversity and Democracy* 18, no. 4 (2015); Sylvia Hurtado et al., "College Environments, Diversity and Student Learning," in *Higher Education: Handbook of Theory and Research*, ed. J. C. Smart (Dordrecht: Springer, 2003), 145–189; Patricia Gurin, Biren Nagda, and Nicholas Sorensen, "Intergroup Dialogue: Education for a Broad Conception of Civic Engagement," *Liberal Education* 97, no. 2 (2011): 46–51; Ximena Zúñiga, Biren A. Nagada, Mark Chesler, and Adena Cytron-Walker, "Research on Outcomes and Processes of Intergroup Dialogue," in "Intergroup Dialogue in Higher Education: Meaningful Learning About Social Justice," special issue, *ASHE Higher Education Report* 32, no. 4 (2007): 59–73; Adrienna B. Dessel and Noor Ali, "Arab/Jewish Intergroup Dialogue Courses: Building Communication Skills, Relationships, and Social Justice," *Small Group Research* 43, no. 5 (2012): 559–586.

136. See Beth McMurtrie, "These Professors Help Students See Why Others Think Differently," *Chronicle of Higher Education*, September 22, 2019.

137. Susan Price, "An Open Mind," *Claremont McKenna College Magazine* (Spring 2019): https://www.cmc.edu/magazine/spring-2019/open-mind.

138. Quoted in McMurtrie, "These Professors Help Students."

139. See George R. La Noue, *Silenced Stages: The Loss of Academic Freedom and Campus Policy Debates* (Durham, NC: Carolina Academic Press, 2019).

140. George La Noue, "Promoting a Campus Culture of Policy Debates," Heterodox Academy, November 20, 2017, https://heterodoxacademy.org/blog /faculty-responsibility-for-on-campus-policy-debates-with-diverse-viewpoints/.

141. Katherine Morgan, "Controversial Speaker, His Event Canceled by Middlebury College, Finds an Audience in a Campus Seminar," *Chronicle of Higher Education*, April 19, 2019, https://www.chronicle.com/article/controversial-speaker -his-event-canceled-by-middlebury-college-finds-an-audience-in-a-campus-seminar/.

Conclusion

1. Clark Kerr, *The Uses of the University* (Cambridge, MA: Harvard University Press, 1963), 15.

2. In this respect, I believe that the university serves in stark contrast to private sector corporations, where the impediments to change are much weaker up front. In this setting, chief executives have much greater latitude in proclaiming new strategies and priorities without having to conduct extensive ex ante consultation that is the hallmark of the university. Having avoided these consultation costs up front, however, they then have to confront and surmount organizational resistance after their strategy or priority has been declared.

INDEX

Abella, Irving, vii

Abella, Rosalie, 12

Academia.edu, 177

academic disciplines: generally, 102, 120,
129, 138–39, 143, 154, 166, 173–74;
humanities and social sciences, 104–5,
107, 136, 157–58, 160, 293n90;
sciences, 102–4, 142, 163, 170–71,
224

academic freedom: assaults on, 4–5,
156–57; declaration of principles of,
149–50; students' perception of,
87–88; university statements on,
230–31

ACT, 66, 68

Adams, James Truslow, 85; *The Epic of
America,* 31

Addams, Jane, 114

admissions policies: "barbell effect," 70;
in Canada, 67; current trend, 21;
demonstrated interest practice, 65–66;
early decision practice, 65; exam-
dependent, 52–53; legacy preferences,
24, 29–30, 54; legal challenge of, 6;
need-blind, 61, 62; open-ended
approach, 53; at private colleges,
51–52; promotion of diversity in,
26, 47, 52–55, 81–83, 210–11,
214–15, 219, 242; "selective," 53–54;
standardized tests and, 52, 66

African American studies, 112

Alcorn State University, 267n63

Allen, Danielle, 90, 127

Allen, Raymond, 156

Alpha Phi Alpha, 208

American Association of Community
Colleges, 115

American Association of University
Professors (AAUP), 149

American Dream, 31, 35–36, 85

American Education Society, 43

American higher education: accessibility
and affordability of, 58–59; cost of,
69; democratic values and, 19, 111;
funding of, 23–24, 39–40, 50, 62, 63,
72; historical evolution of, 18–19;
ideology and, 224–26; key functions of,
21–22, 25; legislation on, 23, 39, 71;
mission of, 22; models of integrated,
202–3; promotion of, 49; as public
good, 71–72; public perception of,
6–7, 43, 78, 225; racial gap, 38; social
mobility and, 36–37, 39, 42–43;
stratification of, 24; studies of, 22

American Historical Association, 105

American Journal of Mathematics, 145

American Political Science Association,
105, 106, 127

American Society for Clinical Oncology,
165

American Society of Gene Therapy, 165

Amherst College, 105

anti-institutional sentiment, 15–16
Arbery, Ahmaud, 13
Arendt, Hannah, 1
Arora, Ashish, 291n63
ASAPBio, 186
Association of American Colleges and
  Universities, 127
Association of American Universities,
  50
Aydelotte, Frank, 107

Bakke, Allan, 214
Barthes, Roland, 161
Bayh-Dole Act, 164
Beecher, Lyman, 43
Bemis, Edward, 149
Bennington College, 109
Berea College, 43, 202–3
Black colleges and universities, 76, 204,
  208; development of, 19, 47, 48–49;
  funding of, 6, 267n63; graduation rate,
  48; historically Black colleges and
  universities (HBCUs), 48, 76,
  206, 208; land-grant status, 48
Black students: discrimination against,
  47, 57, 210; financial aid to, 211;
  fraternities, 208–9; graduation rate,
  303n49; growing number of, 202–3,
  206, 208–9, 212; institutional neglect
  of, 208; recruitment of, 211; statistics,
  214–15; unions, 223; veterans, 210
Blau, Peter, 31
Bloom, Allan: *The Closing of the American
  Mind*, 22, 225
Bloomberg, Michael R., 68, 76–77
Bok, Derek, 98, 125, 215
Bolsonaro, Jair, 5
Bosch, Gundula, 174
Botstein, Leon, 62
Bowdoin College, 43
Bowen, William G., 61, 125, 215
Bowman, Isaiah, 53
Boyle, Robert, 170
"brains trust," 148
Brewster, Kingman, 60, 61
Brown, Michael, 188
Buckley, William F., Jr., 60, 225; *God and
  Man at Yale*, 22

Bush, George W., 82
Bush, Vannevar, 151, 152; *Science—The
  Endless Frontier* report, 153, 155

Caesarean democracy, 10–11, 14
California: access to higher education in,
  59–60; state universities, 37, 59
California Institute of Technology
  (Caltech), 82
Calliope (literary society), 201
Cambridge University, 82
Campus Compact, 114, 115, 118, 127
campus life: history of, 198–200, 202–4,
  206–9; pluralism and, 187–90,
  195–97, 215–17, 220–24, 235
campus speakers: controversies over, 196,
  228, 236–37
cancel culture, 228
Casadevall, Arturo, 174
Catholic students, 206, 207
Central European University (CEU):
  human rights archives, 1–2; relocation
  to Vienna, 2–4; reputation of, 3
Chen, Anthony S., 210
Chetty, Raj, 37, 38
"Chicago Principles," 231
China: higher education system, 8–9
Chronicle of Higher Education, 235
citizenship education, 104–5, 107, 242
civic education: assessment of, 127;
  benefits of, 90–91, 93, 104; challenges
  of, 118–20, 122; at colleges and
  universities, 97–100, 103, 120, 121;
  democratic requirement, 24, 90, 93–94,
  122–23, 126, 242–43; evolution of, 24,
  117–18; faculty-leadership collaboration in, 125–26; initiatives, 127–28;
  at the K–12 level, 95–96, 97, 99, 121;
  Liberal Democracy Index and, 91–93;
  neglect of, 113, 118, 119; public
  debates over, 93; roots of, 89; scholarly
  interest in, 90; top countries, 91
civic–political divide, 116
civic values, 93–94
Civil Rights Act (1964), 210
Claremont McKenna College, 234
Clariosophics (literary society), 200
Clark, R. Inslee "Inky," 60–61, 81

classroom indoctrination, 225–27
clinical trials: conflict of interest and, 165–66
Cole, Jonathan, 140
Coleridge, Samuel Taylor, 199
college admissions bribery scandal, 30–31, 66
College Entrance Examination Board (CEEB), 52–53
Columbia University: democratic learning, 109, 123–24, 126; general education curriculum, 108–9; Jewish students, 53
Committee on Special Education Projects (COSEP), 211
Committee on Un-American Activities, 156
community colleges, 23, 26, 51, 59, 111, 115. *See also* junior colleges
Cooper Union (New York City), 43
Cornell, Ezra, 46
Cornell University: admissions policies, 46; Afro-American Society (AAS), 212; Black students at, 208–9, 210; campus atmosphere, 211; establishment of, 45; financial aid at, 211; racial tension at, 211–12
Coronavirus Aid, Relief, and Economic Security (CARES) Act, 72
COVID-19 Open Research Dataset, 132
COVID-19 pandemic: contact tracing, 132; impact on higher education, 72–73, 131; impact on scientific research, 182, 183–84; interactive dashboard, 132–33; research publications, 181–82; spread of, 133; university response to, 132, 181; vaccines development, 132, 155
critical junctures, 27
Crockett, Molly, 193
Crucible Moment, A (report), 126
culture of fact, 136
curricula: citizenship formation and, 100–101; classical, 100–101, 103, 105; democracy and, 123–24, 127–28, 242–43; distribution requirements, 223–24; elective, 103, 105–6; general education, 108–9; interdisciplinary, 112–13; reproducibility and, 174. *See also* K–12 schools

DACA (Deferred Action for Childhood Arrivals) program, 6
Daily Pennsylvanian, 213
Daniels, Mitch, 125
Dartmouth University, 51
Darwin, Charles: *On the Origin of Species,* 102
"Declaration of Principles on Academic Freedom and Academic Tenure," 149
DeFunis v. Odegaard, 305n76
Deming, David, 74
democracy: institutions and, 16–17; liberalism and, 11, 12, 14, 17; public trust in, 94–95, 135; roots of the idea of, 11. *See also* liberal democracy
democratic citizenship, 93–94, 125, 127
Democratic Knowledge Project, 90
democratic learning, 122–25
democratic recession, 15–16, 20, 94–95
Denison University, 233
Denmark: civic knowledge score, 91, *92;* liberal democracy index, 91, *92*
Derrida, Jacques, 161
devolution of general education, 121
Dewey, John, 89, 114
Diamond, Larry, 15
Dickinson, Matthew J., 236–37
diversity: benefits of, 190, 214; challenges of, 231–32; formation of idea of, 197–98; interactional, 195, 218, 222; promotion of, 25–26, 189–90, 194–95, 210, 220, 232–33; structural, 217; studies of, 25, 301n15
Dole, Bob, 81
Dong, Ensheng, 132
Dreber, Anna, 179
Du Bois, W. E. B., 48, 142, 303n49
Duke University, 37, 221, 233–34, 287n125
Duncan, Otis, 31
Duterte, Rodrigo, 16
Dwight, Timothy, 101

educational immobility, 39, 265n33
Educational Opportunity Grants. *See* Pell Grants
Eisenhower, Dwight D., 158
Eisgruber, Christopher L., 257n16

Elbakyan, Alexandra, 177
elective courses, 129, 155
elective curriculum, 103, 105–8, 117
electoral democracy, 11, 95
Eliot, Charles W., 203–4, 205, 209, 210, 219, 220
Elon University, 233
Elsevier: boycott of, 178
Ely, Richard, 148, 149
endowments, 69, 70
Environmental Context Dashboard ("Landscape"), 68
Environmental Protection Agency (EPA), 169
Erdoğan, Recep Tayyip, 5
Espenshade, Peter, 125, 215
Estonia: civic knowledge score, 91, *92*; liberal democracy index, 91, *92*
Everett, Edward, 142

facts: authoritarian regimes and, 135, 138; definition of, 135–36; distortion of, 136; expertise on, 137, 140; interpretation of, 137, 140–41; polarized, 140; in public policy decision-making, 134–35; public suspicion about, 163
faculty: academic freedom and, 8, 88, 149, 230; attacks on, 4, 6, 8, 156–57, 199; as entrepreneurs, 248; ideological views of, 226, 227, 309n111, 309n112; independence of, 144–45; participation in university governance, 101, 124–26, 186, 224; political affiliation of, 225–26; promotion of democratic norms, 88, 107, 148, 197, 234–35, 250; skepticism of, 113, 118, 249; specialization of, 103–5; statistics, 18; terminations of employment, 156–57
fake news, 181, 183, 289n21
Fauci, Anthony, 133
Federal Contract Research Centers (FCRCs), 158–59
Fitzgerald, F. Scott: *The Great Gatsby,* 34
Flexner, Abraham, 105, 106, 145
Floyd, George, 6, 13
fraternities, 201, 208–9
freedom of speech: case studies, 88; claims of crisis regarding, 224–25, 228, 229;

controversies over, 196; debates over, 25, 232–33; limits of, 226; principles, 231; social media and, 228–29; student approach to, 87–88, 228
Fugitive Slave Law, 201

Galston, William, 135
Gardner, Lauren, 132, 133
Garner, Eric, 188
Gelsinger, Jesse, 165
general education: curriculum, 108–9; movement, 108, 109–10, 111–13, 117
General Education in a Free Society, 110
Gen Z students, 228, 229
G.I. Bill, 23, 39, 49, 55–57, 209, 269n95
Gilman, Daniel Coit, 143, 144, 145
"glass floor" phenomenon, 34
Goldberger House, 1–2
Golden, Daniel, 79
"Golden Fleece" awards, 162
Goldrick-Rab, Sara, 219
government-university compact, 75–76, 154
grade point averages (GPAs), 67
Graham, Gordon, 11
Gratz v. Bollinger, 194
Gray, Freddie, 188
"Great Gatsby Curve," 34
Gross, Neil, 226
Gross, Paul, 162
Grossman, Joel, 230
Gue, Benjamin, 44
Gundlach, Ralph, 156
Gurin, Patricia, 194, 301n15

Habermas, Jürgen, 191
Haidt, Jonathan, 22
Harper, William Rainey, 1, 8
Harvard House Plan, 205
Harvard Red Book, 110, 111–12
Harvard University: admissions policies, 52, 53–54; Democratic Knowledge Project, 127; diversity, 198, 203–4; legacy preferences, 54, 81; mission of, 205; mobility rate, 37; out-of-state students, 198–99, 204; political science courses, 105; residence halls, 205;

scholarships, 41, 43; student life, 199, 204–5
Hawkes, Herbert, 109
Henry, Joseph, 141
hereditary meritocracy, 39
Higher Education Act of 1965 (HEA), 23, 39, 57, 58, 75
Higher Education for American Democracy, 111
Higher Superstition: The Academic Left and Its Quarrels (Levitt and Gross), 162
Hillel groups, 223
Hitler, Adolf, 4
Holodomor, 135
Hopkins, Ernest, 51
Hopkins, Johns, 142–43
Horowitz, David, 225
Horowitz, Helen, 199
Houle, Christian, 32
Howard University, 68
Hungary: assault on academic freedom, 4–5; history narratives, 135; political development, 134
Hutchins, Robert Maynard, 56, 109
hydroxychloroquine, 182, 183

Ibn al-Haytham, 169
Ignatieff, Michael, 3–4
illiberal democracy, 14
Illinois Industrial University, 46–47
industrial research laboratories, 151
informational autocrats, 138
Inside Higher Ed, 234
institutions: decline of public trust in, 15–16, 140; democracy and, 10, 12, 14, 16–17, 20, 90, 154, 239–41, 245–46
interdisciplinary studies, 109, 112, 124, 174
intergenerational mobility, 33, 85
International Association for the Evaluation of Educational Achievement, 91
International Civic and Citizenship Education Study (ICCS), 91, 92
international students, 6, 306n89
Internet: freedom of expression and, 228–29; self-segregation and, 193;

social media, 167, 183–84, 193, 221, 243
Ioannidis, John P. A., 170
Iowa State Agricultural College, 44

James, William, 102
Jefferson, Thomas, 19, 49, 59, 89
Jewish students: discrimination against, 52, 53, 79; quotas for, 53–54; societies, 207–8; statistics, 53, 206
Johns Hopkins Black Student Union, 187, 189
Johns Hopkins Coronavirus Resource Center, 133
Johns Hopkins University: academic freedom statement, 230; admissions policies, 30, 53, 82–83; alumni, 83–84; Black Student Union, 188; campus speakers controversies, 230–31; creation of, 102, 142; curriculum, 128–30, 174, 223–24; educational ecosystem, 143–44; first-generation students, 82, *83*; global pandemic and, 131, 132; Hopkins Votes initiative, 129; influence of, 145; legacy preferences, 30, 82–83, *83*; mission of, 143, 144; Pell-eligible students, 68, 82, *83*; press, 144; promise of purposeful pluralism, 237–38; public forum on diversity, 188–89; research activities, 20, 143, 144; science disciplines, 102–4; student protests, 187, 189
Johnson, Lyndon B., 57, 246
Jordan, David Starr, 149
Journal of General Education, 110
journals, scientific: COVID-19 and, 182–83; disclosure rules, 165; path to open access, 186; publication of research outcomes, 173–74, 183. *See also* scientific research
junior colleges, 51

K–12 schools: civic courses, 96, 97, 99; college enrollment and, 49; democratic values and, 95–96, 242; inequalities, 38
Kaczyński, Jarosław, 16
Kennedy, Ted, 81
Kerr, Clark, 59, 60, 248

Kipling, Rudyard, 136
Kissinger, Henry, ix
Korean War, 157
Kronman, Anthony, 22
Kuhn, Thomas, 161

Lacan, Jacques, 161
Lancet, The, 182–83, 184
land-grant colleges and universities:
    enrollment of African American
    students, 47; establishment of, 19, 44,
    45–48; mission of, 45–46; social
    mobility and, 46
Landon, Alfred, 148
"Languages of Criticism and the Sciences
    of Man, The" (international sympo-
    sium), 160–61
La Noue, George, 235
Latour, Bruno, 162, 163, 164
Lattimore, Owen, 156
Lazarsfeld, Paul, 225
legacy admissions: credibility of colleges
    and, 85; criticism of, 81; defenders of,
    82–83; elimination of, 81–82, 84,
    241–42, 247; history of, 60, 78–79;
    in private colleges, 275n172; statistics,
    80–81, 82–83; tradition of, 29–30,
    54, 79
Legutko, Ryszard, 237
Levinson, Meira, 97
Levitt, Norman, 162
LGBTQ students, 13, 222, 223
liberal arts colleges, 26, 45, 109, 144
liberal democracy: core dilemmas of,
    viii, 14, 27, 190–91; definition of,
    9, 11; diversity and, 190; economic
    standards, 13; education in, 89–90, 95;
    etymology, 10; evolution of, 12–13;
    fragility of, 118, 240–41, 250; income
    disparities and, 13–14; outside actors,
    138; pluralism of, 134; promotion of,
    245; prospects of, 250–51; skepticism
    about, 121; social mobility and, 84–85;
    spread and decline of, 15; universities
    and, ix–x, 10, 17–20, 22–23, 28, 241,
    245–46, 249–50
liberalism, 11, 12, 14
Life Magazine, 49, 216

Lincoln, Abraham, 11, 19
literary societies: decline of, 201;
    emergence of, 199–200; mission of,
    200, 201–2
loan forgiveness programs, 275n166
Louis Napoléon, 11
Lowell, Abbott Lawrence, 53, 205, 220
low-income students: college enrollment,
    37, 40, 76, 81, 264n24; federal grants
    and, 58, 62–63, 75, 270n118;
    graduation rates, 70–71, 76; legacy
    preferences and, 81. *See also* social
    mobility
Lukianoff, Greg, 22

Madison, James, 100
Maine State College of Agriculture and
    Mechanical Arts, 47
Markovits, Daniel, 77, 78
Massachusetts Institute of Technology
    (MIT), 37, 82, 83
mass media, 138, 180
Master Plan for Higher Education in
    California, 59, 60
Max, Tucker, 230
McCarthy, Charles, 147
McCarthy, Joseph, 156
Meisel, Wayne, 114
Melvin Club, 207
Menorah Journal, 207–8
Menorah Societies, 207, 209, 223
meritocracy: criticism of, 38, 77, 78
MeToo movement, 13
Mettler, Suzanne, 56–57
Miami University, 43
military service: education attainment
    and, 285n102; training courses, 107–8
Mill, John Stuart, 12, 191
Miller, Michael, 32
Miłosz, Czesław, 135
Montalembert, Charles de, 10–11, 12, 14
Montesquieu, Charles-Louis de Secondat,
    89
Morrill, Justin Smith, 44
Morrill College Acts, 19, 39, 44–45, 47,
    50, 54, 139, 267n63
Mounk, Yascha, 14
Mowlson (née Radcliffe), Ann, 41

Mundheim, Robert, 212
Mussolini, Benito, 4
Myers, Vernā, 232

Napoleon III, Emperor of France, 11
National Center for Education Statistics, 39
National Defense Research Committee (NDRC), 151
National Endowment for the Humanities (NEH), 154, 160
National Institutes of Health (NIH), 154, 158, 175
National Science Foundation (NSF), 153, 157, 158
National Task Force on Civic Learning and Democratic Engagement, 126
national university: idea of, 100, 198
Nearing, Scott, 149
New England Journal of Medicine, 183, 184
Newman, John Henry, 207
Newman Clubs, 206–7, 209, 223
New York Times, 180
New York University, 311n134
Norway: civic knowledge score, 91, *92*; liberal democracy index, 91, *92*
Nosek, Brian, 171

Obama, Barack, 6, 118
Oberlin College, 202, 216
O'Connor, Sandra Day, 89
Office of Scientific Research and Development (OSRD), 152, 153
open science, 173, 176–77, 178–79, 181, 243
Orbán, Viktor, 2–3, 4–5, 135
Oreskes, Naomi, 169
Organisation for Economic Co-operation and Development (OECD), 60
Oxford University, 82

paideia: concept of, 89
PBS, 180
peer review: external, 153–54, 166, 179, 183, 185–86; open, 179, 300n174
Pell Grants: amount of, 63; eligibility for, 68, 74, 269n112; government

investment in, 73, 241; introduction of, 58; stagnation of, 62–63
Pence, Mike, 239
Perkins, James A., 210, 211, 212
Peters, Absalom, 42
Peterson, Chris, 83
PhD degree statistics, 142, 146
Philomathean Society, 200
PLOS One, 173
pluralism: Civil War's impact on, 200–201; complexities of, 218–19, 229–30, 237–38; importance of, 190–94; limits of, 201; promotion of, 26, 195, 231–38; purposeful, 196, 233, 234–35, 237–38, 244; university role in cultivating, 197
political science courses, 105, 106, 237
populism, 246, 247
post-structuralism, 160
Powell, Lawrence F., 214
Princeton University, 6, 54, 61, 257n16
private colleges and universities, 51–52, 54, 62, 69
ProPublica, 180
Protestant colleges, 52, 53
Proxmire, William, 162
public colleges and universities, 23, 37, 44, 49–50, 54, 58, 63, 72, 75–76, 146, 175, 222. *See also* land-grant colleges and universities; Morrill College Acts
public intellectualism, 167–68
public sphere, 191, 192, 193
Purdue University, 125
Putnam, Robert, 222

racial injustice, 13, 187–88
Radford, Alexandra Watson, 125, 215
ranking of colleges and universities: admissions policies and, 65, 66; algorithm for, 64–65, 68–69; development of, 64; global, 8; publications of, 64, 68
Rawls, John, 134
Reagan, Ronald, 62
Reeves, Richard, 34
research. *See* scientific research
ResearchGate, 177

research papers: citation, 292n63; peer review, 300n174
research universities: emergence of, 25, 27, 139; evolution of, 150–51; national security and, 151–52; open initiatives, 186; promotion of pluralism, 26; public trust in, 133; responsibilities of, 140
Rév, István, 2–3
Rockfish Gap Report, 97
Roosevelt, Franklin Delano, 55, 57, 148, 151
Rosen, Jay, 180
Rosenfeld, Sophia, 136
Ross, Edward A., 149
Rush, Benjamin, 100
Russia: civic knowledge score, 91–92; liberal democracy index, 91–92; regulation of universities, 5
Rutgers University, 72

Sandel, Michael, 38, 77, 78
Sarah Lawrence College, 109
SAT, 66, 68, 80. *See also* standardized tests
Saturday Evening Post, 56
Savio, Mario, 113
Sawhill, Isabel, 34
Schaper, William A., 106
scholarly societies, 139
scholarships: history of, 41–42, 43
science: citizenship and, 104; expansion of, 159–60; open approach to, 180; politicization of, 183; progress and, 161
"Science as an Open Enterprise" report, 177
science wars, 162, 163
scientific research: access to, 179–80; communication of, 168, 185; conflict of interest, 165; corporate influence on, 167, 294n105; dissemination of, 141, 181; federal support of, 139; file-drawing practice, 170; foreign influence of, 167; funding, 176; grant proposals, 175; with negative findings, publication of, 173; new technology and, 184; in the nineteenth century, 141; open initiatives, 181, 183–84, 185, 186;

p-hacking practice, 170; preregistrations, 173; public skepticism about, 180–81; rapid corrections to, 182–83; recognition of, 185; reforms of, 176; reproducibility of, 25, 164, 168, 169–71, 172–73, 176, 179
Sci-Hub, 177
Sen, Amartya, 13
service-learning movement, 113–14, 115, 116–17, 120
The 1776 Report, 5
Shapiro, Barbara, 136
Shapiro, Ben, 225
Smith, Lamar, 169
Smith College, 105
Smithsonian Institution, 141
Snedden, David, 103
SNF Agora Institute, 129
social mobility: challenges of, 34–35, 38; comparative perspective, 33; democracy and, 23, 31–32; evolution of, 32–34; higher education and, 33, 71; immobility and, 39; inequality and, 34; land-grant colleges and, 46; liberal democracy and, 84–85; public perception of, 31, 35; relative mobility, 33, 37; universities and, 26, 36–38
social science disciplines, 104–5
Social Science Research Program, 154
soft despotism, 14
Sokal hoax, 162
Sophocles, 89
Soros, George, 2
standardized tests: admissions policies and, 271n128; adversity score, 272n136; alternatives to, 67; benefits of, 66–67; college rankings and, 66; criticism of, 66, 67
Stanford, Jane, 149
Stanford University, 37, 123, 149
State Student Incentive Grants, 75
State University of New York, 37
statistics: manipulation of, 171–72; *p* values calculation, 172
Stavros Niarchos Foundation, 129
student aid: federal programs, 73–74, 241–42, 270n118, 275n165; Lady Mowlson's scholarship, 71; national

free-tuition program, 75–76; no-loan programs, 69; recruitment and, 69–70; state programs, 241–42; university competition in, 273n143

Student Army Training Corps (SATC), 107

student debt, 24, 69

students: affinity groups, 206–7, 209, 222–23; anti-war protests, 210; commitment to democratic citizenship, 87; community outreach, 87; diversity of, 205–6; dropout rates, 74; enrollment statistics, 40, 49, 73, 99; housing, 201, 216–17, 220–21, 222, 233–34; ideological views of, 226–27; intolerance for controversial views, 228–29; low-income, 37, 43, 52–53; online communities, 221; pluralism, 26; political engagement, 99; self-segregation, 219, 221–22; skills development, 9, 98–99; social activism, 113–14; social opportunities, 195–96, 222–23, 234–35, 244; statistics, 18; veterans, 111, 209–10

Stulberg, Lisa M., 210

Sunstein, Cass, 191

Sweden: civic education model, 92–93; civic knowledge score, 91, *92*; liberal democracy index, 91, *92*

Sylvester, James Joseph, 145

Taylor, Breonna, 13

tests. *See* standardized tests

Thelin, John R., 210

Thielens, Wagnar, 225

Ticknor, George, 199

Title IX, 216

Tocqueville, Alexis de, 12, 14, 31, 32

Tough, Paul, 74

Trebilcock, Michael, 27

Trilling, Lionel, 207

Troper, Harold, vii

Truman, Harry S., 19, 111

Truman Commission, 111, 112, 117–18

Trump, Donald J.: attacks on institutions, 16, 239; environmental policy, 169; higher education policy, 5, 6, 257n16; immigration policies, 5–6; populism of, 7–8, 135

Trump, Donald, Jr., 5

truth decay, 140

tuition: federal grants and, 56, 58; financial aid and, 43; at public *vs.* private colleges and universities, 50; rise of, 58, 72–73

Turkey: assault on academic freedom, 5

Twain, Mark, 136

undemocratic liberalism, 14

United States: political division in, 192–93

universities: anti-Communist campaign, 156; authoritarian states and, 4–5, 8; campus life, 199–200; civic education leadership, 98–100, 108, 118; Cold War era, 157–58; competition between, 63–64, 69–70; critique of, 38–39; diversity at, 44, 47–48, 57, 82, 188, 194–98, 204, 206, 209, 210, 211, 214–19, 231–32; elitism of, 40–41; enrollment, 37, 72–73, 260n56; expert-generating function of, 24–25, 138–39, 243; finances, 40, 72, 74–75, 175, 210; global rankings, 8; imbalance within, 160; industry relationships, 164–65; inequality and, 71; liberal democracy and, viii–x, 8, 10, 17–20, 22–23, 193–94, 245–46, 249–50; military training courses, 107–8; mission of, 18; pandemic response, 131–33, 181–82, 257n16; partisan perceptions of, 6–7; as path-dependent institutions, 26–27; pluralism of, 194, 195, 196, 197, 209, 233–34; populist hostility to, 7, 246, 247; post–Cold War, 162–63; *vs.* private sector corporations, 146, 312n2; public good and, 9; racial tension at, 206, 211–12, 214–15; reform agenda, 247–49; research function of, 159, 166, 167, 168; responsibilities of, 40, 140–41; social function of, 9–10, 18, 19, 20, 36–38, 39, 104; statistics, 18; structure of, 120, *121*; Trump presidency and, 5–7; World War I and, 107–8

University of California, Berkeley, 82, 157, 215–16

University of California, Riverside, 68

University of California Regents v. Bakke, 214

University of California system, 59, 177–78

University of Chicago, 109–10, 231

University of Colorado Boulder, 227

University of Illinois, 50

University of Michigan, 50

University of Missouri, 187–88

University of North Carolina, 199

University of Pennsylvania: Black student enrollment, 212; diversification at, 210, 212; liberal-pluralist movement, 213–14; racial clashes at, 212–13

University of South Carolina, 203

University of Texas, 37

University of Toronto: admissions policies, 29–30

University of Virginia, 124, 199, 221

University of Washington, 156

University of Wisconsin: Catholic club at, 207; community engagement, 147; Extension Division, 50; innovative ideas of, 146; Legislative Reference Library, 146–47; research activities, 149

university presses, 145

US Capitol riot, 98, 239–40, 250

U.S. News & World Report, 64

Vanderbilt University, 221

Varieties of Democracy: Liberal Democracy Index, 91, 92; Project, 15, 33

veterans: college enrollment, 56–57, 111, 209–10, 285n102

Vietnam War, 113, 159, 210

volunteerism, 116

voter turnout, 95

Wake Forest University, 127–28

Washington, George, 19, 100, 121, 198, 199, 205

Washington Post, 180

Weinberg, Adam, 233

Wellesley College, 105

White, Andrew Dickson, 46

Williams College, 43

Wilson, Woodrow, 107

Wisconsin Idea, 146, 147

women's colleges, 105, 109

women's studies, 112

women students: admission of, 216; discrimination against, 216, 222; living arrangements, 216–17

World Health Organization, 183

Xi, Jinping, 8–9

Yale University: admissions policies, 54, 60–61; classical curriculum, 101–2; Linonian Society, 201; mobility rate, 37; out-of-state students, 198–99; Pell-eligible students, 68; publications of, 201; Sheffield Scientific School, 45; women students at, 216

Zakaria, Fareed, 14

"zero tuition" policy, 75

Zimmer, Robert, 231

Zukin, Cliff, 116